D1031753

Building the Body Politic

Building the Body Politic

*Power and Urban Space
in Washington, D.C.*

MARGARET E. FARRAR

University of Illinois Press

URBANA AND CHICAGO

© 2008 by Margaret E. Farrar
All rights reserved
Manufactured in the United States of America
C 5 4 3 2 1

∞ This book is printed on acid-free paper.

Library of Congress Cataloging-in-Publication Data
Farrar, Margaret E., 1970–
Building the body politic : power and urban space in Washington, D.C.
/ Margaret E. Farrar.
p.   cm.
Includes bibliographical references and index.
ISBN-13: 978-0-252-03227-1 (cloth : alk. paper)
ISBN-10: 0-252-03227-6 (cloth : alk. paper)
1. Sociology, Urban—Washington (D.C.) 2. City planning—Washington
(D.C.) 3. Public spaces—Washington (D.C.) 4. Political sociology.
I. Title.
HT168.W3F37   2008
307.7609753—dc22   2007044079

Contents

Acknowledgments

I always admire authors who offer gracious and spare acknowledgments that capture enormous gratitude in a few lines. Unfortunately, I can't do that. There are simply too many people who have been too good to me as I've worked on this project.

From the first, Nancy Love has been incredibly generous with her time, suggestions, and patience in reading the manuscript, and she has modeled both creative scholarship and engaged, responsive listening for me throughout this process. Lorraine Dowler was a tremendous resource as I began to explore how my own concerns overlapped with those of geographers. She also always offered excitement about the project at exactly the right moments. Chad Lavin, Michael Lipscomb, Jamie Warner, and Gary Weisel saw these ideas in their early stages, and helped to shape the manuscript's growth and direction through their perceptive questions and critiques. The Research and Graduate Studies Office at Pennsylvania State University supported early work on this project through a grant that funded my trips to Washington, D.C.

Augustana College has been an incredibly supportive and creative community for teaching and writing. The dean of the college, Jeff Abernathy, has been a true advocate for faculty, and helped to provide the resources for finishing the manuscript in a timely manner. Through two Augustana Faculty Research Grants I was able to fund additional trips to Washington, and with the support of a summer research grant, I was able to hire my indefatigable student assistant, Rebecca Richardson. Becca's superb research instincts and impressive organizational skills made the final stages of this project much less painful than they would have been if I had been left to my own devices. Two of my colleagues at Augustana, Peter Kivisto and Kristy

Nabhan-Warren, deserve special thanks. Kristy has been a continual source of advice, encouragement, and much-needed humor throughout the revision process. Peter has been especially tolerant in enduring regular interruptions of his work because of my frequent visits to his office to ask questions about the research and publication process; that is to say, he's been an excellent mentor, and I'm deeply grateful to him for sharing his expertise.

Since he first introduced me to the study of political theory, Mark Weaver at the College of Wooster has offered superb insight and valuable guidance about all things professional. From Mark I've learned that a professor never stops being an "adviser" to his or her students, and I can only hope that I'm living up to the high standard he set as I now advise my own students.

I also want to thank the skilled and helpful people at the University of Illinois Press, who have been wonderful in helping me navigate the murky waters of first-time authorship. I am especially grateful to Kerry Callahan, who assisted in the early stages of publication, and to Bill Regier, who took the book to completion. I recently learned the identity of one of the anonymous readers of the manuscript, and I am delighted to be able to thank Clarissa Hayward for her careful, incisive comments, which truly challenged me to produce a better book. I would also like to thank my other (and still anonymous) reader; I simply couldn't have asked for more helpful and constructive criticism.

My family has been a constant source of support and understanding in my academic undertakings. They have seemed to know exactly when to ask about progress on the book—and when not to ask anything at all! (They also know enough not to ask the question, "Don't you get summers off?") I would especially like to thank my mother, Mary Farrar, for showing me what it means to give your best to every project you undertake.

Finally, in the middle of all this, I met my husband, Jeffery Glasen. I have so much to thank him for, really, but perhaps his most important gift to me is his unshakeable (and perhaps somewhat irrational) confidence in me. I am deeply indebted to him for his endless patience and good humor, and for reminding me, ever so gently, that there is more to life than books.

1. The Infrastructure of the Political

Make no little plans; they have no magic to stir men's blood, and
probably themselves will not be realized. Make big plans; aim high
in hope and work, remembering that a logical, noble diagram once
recorded will never die, but long after we are gone will be a living
thing, asserting itself with ever-growing insistency.

—D. H. Burnham, on the Senate Park Commission Plan
    for Washington

Several months ago, I sat in a darkened auditorium as faculty, students, and
staff discussed the new campus master plan. The plan called for renovating
dormitories and creating new parking facilities, as well as restoring several
historic buildings. That night, though, the conversation was about the new
student center. The student center would be the jewel in the campus crown,
the architects informed us, with ample meeting room for student organizations, dining facilities, a coffee shop, and perhaps a pub. The audience nodded
and murmured appreciatively, already tasting that first cup of bistro coffee,
or the first swill of legitimate on-campus beer.

Then a veteran of several past master plan campaigns raised his hand.
"Can we talk," he asked warily, "about where the new student center will
be located?" Immediately my generally genial college community divided
into two warring camps. Placing the student center near the dorms on the
outskirts of college property, one group argued, would make students more
likely to utilize the facility, since the building would only be steps away. The
students needed a place to call their own, where they could have some respite
from the pressures of school. Moreover, the center could serve as a bridge
between the campus and the surrounding neighborhood, and go some way
toward healing the traditional town-and-gown divide. The second group
favored situating the student center on the quad; such a central location, they
argued, would engender more student-faculty interaction and rejuvenate the
heart of campus. As the discussion grew more intense, each side predicted
dire consequences if the other's plan prevailed.

Our lives are given shape and meaning through the spaces we inhabit. Where we work, sleep, study, congregate, meditate, worship, govern, or protest shapes not only how we undertake these activities, but also who we are as we perform them. Decisions about the best ways to make space have high stakes, because they are ultimately decisions about the kinds of people we imagine ourselves to be. In the case of the proposed student center, the first group expected college students to be motivated primarily by inertia, unwilling to exert more than a minimal effort in their extracurricular pursuits. Further, this group postulated that the division between the college and the surrounding community was the paramount problem that the new student center should address. The second group, by contrast, assumed that students require and desire more casual contact with professors, and that creating a close-knit college community should take precedence over strengthening the college's ties with its host city. The evidence one might collect to support each of these assertions would hardly be definitive, as each is rooted in fundamentally different ways of seeing the roles of students, faculty, and even the college itself.

Decisions about making space reflect assumptions about who we are, but at the same time, these decisions are also about who we hope to be. That is, we make changes in the built environment because we wish to make things better. Our criteria for "better" spaces are as varied as the spaces themselves; in different contexts, we might want to create spaces that are more efficient, welcoming, beautiful, exclusive, ecologically sound, intimidating, edifying, refreshing, or manageable. What is more, we create "master plans" for campuses, towns, and cities because we believe that in so doing we are not only shaping spaces but the people who inhabit them. Again, in different circumstances, we might want people to become more industrious, friendly, cerebral, militant, relaxed, or obedient. As Burnham's remark at the beginning of this chapter indicates, we devise such "noble diagrams" because we hope that changes in the built environment will stick, that the careful arrangement of streets and buildings, avenues and green spaces, will make our desires less ephemeral. Making changes in the built environment lends permanence to our aspirations about how we should live together. Thus the language of space is also the language of politics, as both try to get at the ways we should organize our collective existence.

This book is about the interaction between discursive and material space, between how we think and speak about space and the ways in which these thoughts and words bring the world into being. It emerged out of a series of questions that interrogate the role of space in political life. At the most metatheoretical level, these questions include: What accounts for the decidedly spatial turn taken in our theoretical vocabulary? What do we gain, or lose, by employing spatial metaphors in our descriptions of political life? My attention then turned to the effects that language has on how and what we build, what we choose to preserve and destroy. How does this built space—as it is imagined, mapped, divided, developed, appropriated, dominated, and lived—influence our ability to live and work together? How does our understanding of past and present space(s) enable or constrain our abilities to envision political change or to describe alternative political futures?

Building the Body Politic examines the connections between discourse, space, and subjectivity as they are made manifest in the built environment of Washington, D.C. Since its inception, policy makers, architects, and politicians have created master plans for Washington; these include initiatives to improve sanitation in the alleys of the capital, to create a historical panorama of national memory in the space of the Mall, to eradicate slums and spur urban renewal, and (most recently) to preempt crime and prevent terrorism through the use of an extensive police surveillance system. These seemingly disparate spatial strategies are brought into being through rhetorical strategies, and all aim to *make* citizens out of both a local and a national population, to build a body politic.

The Language of Space

Space Displaced

In some sense, political theory has always been concerned with the politics of space. However, as Sheldon Wolin writes, few theorists have employed this specific vocabulary; instead, they discuss political space through the use of synonyms: the city, the state, the nation.[1] From the parameters of the Athenian *polis* to the contours of a democratic public sphere, the language of space has helped political theorists articulate the appropriate shape for political life.

Space pervades political theory but, as Wolin indicates, it frequently remains largely under- or unthematized. Space most often constitutes the mise-en-scène for political action; as the stage on which political activity occurs, its effects are always felt but not always easily observed, and even more rarely described. Often the explicit analysis of space is left to philosophers (as a question of ontology: what is the nature of space?) or to geographers (who are presumed to have a monopoly on the study of the subject).[2] Considering the myriad spaces that shape political life—borders that (however provisionally) establish nation-states and that are regularly traversed by immigrants, troops, exiles, refugees, and diseases; regions that capital invests in, transforms, and then abandons; places segregated by color and spheres separated by gender; and zones of combat and "economic empowerment," to name only a few examples—neglecting how space contributes to the exercise of power appears especially problematic.[3]

In recent years, some part of this omission seems to have been rectified by what we might call the spatialization of political and social theory. Under the influence of writers such as Michel Foucault, "[t]he language of social and cultural investigation," as Neil Smith and Cindi Katz argue, "is increasingly suffused with spatial concepts in a way that would have been unimaginable two decades ago."[4] Spatial metaphors now pervade social and political theory. One can think of countless examples; some of the most influential include Foucault's concerns with institutional and discursive spaces, as well as his call for local knowledges; Deleuze and Guattari's privileging of the topographical and nomadic movement of rhizomes over the temporal (historical and rooted) growth of trees; and Derrida's spaces of *différance*. Theorists also make ample use of spatial language in more casual ways; through the use of spatial metaphors theorists can "displace" old ideas, "open up spaces" for critical inquiry, describe subject "positions," identify new "locations," or "make room" for new ways of thinking. Other idioms include centers, margins, inclusion, exclusion, borders, peripheries, sites, standpoints, fields, flows, location, and liminality. Each of these terms transposes political, social and/or epistemological ideas into a spatial register. Speaking spatially allows a theorist to ground (you see?) her claims (if only linguistically); spatial language helps give a recognizable order to the ways we think about our political and social relationships.

One possible explanation for the expansion of our spatial vocabulary is a resolutely material one: changes in the nature of space itself and our relation to it. Theorists of postmodernity, such as Fredric Jameson, David Harvey, and Manuel Castells, attribute the recent "spatial turn" in philosophy to changes in the structure of capitalism; postmodernity (by their accounts, which vary in emphasis but are similar in tone) is a historical condition that necessitates (indeed produces) a different form of spatialized consciousness. The transformation of Western democracies from industrial to postindustrial economies, the vast new global division of labor and the increasing importance of transnational corporations, advances in communications technology and the internationalization of finance—all of these changes have resulted in what Harvey calls "time-space compression," Castells calls "the space of flows," and Jameson names "the cultural logic of late capitalism."[5]

The result of these material and cultural shifts has been a collective sense of displacement and disorientation. Jameson, for example, argues that we have lost the critical distance that previously oriented both our aesthetic and our political sensibilities.[6] This is not surprising since, as Manuel Castells contends, the world is in fact no longer organized by its "places" (clearly demarcated territories with geographical boundaries) but rather it is oriented towards a new spatial logic of "flows"—of capital, communication, and culture. Indeed, the phenomenon of globalization generally contributes to our new spatial lexicon, as innumerable commentators inform us that old ways of thinking about time and space do not reflect (and in fact, perhaps they *cannot* reflect) the newly configured dimensions of economics, politics, and culture. For these authors, the recent spatialization of discourse is a response to the postmodern (postindustrial, post-Fordist) global condition.

Feminist scholarship provides a second possible source for theory's recent spatialization. The history of political space is also a history of the exclusion of women from those spaces, and feminist theorists have brought to light the implications of calling some spaces "political" and not others. Moreover, the central questions in late twentieth-century and twenty-first-century feminism have been questions about location(s) and displacement(s)— disciplinary, cultural, racial, and sexual—all of which require us to interrogate the variable spaces (ontological, epistemological, and political) of "woman." Consequently, feminist theory has produced a plethora of spatially charged conceptual innovations, such as Rosi Braidotti's nomadic politics, Donna Haraway's situated knowledges, Nancy Hartsock's feminist standpoint theory, and Kathy Ferguson's mobile subjectivities.[7] Using these new tools, feminist theorists have questioned not only who has controlled the spaces of knowledge and power through most of human history, but also how these spaces have been represented, which spaces are privileged over others, and which sorts of political actions are possible in the current configurations of domination and resistance.

It is beyond the scope of this project to trace out the myriad influences that have contributed to the spatialization of theoretical discourse in great detail. I merely want to point out that the ways in which we talk about politics have become increasingly saturated with spatial metaphors; our political imagination is now deeply reliant on our geographic imagination. At least in part, this fascination with spatial concepts may result from what Ilana Silber describes as "a groping for a new language perhaps pointing toward an alternative perception of things."[8] Such an "alternative perception" may reflect a move toward quasi-foundationalism (in Stephen White's descriptive phrase, the need for a "weak ontology")[9] at a moment when we are wary of such foundations. Indeed, as Philip Wheelwright describes it, metaphorical language helps us negotiate "the tensions that [we feel] in existence"; metaphors help us grapple with the tumult we feel both within and outside of us.[10]

More often than not, however, the relationship between how we talk about space and the kinds of spaces we create goes unexamined. "Most metaphors," Eugene Miller observes, "are 'hidden' at first, especially for the hearer."[11] It is not sufficient to employ uncritically spatial metaphors without adequately examining their implicit materiality. In fact, the use of spatial concepts does not ensure—and in fact may even work against—a sustained analysis of how discursive and material spaces are bound up with each other in any field of power relations. As one of the first people to interrogate the relationship between language and space, Henri Lefebvre complains about this tendency in this way: "We are forever hearing about the space of this and/or the space of that: about literary space, ideological spaces, the space of the dream, psychoanalytic topologies, and so on and so forth. Conspicuous by its absence from supposedly fundamental epistemological studies is . . . the idea of . . . space—the fact that 'space' is mentioned on every page notwithstanding."[12]

For Lefebvre, there are two fundamental errors one can make in the analysis of space. The first is to succumb to "the lure of binarism": assuming that (what Lefebvre calls) "mental" and "material" spaces are closed categories that exist only in opposition to one another.[13] This strategy often results in the absolute dichotomization and hierarchicalization of these two kinds of space, where material space is assumed to be "real" space, and cultural, metaphorical, and symbolic spaces assume secondary status.[14] The second error is to simply collapse the two; Lefebvre argues that the unproblematic way in which many contemporary theorists conflate "mental" and "material" spaces has significant political and ideological effects, where "the philosophical-epistemological notion of space is fetishized and the mental realm comes to envelop the social and physical ones."[15] In other words, spatialized language comes to imply or even stand in for engagement with actual spaces. By refusing to elaborate the *relationship* between discursive space and material space, we cannot fully understand the effects of either.

Discursive Fields Forever

Rather than treating discursive and material spaces as *either* wholly independent of *or* as indistinguishable from one another, I want to examine them at their points of intersection and to tease out their interaction. Following Foucault's institutional studies, I examine the production of spaces and subjects through the discourses of urban planning, exploring how the language that we use to describe our sociospatial desires ultimately helps to shape not only the built environment but also the very subjectivity of its inhabitants, creating both a class of citizens and its other.

Discourse connotes the language through which knowledges (especially those of the human sciences) are put into circulation and establish conditions of truth. In these circumstances, as Hubert Dreyfus and Paul Rabinow argue, judgments about truth "have serious social consequences."[16] For example, if I make an assessment regarding someone's dubious mental health (e.g., "He's completely insane."), this particular statement carries little weight outside my narrow circle of friends. However, if a psychologist makes a similar determination, the statement is bound up in an entire *discursive field* (in Foucault's terminology)—replete with historical precedents, professional standards, methodological requirements, and occupational expertise—all of which endow that statement with a greater claim to "truth," and potentially much greater ramifications.

It is important to study this type of language because of its constitutive function. Rather than simply describing a reality "out there," expert discourses help to construct reality by creating ideas, concepts, and rationalities that structure and channel our ways of looking at that reality. As James Duncan describes it, a discourse is "the social framework of intelligibility within which all practices are communicated, negotiated, or challenged."[17] Discursive fields erect the boundaries for what it means to think a person, institution, or practice is "normal" or "natural," and constitute the limits outside of which it is (nearly?) impossible to think.

Looking at discourse thus requires us to bracket intra-discursive concerns (e.g., Is he *actually* insane? Does he suffer from bipolar or borderline personality disorders? Which school of thought will better explain and correct his erratic behavior?) in favor of examining the ways discourses define the horizon of possible understandings of the world. Discourse determines not only how we think about problems, but also what can count as problems; a discursive field offers us illumination about a set of phenomena while simultaneously and systematically ensuring that there are blind spots in our vision. As a result, discourse steers our choices about appropriate courses of action; in so doing it helps to forge the parameters of the political. Taking a close look at how particular discursive fields operate, then, allows us to interrogate how patterns of unexamined language work both to restrict and to expand our political imagination.

Implicit in the idea of discourse analysis is the suggestion that a discursive field is also comprised of nondiscursive elements. Geographers have used this insight (as well as ideas from structuralist and poststructuralist literary theory) to argue convincingly that discourses also include maps, photographs, and landscapes; we can "read" each of these as part of a system of signification that communicates ideas about the social order.[18] I will elaborate further on the importance of problematizing the dichotomy between discursive and nondiscursive practices (i.e., between words and things) through the practices of genealogy in Chapter 2.

By showing how the built environment is shaped by discursive practices, we can demonstrate (rather than merely assume) the recursive relationship between ideational and material spaces, between ways of knowing the world and ways of being in the world. Rather than merely (and less than carefully) using spatial metaphors to enhance our writing and thinking, we can study the specific relationships that exist between space and language. In so doing, we can better articulate the ways in which specific configurations of power-knowledge shape our existence, and the ways in which our lived experiences might overflow or subvert the constraints imposed on them by both discursive and built spaces.

The Space of Power

I begin from the assumption that space matters in the study of power; we need to be attentive to the role of the built environment in creating and sustaining contemporary power relations. This is not a claim that we must now take the "context" of politics into account in our analyses; rather, it means that the effects of power are made material in the built environment as economic, cultural, and political resources are consolidated and represented in spatio-symbolic forms. Rather than being merely the *result* of political activity, in other words, space is also part of its *production*. Power is reflected in and exercised through the production and organization of space; understanding how space is imagined, represented, distributed, and utilized is vital for any study of political life. As Sheldon Wolin states, spaces "mark out the paths along which human motions can proceed,"[19] opening up certain political possibilities and foreclosing others by virtue of their arrangement.

Even in our most systematic studies of power, though, the spaces of power often serve only as its neutral backdrop, the mise-en-scene in which the activities of the powerful and the powerless are played out. None of the epicenters of the power debate (for example, Bachrach and Baratz's Baltimore, Maryland; Crenson's Gary, Indiana; Dahl's New Haven, Connecticut; or Gaventa's Clear Fork Valley) are recognized as such.[20] Political theorists who employ these authors' definitions of power are exclusively concerned with its theoretical validity; they rarely acknowledge the space in which that power is employed as being significant to the analysis. Furthermore, the authors themselves never explicitly discuss the role of the built environment in shaping, channeling, and reinforcing the operations of power. Space is treated as a mere container, an empty vessel that is then filled with political actors and actions, but which is itself devoid of any political qualities.

Space and Power in New Haven

Briefly reviewing one of the central texts in the debate on power, Robert Dahl's *Who Governs?*, illustrates what we gain by employing a spatial perspective in our analysis. In many ways, Dahl's work anticipates the "spatial turn" taken in contemporary political theory; the power relationships he describes are thoroughly implicated in and structured by sociospatial relationships— although he does not acknowledge them as such. In his study of New Haven, Dahl privileges narrowly defined political spaces while systematically overlooking the more significant impacts of spatial politics in the city. This inattention to the politics of space renders his theory unable to account for aspects of how power operates in New Haven.

To answer the question posed by the book's title—who governs in a pluralist democracy?—Dahl examines the evolution of the political system in New Haven and documents the rise to power of different groups over time. After studying three issue-areas he deems particularly salient to the community (nominations by the two political parties, urban redevelopment, and public education) Dahl concludes that a single elite does not monopolize decision making in the city. Neither the group he calls the Social Notables nor the Economic Notables[21] dominates the political process or controls all available political resources. In fact, rather than becoming increasingly concentrated, Dahl contends that resources in New Haven have become more and more dispersed throughout the population over time, marking "a shift from cumulative inequalities in political resources . . . to noncumulative or dispersed inequalities."[22]

In addition, these dispersed inequalities are modified by their placement in a democratic system "where key offices are won by elections . . . and where nearly everyone in the political stratum publicly adheres to a doctrine of democracy."[23] Decision makers are continually constrained by the indirect influence exerted by their constituents, whose principal and powerful resources include numbers and votes. The diffusion of political resources over time combined with the ability of a majority of disgruntled constituents to oust an official from office work together to ensure that power never congeals in one place for very long without the consent of the governed. Dahl finds that many different groups in New Haven share influence and resources in a complex process shaped by many different actors. Dahl concludes from this that for the past half century, New Haven has been a "highly stable" and open democratic system.[24]

A Spatial Unconscious

Dahl's highly stable and open democratic system was rocked by the outbreak of serious civil disturbances (more pejoratively labeled "race riots" by some) less than a decade after *Who Governs?* was published. Arguably, this "typical" American city, like the others that were sites of similar disturbances during that period (for example, Washington, D.C.), is still recovering from them. My point here is not to chide Dahl for his theory's lack of predictive power. We can, however, use Dahl's work as a touchstone for our analysis by rereading New Haven with a sociospatial lens. In so doing we realize that Dahl's failure to more broadly theorize the politics of space led him to omit important aspects of power—tensions built into the very structure of the city—from his analysis and thus to overestimate the presence of a healthy pluralism in New Haven.

Indeed, the role of space occupies a paradoxical position in *Who Governs:* although Dahl ignores space as a potential political resource or category of analysis, the politics he documents are resolutely spatial. Consider the issue-areas that Dahl chooses for his study. Two of them—urban redevelopment and public schooling—are explicitly spatial problems. In the first, the very shape of the city is at stake; the outcome of political battles in this instance will be embedded in the urban landscape, which will in turn define the scope and breadth of future political problems and issues. In the second, spatial patterns of living and working form the contours of the dispute just as surely as they delimit regions in the city. In both instances, racial and socioeconomic differences are built into urban space in a way that Dahl first acknowledges and then systematically disregards.

Dahl's implicit recognition of the importance of spatial politics is linked to his explicit (but severely underdeveloped) account of racial politics.[25] Against those who would hold that "ethnic politics" is merely class politics in disguise, Dahl argues that this view undervalues the independent force of ethnic feelings. "An awareness of ethnic identification is not something created by politicians, it is created by the whole social system," Dahl contends. "Ethnic similarities are a palpable reality, built into the everyday awareness of the ethnic from early childhood to old age."[26] Taking this cue from Dahl, we might ask *how* the "palpable reality" of ethnicity is "built into the everyday awareness" of individuals. It is my contention that the built environment contributes to this "palpable reality" by creating a spatiosymbolic order that legitimates some groups and interests while marginalizing or excluding others. Creating a spatial order in the city not only exacts transformations in the urban landscape but also shapes the lives of those inhabiting those spaces.

Thus Dahl refuses to acknowledge the impact of what is in reality a spatial politics: politics that divides cities by race and income; communicates symbolically the consolidation of political, economic, and cultural power; and sets the parameters for the city's present and future decisions. The presence or absence of political efficacy, the relative importance of various constituencies, and the tensions that undergird Dahl's pluralist utopia are manifest in the structure of New Haven's built environment. In *Who Governs?*, however, the decisions one makes in Dahl's preordained political spaces (the legislature, the voting booth, the party convention) get called "politics" whereas the material effects of those decisions do not. As soon as they make the transition from Dahl's narrow political spaces out into the larger community of New Haven, these decisions cease to be called politics and instead become part of the built environment, part of the neutral arrangement of space that Dahl sees in a "typical" American city.

* * *

Nearly half a century after Dahl first published his study of New Haven, political theorists have begun to investigate explicitly the spatial dynamics of power and the relationship between space and democratic life. Margaret Kohn's *Radical Space,* for example, draws attention to the ways in which political dissidence and oppositional practices are fostered through spaces of resistance. Susan Bickford and Clarissa Hayward, in different ways, explore how inequalities are established and reinforced through practices that encourage and perpetuate economic and racial segregation.[27] When we make decisions that affect changes in the built environment—whether they are decisions that provide safe spaces for oppressed groups, limit the routes taken by public transit, establish the legal boundaries of a particular historic neighborhood, or increase the points of entry to a particular facility—we are making decisions that legitimate and reinforce some groups and interests while often (consciously or unconsciously) rendering others "out of place." In this way, space is never only the stage on which political dramas are played out; instead, it is always an active part of the cast.[28] The construction of the spatiosymbolic order helps to establish and sustain relationships of power and powerlessness, domination and freedom.[29]

Bodies Politic

Discursive fields, then, have material consequences. The ways we think and talk about space make (im)possible the creation of particular types of architecture and not others, and bestow legitimacy on some forms of social organization while determining alternative configurations to be illogical, unnatural, or utopian. However, it is not only space that is produced through these conversations, but also subjects. At the intersection of planning discourses and the built environment is the production of subjectivity.

The production of subjectivity occurs at two different moments in this process. First, subjects are constructed by and through the assumptions that we make about those who are the inhabitants of that space, the targets of our plans. If we return to the example of the new student center on campus, we can recall the suppositions at work in both sides of the argument: in one version, students prefer some distance between their academic and social worlds; in the other, students welcome opportunities to integrate their scholarly and extracurricular lives. We cannot demonstrate that one description of college students and not the other is "true"; by making one or the other set of assumptions, we reify these traits, bring them into bold relief, give them justification, and provide them with a material infrastructure.

Even if we could assess the truth about college students (for example, with a survey asking about their preferences), this assessment is disrupted by the fact that our plans for the new building are not only about what the college is at present, but what we hope it will be decades from now. This is the second point at which subjects are constructed through planning practices: what is planned and built (we hope) will produce effects. Even if students are *currently* unenthusiastic about trekking back and forth between their dorm rooms and the center of campus, for example, they could be persuaded to think otherwise with the right enticements; "if you build it, they will come" in this case means that the built environment shapes attitudes, habits, and behaviors. Planners and architects frequently employ this logic (and with good reason): a new stadium will spawn sports fans; a downtown festival marketplace will reprogram suburban shopping habits; mixed-use zoning will result in a more cosmopolitan urban experience. We plan for the subjects we have; we also plan for the subjects we want.

The production of subjects, moreover, is both discursive *and* corporeal; discourse is effective when it is made material at the level of the individual body. Subjects are produced and trained via the manipulation of their bodies, in the habits and behaviors made possible by specific architectures of power. The gridlike organization of the military camp, the arrangement of desks in a classroom, and the strictures of quarantine all contribute to what Michel Foucault names a "political anatomy of detail" in which power serves to fix individual bodies (and souls) in space: into rows, classes, cell blocks, cubicles, and wards. Especially in *Discipline and Punish,* Foucault demonstrates how power inheres in and cannot be separated from spatiality, how certain spatial arrangements shape both individual bodies and the social body writ large.

Planning discourses, especially, can produce a transformation in consciousness through a transformation in practice. Changes in the built environment, for example, might exact changes in how we comport ourselves by making us feel safe or threatened, at home or out of place. Such bodily reactions are evident in the motions of a bank teller who works under the watchful eye of the surveillance camera; in the woman who unconsciously avoids making eye contact with men she passes on the street at night; in pedestrians and cyclists trying to negotiate cities planned for automobiles; in the student who trods the same worn path across the grass to her classes every morning. Subjectivity is seared into corporeality through repetition and practice; Nietzsche calls this "mnemotechnics," the little things, the bodily things, which get written into memory.[30] As Foucault puts it, "nothing is more material, physical, corporal than the exercise of power."[31]

Captial City as Citizen Machine

The phrase "body politic," of course, implies something more than an aggregation of individual bodies; it suggests the production of a collectivity, specifically a nation-state and a national identity. Urban planning discourses not only create subjects but also create citizens, especially (but not only) in capital cities.

Washington, D.C., enjoys (or as its residents might claim, endures) an atypical position among American cities.[32] Unlike most American cities, Washington was not developed as an industrial or commercial center, and its history has been marked by a relative absence of manufacturing activity. Also, unlike many other national capitals that were important trade centers before they became centers of government, Washington was specifically designed *as* a capital city, a "symbolic city where the values of the Nation are on public display."[33] As such, in many ways it has more in common with other planned capitals, such as Canberra or Brasilia, than it does with London, Paris, or Rome.

As the nation's capital, though, decisions about its location, construction, evolution, and restoration are (and have always been) especially self-conscious and deliberative. Washington represents the United States' first real attempt at comprehensive city planning; seen as a model for the nation, planning decisions over the city's two-hundred-year history have reflected and magnified national trends in urban planning.[34] That is to say, some of the most significant transformations in Washington have served as model programs for other American cities. At the turn of the century, for example, the architects of the City Beautiful movement who helped to produce the Washington Mall also were instrumental in redrawing city centers in Cleveland, Chicago, Denver, Harrisburg, Kansas City, and San Francisco (although these plans met with varying degrees of success). The alley sanitation movement that galvanized social reformers in Washington at this time mirrored Progressive ideas about cities and their residents nationwide, most notably the tenement reform campaign led in New York by Jacob Riis. At midcentury, the city's urban renewal effort in Southwest Washington was considered a model for other redevelopment projects across the country. Finally, both the new comprehensive plan for monumental Washington and the city's expansive surveillance system reflect current preoccupations with both collective memory and security in cities nationwide.

What some might see as the contradictory character of Washington (or any city planned specifically as a capital) often results in the depiction of Washington as "schizophrenic," a city which "must shelter inhabitants satisfactorily and accommodate their working places as well as furnish a suitable setting for the 'Seat of Government.'"[35] Commentators on the city often invoke its "dual personality" in their writing; there is "Washington" (the site of our federal government, its landscape punctuated by monuments and cherry blossoms), and then there is the "other Washington" (the site of urban life, where people must be housed, taxes paid, water mains repaired, neighborhoods policed, and trash collected).

In fact, *all* cities must endure this tension between their symbolic spaces and their spaces of everyday life; all cities must negotiate, to some extent, the dual function that is often attributed as unique to Washington. It is precisely the purpose of a city to be both; these functions make the city (in Lewis Mumford's words) "the point of maximum concentration for the power and culture of a community . . . [where] human experience is transformed into viable signs, symbols, patterns of conduct, systems of order [and] where the issues of civilization are focused."[36] Through their civic squares, government buildings, monuments, thoroughfares, and cultural centers, a coherence of identity is built into the city by providing its citizens with common landmarks and places of collective memory. Washington is simply an especially clear case of the city's dual function. Moreover, these functions are not independent of one another but are instead inextricably linked; that is, the city's symbolic spaces are defined against and in relation to space that is considered peripheral to or deviating from this idealized vision of citizenship.

Washington's symbolic functions, however, also go far beyond those of other urban areas. In the case of a capital city, the "little things" of the body described above become more than that; they become part of what Lauren Berlant calls an "official technology of memory" designed to educate people about their membership in, as well as their responsibility to, a nation-state.[37] More than any other place, the architecture and design of a capital city has as its principal function to *create citizens,* much as a factory should forge workers, a prison should fashion prisoners, or a school should produce students. My understanding of citizenship here implies that it is more than a matter of nationality or legal status. Drawing on Judith Shklar's ideas about citizenship as standing, it suggests that the category of citizen acquires meaning only through its dependence on a class of noncitizens, a group of people to whom the rights and privileges of citizenship are denied.[38] In U.S. history, of course, noncitizenship has been ascribed at various points to Native Americans, slaves, women, and immigrants. Citizenship, then, is a site of contestation, a signifier whose contents are often defined and negotiated by way of race, class, and gender. As Barbara Cruikshank argues, "The citizen is an effect and instrument of political power rather than simply a participant in politics."[39] In other words, the contrast often drawn between subjects and citizens is not as stark as it may originally appear.

Whether citizens actively contribute to or passively comply with the decisions of the community; to what degree they expect and utilize their rights and liberties; if they feel entitled to seek justice; which of them might feel "more equal than others" in the eyes of the state—all of these components of citizenship are communicated by and in part facilitated by the built environment of the capital city. A capital city is a crucial component of the "technologies of citizenship" that delimit the parameters of political action.[40] A capital city, then, is a citizen machine:[41] it defines the field of civic life, helps forge ties between disparate groups, and makes material the vision of a shared political identity.

Building the Body Politic, then, examines the ways in which planning discourse produces spaces, subjects, and citizens. The sources for this discourse are multiple, as "planning" is claimed to be the purview of architects, politicians, planning professionals, charitable organizations, and social reformers.[42] Each of these contributes to what Foucault would call the "field of entangled and confused parchments" that are the raw material of genealogy.[43] In examining these discursive formations I ask what types of citizens are forged, reinvented, reinforced, or discouraged through Washington's planning discourses and their attendant practices. As architects and planners set out to describe and transform the space of the city, they map out the coordinates for certain forms that the body politic can take.

Chapter Overview

In Chapter 2 ("Making Space for Power"), I develop a theoretical framework for examining some of the connections between discourses, spaces, and subjects that will undergird my discussion of Washington. I focus on what I call interstitial spaces: the spaces that intervene, interrupt, and unsettle conventional spatial binaries. Foucault's conceptualization of disciplinary power offers us a rich account of how discourses, spaces, and subjects exist in mutually constitutive relation to one another, and how all three create the conditions for the exercise of power. However, although Foucault's work provides important insights into the disciplinary production of subjects and spaces, I will argue that it is insufficient for two reasons. First, although genealogy can pinpoint how power relationships help to produce both space and subjectivity, Foucault's method is less helpful in demonstrating how power is consolidated over time to serve the interests of specific groups or classes; in other words, we need more than genealogy to examine how planning discourses create and perpetuate the conditions of domination. Second, it neglects powerful symbolic aspects of the built environment. Our analysis cannot be limited only to the institutions and practices that Foucault's work foregrounds, but also must engage the extra-disciplinary spaces that constitute the larger topography of our collective life.

Chapter 3 ("Nation Building and Body Building in Washington, D.C."), is the first historical chapter of the analysis. I use the theoretical insights from Chapter 2 to study turn-of-the-century Washington. Specifically, I examine the Senate Park Commission Plan of 1902 for Washington, D.C., and compare it with the alley and tenement reform movement that took hold around the same period. The contrast between these two reform movements serves to illustrate two very different—but by no means opposed—modes of deploying power in the city. In the first, social control is achieved through "aesthetically correct" built space: through the erection of monuments, museums, and a uniform skyline of federal buildings; through the exaltation of beauty as the highest civic good; through the privileging of very visible public space (the Mall) to the detriment of the hidden, quasi-public spaces of the alleys. In the second, the nascent social sciences are engaged to observe, count, and correct or quarantine the deviant, diseased populations in the city. Both of these function through mechanisms of visibility: in its first mode of deployment, power operates via the construction of spectacular, symbolic spaces to be seen both by the indigent population of the city and the nation; in its second mode, the urban population is the object of a medical-managerial gaze that seeks to expel diseased or defective bodies from the space of the body politic.

Chapter 4 ("Remaking Washington at Midcentury") describes the next major structural transformation of Washington. By midcentury and with the passage of the District of Columbia Redevelopment Act, urban planning discourse had undergone several significant modifications. First, discussions of "alleys and alley dwellers" largely disappeared as the term "blight" became pervasive in policy makers' discussions about the shape of the city. Second, turn of the century concerns with morality and immorality were married to a calculus of profitability as the symbolic spaces of democracy were equated with the spaces of consumerism. Similarly, whereas earlier urban spaces were characterized as "healthy" or "unhealthy," mainly signifying the presence or absence of physical disease or moral turpitude, at midcentury, cities' "health" or "obsolescence" came to stand for economic viability. Recasting urban problems in this way metaphorically and literally displaced subjects from urban planning practices and helped justify ever more sweeping attempts at removing "dead" spaces from the living tissue of the city.

In Chapter 5 ("Millennial Space"), I examine contemporary urban planning practices, where an abundance of both commemorative and surveilled spaces defines the twenty-first-century landscape. Both the aesthetic arrangement of memory and the construction of new disciplinary infrastructures, I argue, ensure that urban life is increasingly *made visible*. From the burgeoning number of memorial and museum sites in Washington to the new technologies of surveillance that are becoming increasingly a part of urban life, new modes of making public space create and support the infrastructure for an intensely scopophilic politics. By this I mean a politics where citizens are those who are willing to watch and be watched, and where spaces and people not conforming to certain aesthetic and ideological aims are considered deviant or criminal. Moreover, I conclude, the practices of spectacle and surveillance are becoming increasing intertwined and indistinguishable as they are made material in contemporary urban life.

* * *

"The body politic" is a metaphor by which we identify our political collective, our *demos*. At the same time, though, the body politic is *more* than a metaphor; it refers to the conscious and often material construction of a national identity: the assemblage of various narratives, rituals, histories, memorials, and practices that together comprise what Berlant terms the "National Symbolic," which together generate "an alphabet for a collective consciousness or national subjectivity."[44] Finally, the body politic implies that this national identity is written on and through individual bodies, as they are described in capital city planning discourses, represented in national monuments, and targeted by the state for correction, coercion, and control. *Building the Body Politic* attempts to untangle these threads of power, subjectivity, and discursivity by examining the space of a capital city. In the chapters that follow, I trace how urban planning discourses mark the ways that subjects are constructed in part through the spaces they occupy, and show how these discourses are able to define, curtail, and expand the political possibilities available to cities and citizens.

2. Making Space for Power

The histories of our cities are histories of power and desire, where utopian longings for more perfect spaces collide with the stubborn reality of unpredictable, fleshy, material bodies. Radical changes in urban landscapes are often the result of these collisions. During the nineteenth century in France, for example, Napoleon III sought to create a more modern and more manageable Paris; in 1853 he commissioned Baron Georges Eugéne von Haussmann to build a city more conducive to both public health and social control. The ensuing strategy of "Haussmannization" resulted in sweeping boulevards that cut wide swaths through the dense labyrinth of buildings and alleys that constituted the medieval city; in the process it displaced thousands of residents and decimated their communities through its blueprint for a more manageable urban space. Only a few years later, Frederick Law Olmstead and Calvert Vaux envisioned a public park that would serve as a release valve for social conflict, a place where class tension would be transformed into sympathetic familiarity; the two landscape architects won the competition to design what would become New York's Central Park. Now in the first years of the twenty-first century, the empty husks of the Cabrini Green housing project sit awaiting demolition on the shores of Lake Michigan, while at a construction site in lower Manhattan, the cornerstone has been laid for the Freedom Tower, which is planned to reach 1,776 feet upon its completion at the World Trade Center site.

In any city, the fraught histories of political conflicts are often embedded in its architecture, layered stratum after stratum in the maze of its streets, the arrangements of its buildings, and the ethnic concentrations of its neighborhoods. Here, of course, I do not only mean "political" in the narrow sense of skirmishes over who decides what will be done with whose resources, decisions that are made in council chambers or state legislatures and whose wisdom is evaluated by the voting public in periodic elections. Instead, I am speaking primarily of "political" in the broadest sense: how we imagine, organize, and administer our relationships; what facilitates the use of our talents and capacities; what may nourish our hopes or feed our fears about the possibilities of living well together. What Kojin Karatani calls the "will to architecture" is at once an understanding of the power of spatial metaphors in anchoring philosophical thought, and the fact that (re)making space determines the parameters for the field of power relations.[1]

How might we begin to examine the connections between subjects, spaces, and power, between our utopian yearning for better places and the practical realities of the built environment? In this chapter, I suggest a strategy for analyzing space that will allow us to tease out these interactions. First, I argue that our project must call attention to the *interstitial character of space*. Rather than presuming what we might call singular or absolute spaces (spaces of reason *or* unreason, democracy *or* totalitarianism, freedom *or* domination), this study will focus on the way that many spaces intervene between things, especially things generally considered to be opposites, in such a way as to unsettle them both.

Michel Foucault's work is crucial to this effort because it privileges interstitial spaces, and resists simple spatial binaries. As will become apparent, however, relying on Foucault's work alone is insufficient. Foucault inadequately theorizes how power is consolidated over time to serve the interests of specific groups or classes, and how the built environment affects different bodies differently. This brings us to the second aspect of this strategy: we should be careful to describe how space is implicated in *creating and perpetuating domination*. As David Harvey suggests, accounts of making space need to ask questions about just and unjust spaces, and find ways to ensure the "just production of just geographical differences."[2] If we are interested in creating better spaces, our genealogical curiosity (the desire to know how spaces might have been made otherwise) must be informed by an ability to make meaningful judgments about when spaces are more or less democratic, and allow more or less freedom.

The third aspect of space that the following chapters will elucidate is its role in *producing the symbolic order*: the ways in which the configuration of spaces can communicate authority, legitimacy, and belonging—or weakness, powerlessness, and exclusion. In his insistence that disciplinary technologies have replaced the spectacle of sovereign power in the modern West, Foucault is often inattentive to the symbolic power that inheres in public architecture.

For these reasons, I argue that Foucault's highly suggestive spatializations of power can be more fruitfully deployed when they are supplemented with analyses from theorists such as Henri Lefebvre, Julia Kristeva, and Elizabeth Grosz. Their work provides important resources for theorizing the aspects of spaces, subjects, and power that Foucault either neglects or avoids. By including their voices here, I hope to articulate the dimensions of a new topography of power.

Interstitial Spaces

Foucault's "Spatial Obsessions"

Foucault's work is vital for contemporary studies of space because it has radically challenged the tendency to treat space as a neutral frame for social and political action. Foucault has literally altered the landscape of contemporary political philosophy through his inclusion of factory floors, prisons, schools, and hospitals in our inventory of political spaces.

In "The Subject and Power," an essay published shortly before his death in 1984, Foucault writes that his objective ". . . has been to create a history of the different modes by which, in our culture, human beings have been made subjects."[3] Foucault's books, essays, lectures, and interviews are explorations into subject formation as an effect of power-knowledge. That is, Foucault's project has been to analyze the ways in which we come to know ourselves and how we are subjected by those same knowledges. Much of the work in contemporary political theory has taken up Foucault's project along the axes of power relations and subject formation. Many theorists have utilized Foucault's analyses to extend or reject the discipline's understanding of how power works.[4] Others have employed Foucault to augment our accounts of subjectivity by bringing to light the everyday practices that mold us into being, the knowledges, rituals, disciplines, and institutions that pattern our ways of knowing the world and living in it.[5]

However, as I argued in Chapter 1, little of the work in contemporary political theory gives adequate attention to the term that both grounds and mediates *between* the subject and power: space. From the discursive spaces created for man in the domain of the human sciences to the hospitals, universities, and penitentiaries that translate these knowledges into social and political practice, Foucault's accounts of the subject and power are also always accounts of their emplacement. These spaces are by no means only an incidental part of Foucault's analysis; instead, they occupy a central place in his understanding of how power works in our daily lives. For Foucault, power is a condition of possibility structured very much by the spaces in which we think and act. "Space is fundamental in any form of communal life," he writes. "Space is fundamental in any exercise of power."[6] Rather than being simply convenient metaphors, for Foucault these spaces of power work to shape and delimit the boundaries of intellectual and political practice.

Foucault acknowledges that his work is imbued with these self-described "spatial obsessions."[7] In fact, he argues, trying to separate either subject formation or power relations from their arrangement and deployment in space results in a severely truncated analysis: "I think it is somewhat arbitrary," he writes, "to try to dissociate the effective practice of freedom by people, the practice of social relations, and the spatial distributions in which they find themselves. If they are separated, they become impossible to understand. Each can only be understood through the other."[8]

Foucault's genealogies are histories of sociopolitical and spatial relations. They offer us critical accounts of specific discourses, institutions, and practices that have become (and therefore were not always) "natural" to us, the means by which we construct the truth about ourselves and our past. The legacy of the Enlightenment, Foucault argues, is that we are now brought into being by the knowledges that describe us; at the moment we became both the subjects and the objects of our (human) sciences, he contends, we established new boundaries for thinking, acting, and being in the world, boundaries that are reified through those same discourses.

Foucault argues that power operates largely through disciplinary technologies. Individuals are normalized by being watched, supervised, managed; their movements are regulated, their (dis)abilities are assessed, their records are kept. Whether the appropriate metaphor is the Panopticon (the idea of a ubiquitous and perfect visibility) or (as Thomas Dumm argues) a monitor designed to "provide partial coverage of dangerous spaces,"[9] Foucault's conception of power is based on the subject *being seen,* and being created by those who do the seeing. For this reason, Foucault opposes disciplinary power to what he calls juridical power or sovereign power. Where disciplinary power is exemplified in the space of the modern prison, sovereign power was enacted through the spectacle of a public execution. In instances of sovereign power, the visual mechanism is reversed: subjects are *watching* rather than *being watched;* power is exercised through the manifestation of an extravagant example rather than the subtle intrusion of an internalized gaze. Although Foucault does not argue explicitly that sovereign power is no longer with us, he clearly stresses disciplinary power as the most important and the most insidious form of power in operation today. By Foucault's account, disciplinary power is the principle means by which we are subjected to increasingly intrusive mechanisms of control.

A genealogy of sexuality, for example, demonstrates how we have come to recognize certain sexual practices as normal and other as aberrant; it will ask when "the homosexual" became a specific sort of human being, a biological/ psychological/ sociological profile to be studied, documented, managed, and administered as a specific (deficient or deviant) part of a larger (reproductive) population. What Foucault calls the invention of the homosexual stands in sharp contrast to prescientific ways of conceptualizing sex; the subject of what were once "inconsequential bucolic pleasures" becomes, through the course of the eighteenth and nineteenth centuries, "the object not only of a collective intolerance but of a judicial action, a medical intervention, a careful clinical examination, and an entire theoretical elaboration."[10] Consequently, the invention of the homosexual necessitates the production of a new built environment: the hospital (or prison) ward; the treatment center; the research institute; the network of organizations and Web sites dedicated either to "protecting the family" or to lobbying for gay, lesbian, bisexual, and transgendered (GLBT) rights; the urban geography of gay districts, gay neighborhoods, and "safe" spaces. All of these places are both products and authors of this new form of subjectivity, responses to and continual reinventions of "the homosexual." In short, sexuality is produced and (as Judith Butler might argue) performed through medical, legal, psychological, social, and *spatial* practices.

The Space(s) Between

Foucault's work draws attention to what we might call the *interstitial character of space.* As Dreyfus and Rabinow describe it, this notion of the interstice means that for Foucault, "[t]he play of forces in any particular historical situation is made possible by the space which defines them."[11] Throughout Foucault's work, his focus on liminality, thresholds, horizons, transgressions, and transfigurations mark not so much strict divisions between this space and that space but rather the hazy regions where these spaces overlap, coincide, contradict, or prefigure one another.

This interstitial character of space is illustrated in (at least) three different zones in Foucault's writings: the space(s) between words and things, between knowledge and power, and between domination and resistance. Although I treat each pair as analytically distinct here, none of these spaces is discrete or exclusive. Rather, each intersects with the others as a site of problems, tensions, and energies that Foucault deploys in his investigations. By attending to these interstitial spaces, we will be able to add depth and texture to our analysis of urban space.

BETWEEN WORDS AND THINGS.   In Chapter 1, I described one of the conundrums we encounter in studying space: that very often in our analyses, we either cleave the discursive from the material in an unconvincing attempt to claim they are independent of one another or we conflate them so that there is no analytical distinction at all.

Foucault's work is theoretically persuasive in part because it abolishes this binary relationship; in this case, Foucault theorizes in an intermediate zone between the metaphorical and the material (or between words and things). Foucault deploys potent images of space (for example, the Ship of Fools, the confessional, and the Panopticon) to describe the contours of power in the modern West. These spaces are neither precisely material nor exactly metaphorical; they are ways of condensing complicated, political relationships between specific instances of power, knowledge, and rationality into a single illustrative site. Foucault's "simultaneously mythic and real" spaces, as Gilles Deleuze argues, make Foucault a mapmaker of a very peculiar sort; his maps are meant to be used rather than to mirror the terrain.[12]

The "simultaneously mythic and real" Panopticon is Foucault's best-known metaphor for the power of modern spaces (or the spaces of modern power) in forging subjectivities.[13] Bentham's Panopticon is a design for a prison that was never built, and yet in some sense its principle features were replicated throughout the West as an integral tactic for refining processes of modernization, industrialization, and urbanization. The Panopticon features a central tower with windows on all sides that looks out over a ring of cells that face the tower. Space is organized around vision so that a maximum number of people can be observed at a minimum cost; the authoritative gaze in the Panopticon is both vertical (the guard in the tower looking down at his charges) and horizontal (prisoners watching each other so they can report possible transgressors). In its ideal, most efficient form, this disciplinary machine does not even need the guard in the tower to operate effectively; all the prisoners require to monitor their behavior is the possibility of being watched. One-way glass, for example, can take the place of an actual guard and produce the same results. As an institution that allows for those in authority to see without being seen, the Panopticon fashions subjects that internalize the force of this authoritative gaze.

There are few prisons built on the model of the Panopticon. Rather than a single, historical institution, the Panopticon is instead ". . . a type of location of bodies in space, of distribution in relation to one another, of hierarchical organization, of disposition of centres and channels of power;"[14] it exemplifies a revolutionary spatial technology that was critical to the production of normalized subjects. Its basic structure and logic, moreover, is replicated throughout contemporary urban life. Well-documented in Mike Davis' *City of Quartz,* panopticism is made manifest in Los Angeles and other central cities in the carceral architecture of shopping malls, police stations, libraries, and hotels.[15] As I describe in Chapter 5, the advent of new surveillance technologies and increasingly centralized security procedures have made panopticism simultaneously more dispersed and more thorough, extending to a wider range of places and behaviors. No longer concentrated in individual buildings, panopticism is now a pervasive condition of urban life.

By theorizing power as operating in the interstices between matter and metaphor, we can complicate the relationship between physical and cultural space by mapping a "simultaneously mythic and real" geography,[16] acknowledging that physical spaces are always endowed with cultural meanings that define and exceed their materiality. It is not only the built space of the penitentiary, or the winking eye of the camera on the street corner, but also its ideational architecture that shapes our understandings of freedom and domination, liberty and captivity.

BETWEEN KNOWLEDGE AND POWER.   The second space that Foucault explores is that between knowledge and power. Foucault regards power and knowledge as inextricably linked. "We should admit," he writes ". . . that power and knowledge directly imply one another; that there is no power relation without the correlative constitution of a field of knowledge, nor any knowledge that does not presuppose and constitute at the same time power relations."[17] Any space of knowledge is therefore also a site of power relations and needs to be analyzed as such.

Foucault thematizes the spatialization of power-knowledge in three different ways. First, Foucault contends, knowledge becomes spatialized when it utilizes spatial techniques; the classification schemes of Linneas and the subsequent transcoding of the natural world into the spaces of illustrations in books are two such technologies.[18] These spatial practices serve as the preconditions for knowledge becoming a science; one must be able to catalogue elements of the world into meaningfully distinct categories (element, species, genus, genre, regime, etc.) to build on our knowledge in a systematic way by sorting and separating elements of the world into tables, indices, and matrices.

Second, our disciplinary categories spatialize knowledge by arranging phenomena into narrow, professionalized zones, so that (for example) we look at "the political," "the economic," "the geographic," and the "psychological" as discrete areas of study, parsed out along distinct axes of our existence. Returning for a moment to the first distinction between discursivity and materiality, we can acknowledge that disciplines are not just zones of thought but are territorialized in the very material spaces of journals, conferences, funding lines, and university departments. The phrase "divide and conquer" has purchase here, although it is unclear whether we are conquering (acquiring mastery over these different domains by isolating them according to expertise) or being conquered (by our inability to traverse disciplinary boundaries and examine problems more holistically). Disciplinary constraints thus channel the study of power in specific directions, and blinker our vision of politics in systematic ways.

Third, in his studies such as *The Birth of the Clinic, Madness and Civilization,* and *Discipline and Punish,* Foucault shows that the "human sciences" build knowledges into our modern landscapes in the forms of universities, clinics, mental hospitals, and prisons, all of which serve to spatially segregate certain elements of the population. Thus the human sciences help to produce different aspects of our built environment, just as they help to construct the complex topography of the human subject. These knowledges, their corresponding disciplines, and their attendant institutions work individually and in concert to organize not only ways of knowing but also ways of *being;* they police the borders of modern subjectivity by sorting, classifying, and distributing people in space according to their decent or deviant behavior, by codifying their competence or dysfunctionality. They assign meaning to categories of human existence and assign spaces for those meanings to exist. Disciplined knowledge establishes the bounds for the thinkable and the unthinkable, the real and the fantastic, the true and the false.

BETWEEN DOMINATION AND FREEDOM.   Disciplinary power is never univocal in its spatial practices, however. Rather than being essentially or even primarily spaces of domination, Foucault instead posits these sites as integral to the spatial order of our modern existence, but an order that provides the material conditions of possibility for both subjugation *and* resistance. Sites of disciplinary power—the prison, the barracks, the hospital, etc.—also belong to the category that Foucault calls heterotopias, a specific type of interstitial space.[19] As opposed to utopias (singular and absolute places that are in fact no-places), heterotopias can be found within our already existing spatial order, and act in such a way so as to "suspect, neutralize, or invert the set of relations they happen to designate, mirror or reflect."[20] In other words, heterotopias are those elements of the built environment that both comprise and disturb the social order by mapping and revealing its phobias, obsessions, contradictions, and reversals.

Foucault describes two types of heterotopias: heterotopias of crisis and heterotopias of deviation. The first type are privileged, sacred, or forbidden places designated for socially significant transformational experiences; he names adolescents, menstruating women, pregnant women, and the elderly as among the groups subject to such crisis spaces. These, Foucault argues, are largely disappearing in modern society, or at least are being replaced by the heterotopias of deviation. In addition to the above named disciplinary spaces (prisons, clinics, hospitals, etc.) Foucault also names brothels, carnivals, resort villages, cemeteries, museums, gardens, parks, and libraries as heterotopias of deviance.

Foucault outlines six different principles by which heterotopias operate. First, heterotopias are "those in which individuals whose behavior is deviant in relation to the required mean or norm are placed."[21] The mentally ill, the criminal, the elderly, the dead, the adulterous or otherwise sexually aberrant are all obviously relegated to spaces of deviance, some to the disciplinary institutions that Foucault describes in his other work. But so too are other behaviors existing outside the space-time of the modern, industrialized world: festive, restive, and contemplative behaviors that resist normalization and that can be found in these alternative spaces.

Second, the same heterotopic spaces can function differently over time or in different societies. Foucault uses the example of the cemetery here: until the end of the eighteenth century, he reports, cemeteries were located near churches in the centers of towns, and were characterized by "a hierarchy of possible tombs"; the charnel house housed most of the community of the dead and the few individual graves were located inside the church. As society has become increasingly atheistic, we have focused more attention on the state of individuals' bodies, "the only trace of our existence in the world and in language." From the beginning of the nineteenth century, the space of the cemetery registered this shift by according every person the right to "her or his own little box for her or his own little personal decay"; at the same time, the cemeteries themselves began to be located outside the city.[22]

The third principle of a heterotopia is that is can juxtapose several sites within itself that otherwise might be incompatible. Theaters and cinemas, for example, can bring "a whole series of places that are foreign to one another" into the same room. Similarly, exhibitions such as the Midway in Chicago's White City (and its modern theme park incarnations, such as Disneyworld's Epcot Center) can juxtapose various, disparate cultures (or representations of those cultures) in a new, cohesive space of consumption. Foucault's fourth principle is related to this: heterotopias are always "linked to slices in time," by existing outside of normal time and by creating their own time.[23] A prisoner's sentence, a two-week vacation, and the suspension of time one experiences watching a play or a movie are all examples of heterotopic time. Rather than a rigid and orderly progression, time is malleable, unstable, and modified through spatial practice.

The last two characteristics of heterotopias that Foucault describes illustrate that heterotopias cannot exist in just any space. They necessitate "a system of opening and closing that both isolates them and makes them penetrable."[24] One can enter a heterotopic space if one if forced to do so (in the case of a prison), or one must "have a certain permission or make certain gestures."[25] Finally, heterotopias always have a function in relation to the spaces that they are not; they can never exist alone. Foucault argues that this function ". . . unfolds between two extreme poles. Either their role is to create a space of illusion that exposes every real space, all the sites inside of which human life is partitioned, as still more illusory (perhaps that is the role that was played by those famous brothels of which we are now deprived). Or else, on the contrary, their role is to create a space that is other, another real space, as perfect, as meticulous, as well arranged as ours is messy, ill constructed, and jumbled."[26]

Taking Foucault's description of heterotopias in toto, we can see that they are above all paradoxical spaces, spaces of contestation, contradiction, tension, and reversal. On the one hand, they help to order disciplinary spaces by marking out spaces of difference and deviation; individuals who are placed there (or who place themselves there) are outside the norm of what society considers normal, proper, good, or true. Heterotopias make material the spaces of otherness.

On the other hand, by creating a space for this difference to exist, societies in some sense recognize and endorse this deviance as intrinsic to their operation. As a result, heterotopias always threaten the scaffolding of order and meaning in a society by exposing the places where order and meaning break down. They both reflect the values of a culture and simultaneously distort those values, almost like funhouse mirrors, where the image of one's self is there and recognizable but stretched, contorted, reflected obscurely and obscenely in either hilarious or monstrous ways. For example, the existence of the brothel—a deviant sexual space outside the bounds of "normal" love and marriage—in some sense makes possible modern bourgeois heterosexuality while at the same time undermines the supposed normalcy and reality of purely romantic or procreative sexual arrangements. Heterotopias are politically charged spaces that often provoke conflict over the parameters of subjectivity.

As we will see in the chapters that follow, urban spaces often are perceived as heterotopic spaces: spaces of paradox and contestation, where various forms of identity, morality, and knowledge are produced, challenged, reinforced and disrupted. The labyrinth-like network of alleys that challenged social reformers in Washington at the turn of the last century was at once both integral to *and* deeply threatening to the capital city's architectural and political infrastructure, because it concentrated the poor and dependent in what was supposed to be the heart of the body politic. Similarly, the various attempts to build utopian elements into Washington to correct for the messiness and ambiguity inherent in urban life have created urban spaces that are not unlike theme parks, slices of heterotopic time-space that exist at once both juxtaposed to and as part of the modern city. The McMillan Plan of 1902, the modernist visions of the city advanced at midcentury, and contemporary efforts to secure urban space in Washington all serve to simultaneously constitute and undermine ideals of citizenship by offering a way to interpret the city as coherent and meaningful, while at the same time illustrating precisely where this order and meaning fall apart.

The heterotopia has important implications for exploring Foucault's accounts of freedom and domination. Rather than a neutral arena in which individuals struggle for dominance (that is to say, liberalism's version of what a political space looks like),[27] heterotopias indicate that spaces are never pure, that they are always implicated in and indeed help structure power relations. In short, for Foucault there is no absolute or perfect "space of freedom." "I do not think there is anything that is functionally—by its very nature—absolutely liberating," he concludes. "Liberty is a practice . . . The liberty of men is never assured by the institutions and laws that are intended to guarantee them."[28] Although Foucault criticizes crude attacks on LeCorbusier, he also uses the architect as an example of misplaced hopes in an unequivocally revolutionary architecture. "[I]t can never be inherent in the structure of things to guarantee the exercise of freedom. The guarantee of freedom is freedom."[29]

Domination and Difference

Despite Foucault's adeptness in analyzing interstitiality, his work overlooks or occludes elements of space that I think are crucial to understanding its political character, specifically its role in creating the conditions of domination. In this section, I describe how our analysis of urban planning discourse will need to go beyond Foucault in describing the materiality of oppression and difference inherent in building the body politic.

Making Power Matter

There is no doubt that Foucault's political agenda is subversive, directed at undermining the dangers of political fundamentalism and dismantling the tyranny of ossified self-assurance. Foucault states quite clearly that he hopes the effect of his analyses is ". . . [t]o give some assistance in wearing away certain self-evidences and . . . to contribute to changing certain things in people's ways of perceiving and doing things; to participate in this difficult displacement of forms and sensibility and thresholds of tolerance."[30] However, while Foucault's accounts of disciplinary power are by no means value-neutral, the distinctions he draws between "power" and "domination" are never terribly explicit (Jürgen Habermas criticizes this as Foucault's predilection for "crypto-normativity").[31] For example, rather than conceiving of relationships that are essentially "free" of power (for this can only be an abstraction), Foucault contends that "it would be better to speak of an 'agonism,'—a relationship which is at the same time reciprocal incitation and struggle . . . a permanent provocation."[32]

This ambivalence towards describing an essential freedom is a result of two factors: first, Foucault's leeriness of the will to power inherent in any theoretical enterprise, and second, Foucault's radical redefinition of power. In opposition to most accounts of power, Foucault argues that power is not something one has or doesn't; rather, it is "something which circulates, or rather as something which only functions in the form of a chain. It is never localised here or there, never in anybody's hands, never appropriated as a commodity or piece of wealth."[33]

This formulation requires Foucault to downplay the ways in which the sites of disciplinary power are *not* dispersed randomly throughout a society but whose impact is instead absorbed most often by disenfranchised populations, and whose effects perpetually reinforce each other. That is, if we agree that the built environment legitimates some people while disenfranchising others, we are acknowledging that power and its effects can be consolidated and concretized. Modern cities, for example, perpetuate economic and racial segregation, through transportation, zoning, and housing policies. Mobile capital leaves urban landscapes decimated but leaves needy populations intact, with limited education and employment opportunities and little hope of moving elsewhere.[34] Limited opportunity makes criminal behavior seem rational, and makes an individual's entry into the prison system more likely, which in turn sets in motion other normalization machines: mental health evaluation, state social services and welfare, and an even more limited range of possibilities for education and employment.

A critical theory of space, then, should be able to articulate when spatial arrangements are more or less emancipatory, more or less oppressive, and create better or worse conditions of existence. In short, we need to be able to talk about justice and injustice, liberation and domination—while at the same time understanding that none of these terms can ever be extricated from the play of power relations. Foucault's justified suspicion of the will to power inherent in both critical political theory and efforts at social reform does not trump the need to make reasoned political judgments about the quality and inequality made material through the built environment.

Mapping Corporeality

As Foucault would surely agree, the built environment has different impacts on specific populations. The "body politic," as I will show in the chapters that follow, is an obvious misnomer; this body was never singular, whole, unified, or indivisible, despite an enormous amount of effort to render it as such. Rather, political bodies are not only differentiated along the various axes Foucault identifies (healthy/sick, sane/insane, law-abiding/criminal, heterosexual/homosexual, normal/abnormal), but are also always cross-cut by race, gender, and class.[35]

Henri Lefebvre's work foregrounds the ways in which identity and difference are inscribed in space. Subjectivity cannot be analyzed apart from the spaces in which it is produced, he argues, because ". . . groups, classes or fractions of classes cannot constitute themselves, or recognize one another, as 'subjects' unless they generate (or produce) a space."[36] Said another way, space brings subjects into being, makes them real, makes them matter. However, Lefebvre argues, confronting the materiality of space necessitates confronting the materiality of the body, which "at the very heart of space and of discourse, is irreducible and subversive."[37] Unlike Foucault's description of the thoroughly disciplined (and therefore somewhat abstracted) body, though, Lefebvre's body is "a practical and fleshy body" with "spatial qualities (symmetries, asymmetries) and energetic properties (discharges, economies, waste)."[38] This active, vital body upsets any theory that strives for closure—or, for that matter, disclosure. No matter how totalizing systems of oppression become, and no matter how insistently theorists strive to understand them, the body remains partly unpredictable and opaque, producing unanticipated effects. Unlike Foucault, then, for Lefebvre the body exists at least in part "[p]rior to knowledge, and beyond it" in its actions and sensations, in its capacities for pleasure, pain, and survival.[39]

Rendering the body in its specificity has important implications for the gendered aspects of space and power, and it is here that Lefebvre's work can be usefully read with that of feminist theorists of the body such as Elizabeth Grosz. For Grosz, a "practical and fleshy" body is also a sexed body, a body whose sexed difference is fundamental and material (even as it is manifested in different modes in different historical and cultural circumstances). As Grosz argues, the sexed body is less like a blank page for writing than a copperplate for etching; it has a texture, a materiality that has a role in the production of subjectivity and power.[40] The body's materiality needs to be accounted for in analyzing the corporeal aspects of power, and the kinds of sexed subjects that are produced through each.

Returning to the heterotopic space of the brothel may help illustrate this point. Although Foucault argues that heterotopias are spaces of contradiction and contestation, he seems to suggest that these contradictions occur only between two poles: the dominant cultural values and the alternative values that may be carved out and illuminated in heterotopic space. Foucault does not acknowledge how multifaceted and unequal such contestations can be. Foucault cites the brothel as an "other space" presumably because it contradicts the institution of bourgeois marriage by providing a space for erotic imagination and transgression. In fact, Foucault argues in another forum, the brothel is not unlike another heterotopic sexual space: the public baths, the "cathedral of pleasure" in the center of the city. "One can directly compare the bath and the brothel," he states. "The brothel is in fact a place, and an architecture, of pleasure."[41]

Yet it is unclear that the brothel is a space of pleasure for everyone present. Foucault goes on to note that in this community of pleasure, men "were tied to one another by the fact that the same women passed through their hands, that the same diseases and infections were communicated to them."[42] What might be said of the women in such a "community"? What might be said of their erotic imaginations and sexual transgressions? Foucault's account renders them as only objects, passed (not coincidentally, like the diseases themselves) among men.

Taking the materiality of differently sexed bodies into account, we might find that for many (if not all) of the women, surely the brothel was more a space of employment than a space of pleasure, arguably not very different from any other place of business where women service a paying clientele (like stylists at a hair salon, waitresses in a restaurant, or nurses in a hospital). We might also note that although male clients of the brothel were often legitimate members of the "normal" bourgeois community (the embodiment of a sort of sociosexual schizophrenia), the prostitute's body was made legible through legal, medical, economic, and sexual discourses, all of which testified to her status as decidedly outside social and sexual norms. The body of the prostitute (marked as a poor, sick, criminal, and/or sexually deviant woman) thus unsettles any abstracted or generalized "body" as the locus of disciplinary power. Thus "deviance" and "transgression" are inscribed differently in differently sexed bodies, even as the bodies share the same interstitial space. Ignoring these differences risks obfuscating the reality of domination, a point we shall revisit in more detail.

Acknowledging Abjection

What is more, our relationships to fleshy, material bodies other than our own are bound up in subdiscursive realms, in what Iris Marion Young refers to as the subject's sense of ontological integrity.[43] The construction of race and racism is a case in point here. Although some social science continues to produce "evidence" for the intellectual inferiority of African Americans (as the debate over *The Bell Curve* attests),[44] some of the most insidious forms of racism occurs not so much in what is thought or said, but in the constant negotiation that occurs between our selves and bodies that are markedly, materially different from our own. If I am acutely conscious of the differently colored skin of someone near me, I am experiencing a minor disturbance in my sense of self, and I make adjustments in my comportment accordingly. Often these negotiations are unsophisticated, unreflective, and unconscious; they seem "automatic" to me, and my attempts to explain them may amount to nothing more than ex post facto rationalizations.

Some of the most fundamental challenges to our ontological integrity can be understood through the category that Julia Kristeva calls the abject. At the level of the individual body, the abject is material expelled from the body by the body—mucus, bile, vomit, pus, and excrement—while at the same time being a part of it. From early childhood, what is abject draws us in and repulses us all at once; we experience curiosity at the once-self or almost-self and horror at the same. The corpse is the exemplary case of abjection: a dead body, once living matter, once a living subject, is now an (almost) object, human and not human, dangerously present and terrifyingly absent. What is abject is considered disgusting, abominable, repellent, and uncivilized; it serves to remind us of what is bodily, irrational, and animal about us.[45]

The abject is an ambiguous place that exists at the border of the human and the animal, a precarious *spatial* relationship that establishes "the place where I am not and which permits me to be."[46] By regarding certain bodily functions and substances—most often bodily fluids and feces—as abject, we differentiate ourselves from animals and take our place as human beings.[47] But this is a precarious accomplishment. In its proximity to the border of the self, the abject unsettles the self's sense of order; the abject "draws [us] toward the place where meaning collapses."[48] What is abject continually threatens to span that short distance between the me and the not-me.

Because the self regards the abject as so close, as so threatening, what is abject produces anxious or even terrified fortifications of the self's borders. As Kristeva writes: "Through frustrations and prohibitions, this authority shapes the body into a *territory* having areas, orifices, points and lines, surfaces and hollows, where the archaic power of mastery and neglect, of the differentiation of proper-clean and improper-dirty, possible and impossible, is impressed and exerted."[49]

Utilizing the anthropological work of Mary Douglas, Kristeva contends that abjection also plays out at the level of the body politic. The body, Douglas argues ". . . is a model which can stand for any bounded system. Its boundaries can represent any boundaries which are threatened or precarious."[50] What is considered civilized in a culture—what is appropriate, respectable, and good—is legally, morally, and spatially set apart from that which is considered uncivilized, inhuman, or evil. The space of the social body (the space of civilization)—of the human, the rational, and the clean—is marked and guarded against the space of the abject. Both personal bodily habits and entire social systems are organized around keeping the abject in its place; that is, away from the space of the self.

One of the most important ways the social body, like an individual body, gives itself a fragile order is through its ideas of pollution, dirt, contamination, and purity. As we shall see in the following chapters, defining the body politic often relies on separating the idealized citizen body (one untroubled by its physicality, unconnected to its animality, nominally unsexed but always implicitly male) from its abject other (what had to be controlled, monitored, and/or expelled).

Carefully codifying ambiguous boundaries—whether through personal or political sanitation—reifies indeterminate identities into manageable differences. Douglas asserts: "[I]deas about separating, purifying, demarcating and punishing transgressions have as their main function to impose system on an inherently untidy experience. It is only by exaggerating the difference between within and without, above and below, male and female, with and against, that a semblance of order is created."[51]

Both Douglas and Kristeva acknowledge that the sociospatial relationship between the self and the abject is also often a gendered relationship. Frequently pollution ideas are meant to mirror and exaggerate (and therefore to teach) ideas about the society's sexual order;[52] basic material differences are culturally coded and converted into systems of domination. What is considered a respectable and healthy body—a contained, controlled body, readily separable from its animal functions—is most often identified in European cultures as a white, male, heterosexual body. Conversely, what is considered "repulsive" by a culture—what is most closely associated with sexuality, animality, fluidity, and corporeality—is most often equated with women, or the feminine. Women's bodies have been constructed (as Elizabeth Grosz argues) "not only as a lack or absence but with much more complexity, as a leaking, uncontrollable, seeping liquid; as formless flow; as viscosity, entrapping, secreting; as lacking not so much or simply the phallus but self-containment."[53] Women who belong to what are claimed to be "repulsive" racial groups are accordingly regarded as more sexual, more animalistic, and more bodily than even white women.

In our account of the body politics and the spaces of citizenship, then, any analysis must consider how discourse reasserts and reinscribes the experience of abjection. Moreover, we should be alert to how abject spaces are often rendered feminine, whereas the spaces of authority and legitimacy are anxiously ascribed with masculine traits.

* * *

In short, the spatial order is not as fluid as Foucault's descriptions of power might have us believe. Space—how it is claimed, divided, bought, sold, built up, and torn down—is a "record of deeds done by those who have had the power to build"[54] and those who have occupied those spaces. The domination of space by some groups and not others shapes the world in certain ways, lays down particular infrastructures, and produces substantial changes in the landscape that are not easily reversible or resisted. Although power itself might be fluid, the geographies of power are often less so, embedded in architecture and ensconced in deeds and titles, written on and through particular bodies.

Here Lefebvre's work once again is compelling. Lefebvre wants theory to confront space, as it should confront the body, in its radical materiality. When power is spatialized it is not fluid. Rather, "the subject experiences space as an obstacle, as a resistant 'objectality,'" he writes, "at times as implacably hard as a concrete wall, being not only extremely difficult to modify in any way but also hedged about by Draconian rules prohibiting any attempt at such modification."[55] Space has texture, structure, and substance, and is in many ways resistant to simple transformation. Moreover, Lefebvre insists on specifying the gradations between domination and freedom. Lefebvre distinguishes between the domination and appropriation of space, and the implications of these for political practice. A dominated space, Lefebvre argues, is space that is "closed, sterilized, emptied out"—it is close to being a product, capable of endless reproduction and commodification.[56] Appropriated space, in contrast, is a space "modified in order to serve the needs and possibilities of a group."[57] Rather than being the "realization of a master's project" (dominated space), appropriated space more closely "resembles a work of art"[58] and is a necessary precondition for political resistance. However, Lefebvre does not advocate a simplistic abolition of dominated spaces in favor of appropriated ones; "ideally, at least" he argues, "they ought to be combined."[59] Rather, he argues, the problem is that Western history has been a history of their separation and antagonism, where the victor has too often been dominated space.[60] As the rationalizing forces of the state, the military, and capital have expanded over time, their transformations in space have overtaken much of our spatial practice,[61] diminishing our capacities to creatively appropriate space(s) for ourselves, and limiting our possibilities for fulfilling political life.

The Spatiosymbolic Order

Finally, rather than solely focusing on the networks of disciplinary power in specific institutions, this analysis will foreground what we might call the *spatiosymbolic order:* the ways in which economic, political, and cultural resources are concentrated and communicated in society through the built environment. Thus in addition to looking down—at the microphysics of power that operate at the level of the individual—a theory of spatial subjectification also needs to look up: at the aggregate effects of institutions and at extra-disciplinary spaces as they comprise our built environment. The spatial order of society (who builds, how they build, and what they build) is symbolic as well as disciplinary; it works through spectacle as well as surveillance. Studying the spatiosymbolic order requires an understanding of what Orville Lee calls the power to create "symbolic categories and classifications to represent objects in the social world and . . . the authority to make [these] representations socially binding."[62] It is evident that symbolic power is thus crucial to the production of citizenship.

Rather than seeing subjects as being mainly constituted through disciplinary knowledges and practices, I argue that subjects and citizens are also created through their symbolic representations in our associational life. Some of the most important representations of our cultural and political life are manifested in our urban planning practices and our public architecture. The ways in which we arrange our cities for collective life and the values we choose to make visible in our built environment render power relations literally material. By reflecting and reifying the power of some groups over others, these activities make (in Lee's words) "symbolic practices socially effective."[63] This symbolic function of city planning—the spatiosymbolic order—is not only oriented towards how we are *seen* (as in Foucault's disciplinary power), but also by what we *see;* it is spectacular power, offering us a vision of our social and political life in concrete and steel.

Disciplinary power and symbolic power require different kinds of analysis. For instance, a strictly Foucauldian critique of consumer culture would probably stress the exponential growth of database marketing, techniques by which our purchases are tracked and recorded, statistically modeled and projected, where we accumulate credit histories and purchasing profiles that are also part of some larger market niche.[64] What this analysis ignores (and what is supplemented through an appreciation of symbolic power) is how certain appropriate forms for our lives are sold to us through what we see, advertisements that sell not a specific product but an entire lifestyle. This accumulation of choices, aspirations, and values is a symbolic construction that communicates we are "this kind of person" if we shop at Wal-Mart or Target, drive a Ford or a Volkswagen, wear Dansko clogs or Manolo Blahnik sandals. Although they are certainly not as brutally dramatic as the drawing and quartering of Damiens the regicide, the spectacles of consumer culture teach us through symbolic, not disciplinary, practices.

Urban planning policy and public architecture, then, surely perform disciplinary functions, but they can also serve as conduits of spectacular, symbolic, and sovereign power—especially in capital cities. The skyscraper (in its equation of verticality with social status), the corporate workplace (with its entrenched hierarchy of "cubicles" versus "corner offices"), the monument (with its clear message about whose history is worthy of memorialization), and the department store (with its lush displays of conspicuous consumption)—all serve to make material the values of a culture in easily decipherable signs; together they constitute a "repertoire of symbolic practices" that work in concert to forge subjectivity.[65] Symbolic power communicates social and political relations through this codified aesthetic; it condenses meanings into easily interpretable signals for the viewer to read, absorb, and respond to, often in lieu of rational choices.

Like disciplinary power, though, symbolic power impacts different groups differently. Symbolic spaces make material signs of social cohesion while simultaneously codifying social hierarchy; they communicate who is welcome in certain places (and who is most definitely an outsider) by providing us with stories of belonging and exclusion that are told through the built environment. "Bum-proof" benches at city bus stops, metal detectors in airports, rainbow flags hung outside homes and businesses, through traffic limited by cul-de-sacs and gates, highway billboards that advertise strip clubs at the next exit, and bicycle lanes on city streets are only some of the more obvious examples. For different groups of people, then, a city's symbolic spaces can become alternately sites of pride, patriotism, community, shame, fear, or isolation. Especially in commemorative architecture (monuments, memorials, historic markers, museums), we learn whose histories are legitimate, which narratives are superfluous (or systematically omitted), and which images are embraced as part of our official, national accounts of origins and destiny. We learn who is allowed to speak for history, who is allowed to speak for "us," and whose voices will always be considered marginal to the main event.[66] As Mike Davis argues in *City of Quartz,* while architectural critics are often oblivious to the differential symbolic effects of social spaces, marginalized groups often respond to them immediately.[67]

* * *

In this chapter, I have argued that power is codified and made material in the built environment and that spatial practices help to write power relations into subjectivity. I have outlined how the interstitial character of space, its differential impact on different kinds of bodies, and its role in consolidating symbolic power help to create and sustain relationships of domination. The built environment certainly serves to habitualize us to power through disciplinary techniques (spatial practices that enable observation and segregation). However, power also functions symbolically, by communicating narratives of social hierarchy and cohesion. "Building the body politic"—the production of a specific spatiosymbolic order through the practices of urban planning and public architecture—encompasses both of the disciplinary and symbolic aspects of power.

In the following chapters, I examine historically specific manifestations of the spatiosymbolic order in Washington, D.C., and how the production of subjects and citizens changed over the course of the twentieth century. I explore how both disciplinary power and symbolic power are manifested in Washington's urban spaces, and how they can help us to understand better the impact of spatial relations in the production of subjectivity.

3. Nation Building and Body Building in Washington, D.C.

> Look down on it in the early morning from the pinnacle of the Washington Monument. The geometric pattern of its streets stretches out in the early sun to a rim of blue water and green hills. From this peephole in the sky it looks like an architect's dream, a World's Fair model turned on by an electric switch, a study in shine and shade and movement, a fabulous and incongruous mixture of long, straight modern boulevards and classical pillared buildings out of Greece and Rome.
>
> —James Reston, in *The New York Times Magazine*, 1941

> People bid their wise men . . . to remove and forever keep from view the ugly, the unsightly, and even the commonplace.
>
> —Daniel Burnham, on the Senate Park Commission Plan for Washington, 1902

From it inception two centuries ago, Washington, D.C. was intended to be more than a city; it was imagined to be a symbol of the utopian possibilities available both to the newly founded nation and to the nation's cities. In addition to the endless technical questions implied in city planning and design, the "makers of Washington" continually asked themselves more theoretical questions about bodies and cities, and about the political implications of the built environment: How does one build universal ideals—democracy, freedom, unity, order, and strength—into a particular urban landscape? And how does one simultaneously acknowledge that less than ideal people will

Earlier versions of these ideas have appeared in Margaret E. Farrar, "Making the City Beautiful: Aesthetic Reform and the (Dis)placement of Bodies," in *Embodied Utopias: Gender, Social Change and the Modern Metropolis,* edited by Amy Bingaman, Lise Sanders, and Rebecca Zorach (London and New York: Routledge, 2002) 37–54; and in Margaret E. Farrar, "Health and Beauty in the Body Politic: Subjectivity and Urban Space," *Polity* 33 (Fall 2000): 1–23.

inhabit this landscape, that city space—no matter how perfectly designed—is always *lived* space? How does one educate the citizens of such a place, and make their (imperfect, unpredictable) bodies worthy of the space in which they reside? How does one build the body politic?

In this chapter, I examine the Senate Park Commission Plan of 1902 for the National Mall and compare it with the alley and tenement reform movement that took hold around the same period. Both the Mall and the alley serve as normalizing, heterotopic spaces in Washington at the turn of the century. Both are part of the half-real, half-imaginary geography[1] of city making, interstitial spaces that are at once actual places *and* potent symbols that together constitute the discursive infrastructure of citizenship. By describing the Mall and the alley as complementary efforts to shape urban space, I show how the makers of Washington built the body politic to reflect a certain kind of body, and how they consciously (and unconsciously) struggled with the reality of imperfect, unpredictable, fleshy, faulty, material bodies in their corporeal topography (or urban physiology). Seeking to organize the body politic around a very specific corporeality—a body politic that is built around an idealized (white, male, bourgeois) citizen—Washington's planners quite literally built others out of the spaces of citizenship. Through aesthetic reforms (rebuilding the National Mall) and social reforms (improving Washington's alleys), policy makers sought to reconcile imperfect citizen bodies with the symbolic spaces of democracy.

Monumental Changes:
The Washington Mall and Citizen Bodies

Shortly after the colonies won their independence from Britain, George Washington and Thomas Jefferson commissioned French-born architect and engineer Pierre L'Enfant to draw up plans for a new capital city. The new capital had to accomplish many things. First, it had to unify the then loose confederation of independent, contentious states under the auspices of a national identity. Second, it needed to establish and convey the presence of a strong national government, in a context where a strong central government was suspect. Third, it had to communicate the legitimacy of the new country in the eyes of other nations, and demonstrate America's parity with the European capitals. Finally, Washington, D.C., had to appease those states whose sites were not chosen for the site of the capital city.

L'Enfant's plan met all of these objectives. He designed a city rich in the symbolism of the new nation. Drawing on knowledge of European capitals (especially Paris and the grounds of Versailles), L'Enfant's Washington featured broad, diagonal boulevards and carefully positioned public parks and plazas. Each of the diagonal streets in the city was named after one of the American states, and its proximity to D.C.'s central public buildings indicated its importance in the process of building the nation. Massachusetts, Virginia, and Pennsylvania became avenues central to the city's design, and both Delaware and New Jersey, important for their roles in ratifying the Constitution, were designated as streets that would intersect with the Capitol.[2]

L'Enfant's Washington was also a city of vistas; Washington was to be a city on display, for both the nation and for the world. What could be seen and what was rendered invisible, depending on one's location in the city, were of paramount importance. The Capitol Building, located at the top of a gradual natural incline—which "stands really as a pedestal waiting for a superstructure," according to L'Enfant—was to command the view of the federal city. Other, smaller public squares around the city were also to be "visual focal points," "advantageously and reciprocally seen from each other."[3] Even in L'Enfant's plan, these elements of the visual doubled as mechanisms for social control: wide, diagonal boulevards connected via circular centers were first built into the urban landscape in Haussmann's Paris; their express purpose was to allow the national military to fortify the central circles, making it easy to quell citizens' rebellions (peasants' rebellions) by firing canons down several streets from a central location. Wide streets were not merely an aesthetic consideration but also a military-political one.[4]

Despite almost universal endorsement for L'Enfant's original plan for the area, however, many of his ideas were ignored for decades. Long after he had submitted the final versions of his plans to Congress, Washington remained a relatively small and swamp-infested city; it certainly did not resemble any of the world's great capitals that L'Enfant so admired. There are many reasons for this, but perhaps the most significant is that L'Enfant's plan expressed a national unity and a national spirit that simply did not exist through most of the nineteenth century. Divided over issues of commerce and slavery, the states did not put much trust in a central government or much investment in a national capital.

A turning point in Washington's transformation into a true capital city was the administration of Alexander ("Boss") Shepherd. Shepherd became head of the Board of Public Works in 1870 and became governor of the territory in 1873; under his direction the city paved hundreds of miles of roads, developed a modern sewage system, and constructed over a thousand buildings. Although dramatically changing the profile of the city, Shepherd's initiatives (and substantial cost overruns) caused Congress to abolish the District's territorial government. With the passage of the Organic Act in 1878, Congress put the Senate Committee on the District of Columbia in charge of Washington, beginning a century of direct congressional control over the city.

As a result of Washington's slow growth and its peculiar, unilateral governing structure, policy makers saw much of the area, especially around that of the Mall, as a tabula rasa for future planning efforts. Buoyed by the enthusiasm for urban grandeur displayed in force at the 1893 Columbian Exposition and emboldened by the U.S. victory in the Spanish-American war, politicians began to contemplate resuscitating the dream of a national capital city that could take its place on the world stage.

Lessons from the White City

When the members of the Senate Park Commission took the opportunity of Washington's centennial in 1900 to rebuild the nation's capital, they already had some experience in constructing idealized urban spaces. The array of urban design experts who planned the Washington we know today were the same men who were instrumental in designing the White City built for the Columbian Exposition only a decade earlier in Chicago, and their plan for the capital city bears the imprint of this earlier experiment in city making.[5]

Although most of its buildings were only temporary structures, hastily fashioned out of steel frames, plaster, and spray paint, the sheer scale of the model White City (popularly named both for its luminous appearance and the promise of a utopian urbanism it conveyed) astonished the millions of visitors who came to Chicago during the fair's six-month run on the shores of Lake Michigan. The White City's size was matched only by the scale and intricacy of its displays of scientific, technological, and artistic progress. Each structure erected in the White City served a specific purpose or lauded a specific accomplishment in modern life, from buildings devoted to Administration, Electricity, and Transportation to the behemoth dedicated to Manufactures and Liberal Arts. Even women's accomplishments (in everything from culinary arts to painting and sculpture) were housed in their own building.[6]

Like other world's fairs before it, the Columbian Exposition showcased the triumph of the modern and the urban by contrasting it with the primitive and the exotic, the spaces of civility against the spaces of otherness. Indeed, the spatial arrangement of the White City mapped the interstitial space of power-knowledge, taxonomizing what was central to, and what was peripheral to, Western civilization. The Midway Plaisance (ironically located near the Women's Building, and often omitted from maps of the fair) featured exhibits that offered visitors the chance to experience a street in Cairo or a Javanese village.[7] As Robert Rydell argues, cultural hegemony was inscribed even in the arrangement of the exhibits on the Midway itself, locating more "advanced" nations closer to the center of the White City.[8] Everything, including the others of modernity, had and kept its place within the confines of the fairgrounds.

Most strikingly to many visitors, each aspect of the White City was part of a comprehensive plan. Each component contributed to its total effect: plazas and buildings, of course, but also street signs and street widths, lampposts and bridges, the shapes of the trees used in landscaping and the stones used in building—all of these were legitimately subsumed under the purview of civic art and city beautification. Rather than "mere units of an aggregation," the White City's spaces were planned with an eye towards the whole; for the first time, the city was planned so that each part of its parts was functionally and spatially distinct from the other, while each contributing to the life and beauty of the larger entity.[9]

The White City also elicited praise for its impeccable sanitation. Prevalent water closets, filtered drinking water, and a state of the art sewage treatment system insured that both the "residents" of the model city and the city itself were not only orderly but also clean. One commentator noted approvingly that "for a nickel one could get at frequent intervals clean hands and face and a smooth head of hair."[10] A modern city should provide for the improvement of its citizens' bodily habits and hygiene, and create the conditions for a truly civilized public sphere; as one writer raved: "The substantial macadamized roads were laid as though they were to serve the next generation but were cleaned as though there were to be no tomorrow. The nightly cleaning was followed by the watchful care of the day sweepers."[11] With its uniform, larger-than-life neoclassical buildings, immaculate boulevards, green parks, and decorative fountains, the marvel on the shores of Lake Michigan represented hope and renewal for American cities. Sociologist Charles Zueblin, who traveled the country promoting city beautification, wrote that the White City was "an epitome of the best we had done, and a prophecy of what we could do."[12]

The Columbian Exposition's clean, ordered, functional spaces differed markedly from the chaotic spaces of actual turn-of-the-century American cities. Clearly demarcated zones of activity and identity, populated by clean, middle-class bodies,[13] were a welcome change from the city's usual ambiguity, anonymity, and alterity, and made it a startling visual contrast to the actual city of Chicago: "Both . . . were lapped by the waves of Lake Michigan whose blue-green waters penetrated deep into the heart of each city. In the one case the waters were bordered by ugly docks and warehouses, spanned by hideous buildings, and defiled by the city's foulness, while they flowed under a murky sky. In the other, they were lined by fairy architecture, immaculate docks and strips of verdure and crossed by graceful bridges, while the clearness of an azure sky found reflection in the pure waters."[14]

By mimicking and sanitizing only the best aspects of the urban experience, the White City alleviated many of the anxieties generated by nineteenth-century urban life. The actual city, as one commentator of the time wrote, is "a surprise to its own inhabitants. It grows beyond all prophecy; it develops in unexpected directions; it increases in territory and population at a pace which is scarcely less than appalling."[15] Actual cities were unpredictable and excessive, intemperate and gluttonous: they consumed unprecedented amounts of energy and people, and expelled equally obscene amounts of filth and pollution. "We are tired of polluted air and water, dirty streets, grimy buildings and disordered cities," critics complained.[16] The kaleidoscopic intensities of urban life—in the words of Georg Simmel, the "rapid telescoping of changing images, pronounced differences within what is grasped in a single glance, and the unexpectedness of violent stimuli"[17]—were disorienting and unsettling; residents of the city were constantly being bombarded by external forces, changing circumstances, strange bodies.

Through comprehensive planning, though, the city became less threatening. In contrast to the psychic and bodily threats that urban life posed daily to its citizens, the White City offered its inhabitants the promise of a "delicious safety," an "unspeakable and indescribable relief to move freely in the midst of the great throngs and not feel in imminent danger." Planned cities such as this would breed "well-behaved and good natured crowds," rather than boisterous or disorderly mobs.[18] Viewed next to Chicago (or as the president of the American League for Civic Improvement put it, the Black City)—a "very real and very earthly city, full of faults"—the clean and relatively homogenous space of the White City was a "symbol of regeneration," a rebirth out of the rubble and rubbish that characterized turn-of-the-century urban life.[19]

The Columbian Exposition was a tremendous success, attracting over 700,000 visitors on a single day, and over twenty-two million over the course of its six month run. By offering the public a controlled, clean, attractive "urban" experience, the fair succeeded in bringing back middle-class professionals (who had already begun to move out to the suburbs) back to the "city" (if only an artificial one); comprehensive city planning, it was discovered, also had significant commercial possibilities. As George Kriehn argued in his definitive article on the subject, investment in city beautification as exemplified in the White City *paid:* in tourism, in real estate values, and by "attract[ing] a desirable class" of people.[20] Or, as Daniel Burnham argued, by planning a city with regards to the needs of the middle and upper classes, "the greater attractiveness thus produced keeps at home the people of means and taste."[21]

Yet the "citizens" of the commercialized space of the Columbian Exposition were tourists rather than residents. According to one enthusiastic description: "There was not another place in America where the American citizen could feel so much of the pride of popular sovereignty as he could after he paid his half dollar and become a naturalized resident of this municipality. Once within those grounds he was monarch of all he surveyed. He could go anywhere. He could see anything."[22] From the outset, then, city beautification equated citizenship with consumerism, political agency with purchasing power. Cultural differences were arrayed in what Jim Duncan calls "contrived landscapes" of tourism,[23] spaces rendered simultaneously aesthetically pleasing and politically innocuous. The White City was, above all else, a place for diversion, distraction, and escape from rather than engagement with civic life.[24] Such spaces of "entertainmentality," in Timothy Luke's suggestive phrase, bring people together while simultaneously keeping them apart, suspending them in a particular and highly mediated version of reality.[25]

In the decade following its construction and subsequent dismantling on the shores of Chicago, the White City became a highly charged symbol for urban planning discourse.[26] As a heterotopic space that showcased the best of what cities had to offer, while at the same time not being a city at all, it provided an unambiguous response to anxieties over turn-of-the-century urban life. Like many such projects, its version of an urban utopia—clean, functional spaces, productive of an orderly citizenry—was a no-place desiring a population of no-bodies, or rather (since that particular population does not exist) a population of unproblematic bodies, whose materiality would not interfere with the carefully planned spaces of the perfect city.

White City, Capital City

In what would become known as the City Beautiful movement, proponents of the White City model urged others to pursue similar projects in actual American cities. As Washington's centennial approached, a prominent Washington newspaper (*The Washington Star*) and a new national urban planning magazine (*Municipal Affairs*) both proposed that the nation's capital would be the perfect place to actualize the lessons from the White City.[27] Washington would be the site for the nation's first comprehensive city plan.[28]

On March 8, 1901, Senator James McMillan, then Chairman of the Senate Committee on the District of Columbia, introduced a resolution authorizing the use of the Senate contingent fund to pay planning experts for the development and improvement of the entire park system of Washington, D.C. McMillan's plan, revealed to Congress and the public on January 15, 1902, proposed sweeping changes—one might say, monumental changes—to the center of Washington. Although it took almost three decades to complete and certain aspects of the design were never realized, the plan radically altered the landscape of the capital for the twentieth century and beyond.

The centerpiece of this new plan was the reconstruction of the National Mall. Although the Capitol and the White House were built in accordance with L'Enfant's plans for the city, the Mall in 1900 resembled any other city park. Rather than the original design—an open, majestic space complete with a ceremonial boulevard—the Mall in 1900 remained covered with clusters of trees and winding paths, cross-cut by several small streets and (most tragically, for some) the Pennsylvania Railroad. In short, at the turn of the century, the National Mall was not terribly distinct from the rest of the District of Columbia (see Figure 3.1).

In marked contrast to other sorts of urban parks popular at the time (New York's Central Park, for example), McMillan's plan conceived the Mall as a highly formal public space, combining elements from L'Enfant's original designs with lessons from the Columbian Exposition. The Senate Park Commission plan replaced winding paths with axial walkways, private residences with public edifices. The commission's report described the plan for the Mall in this way (see Figures 3.2 and 3.3):

> By the inclusion of the space between Pennsylvania and New York avenues on the north, and Maryland avenue and the Potomac River on the south, the new composition becomes a symmetrical, polygonal, or kite-shaped, figure bisected from east to west by the axis of the Capitol and from north to south by the White House axis. Regarding the Monument as the center, the Capitol as the base, and the White House as the extremity of one arm of a Latin cross, we have at the head of the composition on the banks of the Potomac a memorial site of the greatest possible dignity, with a second and only less commanding site at the extremity of the second arm.[29]

The results were nothing less than majestic: a careful geometry that included formidable, uniform stone buildings, strategically placed monuments, and reflecting ponds and fountains. The Plan created the grounds for the Lincoln and Jefferson Memorials by filling in portions of the Potomac River, thus closing off formerly open vistas with an identifiable perimeter.[30] Each of these separate components worked in combination to produce impressive views of the national capital. In effect, the commission sought to bring the White City to Washington.

Figure 3.1. The Washington Mall circa 1900. Reproduced courtesy of the Library of Congress, LC-USZ62-26801.

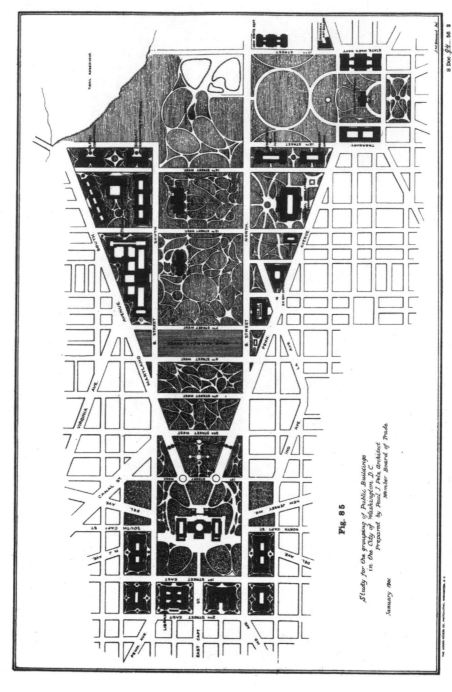

Figure 3.2. 1901 Study for the Washington Mall. Reproduced courtesy of the Library of Congress, LC-USZ62-60169.

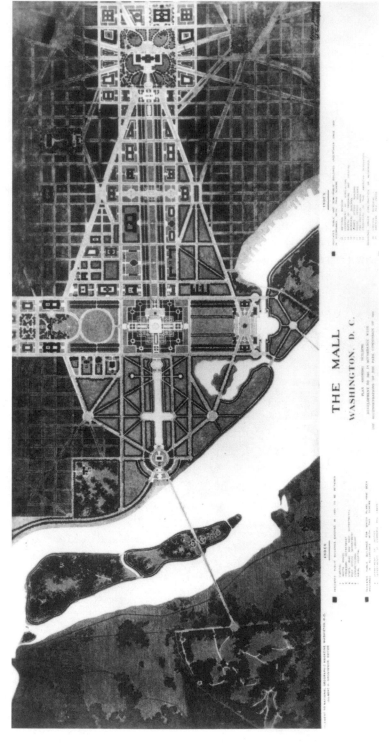

Figure 3.3. The McMillan Plan for the National Mall. Reproduced courtesy of the Library of Congress, LC-USZ62-076235.

Attempting to make Washington a real, functioning White City served three important and interrelated purposes. First, implementing City Beautiful ideals in Washington would provide the city with a much-needed international identity. Especially after the United States' victory in Spain in 1898, rebuilding Washington would be a sign that America could take its place alongside the world's other capital cities.[31] Enduring aesthetic ideals and their realization in beautiful cities were thought to be the necessary outcome of both an individual's and a nation's intellectual and cultural growth. Whereas European countries and their citizens had reached this stage of development centuries before, urban planners in the United States argued that its citizens had at last evolved to this point by the end of the nineteenth century. As Robert Stern argues, closing off expansive vistas through the Potomac landfills represented the closing of the American frontier, a development "key to the nation's maturity."[32] An editorial in *The Century* proclaimed, "We are now at that stage of civilization when . . . we are ready to respond with the fullest appreciation of the best that can be offered."[33]

This was a *telos* that the Senate Park Commission believed could be traced directly to its origins in the Columbian Exposition. As Daniel Burnham declared, "Up to 1893 the American citizen, as a rule, had given little thought to the way that things generally looked around him. Not far then had he advanced in the development of a civic sense of the beauty in the quality, quantity, and relation of the lands and buildings he works and plays in . . . [However,] within him was an instinct groping forward. He wanted an example to give it form, breadth, and a base for grand initiative. He wanted a vision, a picture materializing his yearnings. The World's Fair came, and disclosed what all were unconsciously waiting to receive, a lesson in landscape architecture."[34] While we might snicker at the idea that what every human being wants, in an almost primal and instinctual sense, is "a lesson in landscape architecture," Burnham's narrative reflects the hope that by imitating the classical architecture of Greece, Rome, and Paris, and by drawing on the impulses supposedly awakened by the World's Fair, planners could emulate (and eventually replicate) the cultural heritage and tradition found in European cities.[35]

Second, remaking Washington would help to unify the nation. As Charles Moore argued in an article extolling the virtues of Washington beautification, "[A]ny improvements which Congress may undertake in the District of Columbia will be made not alone for the benefit of the comparatively few permanent residents, but for the much greater number of American citizens who have a just pride in seeing that the capital . . . is made worthy of the advancing power and taste of the people."[36] By financing Washington's reconstruction, Congress would be building a symbol of newly expanded federal power and stronger ideals of national identity in the wake of the Civil War. Its designers wanted to emphasize that "after a full century of misunderstandings, and conflict of interest . . . we were now one people, with common purposes and aims, common ideals, and a common destiny."[37]

Finally, by emphasizing national unity, the rebuilt space of Washington would forge a new kind of citizen, and catalyze unprecedented patriotism. The National Mall would be an instrument for civic education, a built space that made visible—made spectacular—the values and virtues required of its citizens. The Mall would help to (re)create "Americanness:" a "particular persona," as Timothy Luke describes it, "that requires constant reinvention and reaffirmation."[38] Like the art of the City Beautiful movement more generally, the public art planned for the center of Washington was heroic art, nationalist art, where a person could encounter his heroes daily in the sculptures and statues that populated parks and plazas. Strong and vibrant public art, it was postulated, would inspire a strong and vibrant political culture, where ". . . the state, government, the ideals of parties, are no longer abstractions, but are concrete things to be loved or hated, worked for, and done visible homage to."[39]

In short, rebuilding the Mall was not just an exercise in comprehensive urban planning, but rather served the more general purpose of using the urban landscape to cultivate a singular national identity and project that identity to the world. In their annual report issued that year, the Washington Board of Trade made this connection between city, nation, and citizen bodies explicit: "The bloodshed of the Revolution created the Federal Union and the Capital. The bloodshed of the Civil War developed a nation and a national city. The bloodshed of the war with Spain washes out all traces of civil struggle, reunites the national elements, and expands and promotes the nation and the national city."[40]

He Who Runs Must Read

Monuments and monumental architecture were crucial to producing a unified civic identity. "It becomes a part of the education of a people," wrote one commentator, "to have the great events of our history put before them in enduring and beautiful forms, so that 'he who runs must read,' so that every great event will be endeared to each person and made definite and permanent in the mind by a living picture that shall endure."[41] The civic lessons to be built into the Mall were lessons that everyone could comprehend, regardless of his ethnic background or level of education. George Kriehn argued that ". . . monuments teach glory more eloquently than any books," because "[n]othing would be a more effective agent in making good citizens of our foreign population than such monuments. Many of them cannot read English books, but they can read monuments which appeal to the eye."[42] In this way, citizenship would be fashioned through the built environment; a citizen would recognize American values built into the parks where he strolled, the plazas where he lunched, the landmarks by which he oriented himself to his surroundings. Washington's monumental space, like all monumental space, was not just meant to be looked at but was also to be lived; citizenship was enacted through imitation.

Monuments, then, are crucial conduits of symbolic power. Monuments are meant "to inspire the beholder with high ideals and to emulation of deeds of self-sacrifice, valor or patriotism";[43] they are meant to *make* citizens out of an otherwise heterogeneous, unmanageable population. The monumental space of the Mall was supposed to offer every member of the society an image of that membership to imitate; as Henri Lefebvre maintains, a monument is intended to provide a *mirror* of what it means to be a citizen.[44] The act of reading and internalizing the language of monuments is part of the performativity of nationalism, in which national identity is "constituted not by 'a founding act but rather a regulated pattern or repetition.'"[45]

Yet if monuments are meant to be mirrors, they are peculiar mirrors, for several reasons. First, if they are mirrors, monuments are telling for what is *not* reflected in them, and why. As Dietrich Schirmer notes, "the symbolic politics of American nationalism is . . . a politics of omission."[46] Such exclusions are rarely arbitrary or coincidental. Take, for example, the African Americans who, while being denied citizenship and political representation, helped to build the Capitol, the very symbol of America's republican democracy. Ironically (far too weak a word) African Americans also helped to cast the bronze Statue of Freedom that adorns the Capitol dome—a statue that was installed in 1863, before African Americans had achieved the status of full persons in the U.S. Constitution.[47]

When the "others" of citizenship are depicted in monumental architecture, they are often shown only to reinforce their subordinate status. For example, several of the nineteen panels in the Rotunda frieze of the Capitol Building depict the history of Native American–settler relations in the United States as part of the general story of progress and civilization that the frieze narrates. Allegorical figures in the frieze also depict raced and gendered aspects of power. In one panel, America (embodied as a white woman) stands in the center with her spear and shield. To her right sits a young Native American woman with a bow and arrows, who represents "the untamed American continent."[48] In another example, in the fresco in the dome of the Capitol

Building, George Washington is presented as a god sitting in the heavens; gathered around him are thirteen "maidens" representing the colonies.[49] In this schema, men appear as actual historical figures and übercitizens; mythical women may represent nations and peoples, but are not actors in them or on behalf of them in the same way. As Joanne Sharp argues, "The female is a prominent *symbol* of nationalism and honor. But this is a symbol to be protected by masculine agency."[50]

Thus monuments do not actually "reflect" so much as they imagine, mythologize, and distort important characteristics of their subjects. To some extent, this kind of distortion or reduction is inevitable; it is a necessary consequence of any process of representation, whether aesthetic or political. For example, it is not surprising to us that representations of "Americans"—from the imposing figure of Lincoln to the figures sculpted into the edifice of the Capitol Building—are almost always members of the dominant class (white, wealthy, able-bodied men). In this way, the many (bodies, in all their particularity and plurality) are reduced to the one. Such symbolic, physical representations of citizenship in this case are part of what David Roediger refers to as the "wages of whiteness"; in the words of W. E. B. DuBois, "a sort of public and psychological wage," a privilege granted by virtue of skin color.[51]

Yet even the impressive figures that are included in the American pantheon of monumental citizens aren't *themselves;* their identities are often strangely contorted to suit particular, political purposes. James Loewen describes a striking example of this in the Jefferson Memorial. By altering or misleadingly juxtaposing diverse quotations from Jefferson's writings and etching them into marble, Loewen argues, the Memorial represents Jefferson as a proto-abolitionist who rallied for racial equality instead of as a slave owner whose attitudes and actions towards African Americans often contradicted his otherwise democratic sensibilities. The point is not simply to replace a hagiographic version of history with something that exposes the flaws of our heroes. Rather, Loewen writes, the Jefferson Memorial erases the complexity of an important American problem—the reality of racial injustices perpetrated in an ostensibly democratic system—and replaces it with a convenient and simplistic narrative of national progress.[52] As Jenny Edkins contends, it is in this way that "dominant powers can use commemoration as a means of *forgetting* past struggles," obscuring the strife and violence entailed in maintaining civil order.[53] In this case, the monument does not mirror but (re)constructs identity, history, and citizenship, by reinforcing the nation's symbolic unity at the expense of a potentially productive dialogue.

These examples might not be considered particularly troublesome in themselves because as our country evolves, as more rights are extended to different populations, as the dominant class becomes more diffuse, and as the category of "citizen" becomes more diverse (the reasoning would follow), monuments-as-mirrors will become more accurate, and the images of important others— whose bodies do not conform to the white, male able-bodied image—will become incorporated into our national hagiography. More importantly, these others will be represented as actors in history, rather than as those on whose behalf the "real" subjects of history acted.

In fact, as we shall see in more detail in Chapter 5, monumental space *has* become more reflective of more varieties of citizens, as African Americans, women, and Asian Americans (to name a few such groups) have all claimed access to symbolic space. Yet this development also demonstrates the limits of identity politics; as more groups (rightfully) demand representation in what Judith Baca calls the "cannon in the park"[54]—and the space for these representations is finite—we are forced to confront thorny political questions that accompany a simplistic pluralism: which groups have a "right" to symbolic space? How can we allocate symbolic space for underprivileged groups without—often literally and spatially—marginalizing them? And how do we inventory the groups "worthy" of symbolic representation (African Americans, women, Asians, gays and lesbians, persons with disabilities . . .) without devolving into what Judith Butler has called an "embarrassed et cetera"?

Understanding monuments as mirrors is also problematic, though, because of what this implies about the nature of identity, agency, and symbolic power. For the proponents of the City Beautiful movement, the symbolic power generated through monumental architecture was unidirectional; that is, monuments were meant to be read, their meanings unambiguous, their professed values internalized, and these values then acted on. The images of citizenship that monuments offer us by this account are ossified images; monuments are meant to fix the citizen-body and national identity in space and time. Monumental space—at least the neoclassical variant envisioned in the Park Commission plan—reflects the desire for certitude and finality, serving (or hoping) to, as Steve Pile argues, "make space incontestable, both by closing off alternative readings and by drawing people into the presumption that the values they represent are shared."[55] For the architects of the Mall, monumental space would literally write a particular version of citizenship into stone, thus erasing the ambivalence of history and the instability of identity.

Clearly, this formulation implies a rather simplistic relationship between the signifier (monumental forms) and the signified (whatever values, histories, or peoples the monument is said to represent).[56] Monuments, rarely (if ever) convey only one meaning, even when their symbolism seems especially clear. Monuments always require an interpretive act on the part of the spectator. For example, a white Southerner (schooled in the primacy of states' rights and the concerns over commerce that were the catalyst for the Civil War) climbing the impossibly steep steps of the Lincoln Memorial and standing next to Lincoln's giant stone knee will likely experience that space differently than a Northerner (schooled in the difficult, yet inevitable, moral triumph of the abolitionist cause). Or, an African American may respond to Richmond's Monument Avenue, replete with enormous statues of confederate Civil War heroes, differently than a white native of that city.[57] What Lauren Berlant calls "the fantasy-work of national identity" is just that: a myth of common origins, a fiction of a shared destiny.[58] Because there is no singular "American experience," people bring their own identities, histories, values, and understandings to these sites, interacting with them rather than simply being acted on by them.

Second (and related to the first point), all monumental space is not created equal. Maya Lin's Vietnam Veterans Memorial (VVM) is cited frequently as an example of monumental space that eloquently—and deliberately—communicates ambivalence and ambiguity rather than certainty and finality.[59] When the Vietnam Veterans Fund sponsored the competition to create an appropriate memorial, it gave explicit directions that the design should not include the "politics" of the war. Yet from the very beginning, this built space was fraught with political struggle. As Lin herself describes it, despite her best efforts to create an "apolitical memorial"—one that did not "take sides" in interpreting the conflict—even the most basic building decisions regarding the VVM became highly politicized: "For instance," she writes, "the granite [used in the memorial] could not come from Canada or Sweden. Though those countries had beautiful black granites, draft evaders went to both countries, so the veterans felt we could not consider their granites as options. (The stone finally selected came from India)."[60] Indeed, many people objected to using the color black for the walls of the monument at all; Lin was told that "the color black was called the 'universal color of shame and dishonor' . . . It took a prominent four-star general, Brigadier General George Price, who happened to be black, testifying before one of the countless subcommittee hearings and defending the color black, before the design could move forward."[61]

Lin consciously tried to avoid interpreting the conflict for visitors, but in so doing she also created a space where people could create their own interpretations, either individually or as part of a community. For example, Lin designed the memorial to encourage interaction between the structure and its audience; she writes that in the VVM she sought "to create an intimate dialogue with the viewer, to allow a place of contemplation."[62] To facilitate this

sort of "intimate dialogue," Lin chose to use the smallest available typeface—
one that requires the viewer to come up very close to the monument—to
list the veterans' names. Although the complete list of the dead and missing
was initially a requirement by the Veterans Memorial Fund that sponsored
the project, Lin eventually concluded that "the need for the names to be on
the memorial *would become* the memorial; there was no need to embellish
the design further."[63] As a result, Lin says, "the work [has] a tactile quality.
. . . This active participation with my work involves the viewer in a direct
and intimate dialogue with the work."[64] On any given day one can see people
standing close to the wall, touching the names of the veterans, or making
pencil rubbings of them. The VVM is visited by over one million people
every year, and surely its popularity is due in part to Lin's design choices.

However, one of the most powerful aspects of the VVM is not in viewing the sculpture itself but looking at what people have left behind there.
At the base of the wall, one can often find letters, poems, and photographs;
stuffed animals and service ribbons; mortarboard tassels; Bibles or Hershey's
kisses. Since its completion in 1982, over thirty thousand objects have been
left at the wall; they are collected each day by the National Park Service and
housed in the Vietnam Veterans Memorial Collection.[65] This spontaneous
and fluid "monument" exists alongside and in conjunction with the original
sculpture—and in no way could it have been predicted by Lin or mandated
by her design. Instead of creating a space devoid of politics, then, Lin's design
allows for competing perspectives to exist simultaneously. That is, rather than
closing off interpretation and speculation about the work's meanings, more
democratic monuments might open them up.

Finally, even a widely shared interpretation of a monument can change
over time. Despite the best intentions of their creators, as Jenny Edkins writes,
"memorials in stone are not permanent, and their intended message—whatever
it is—can change as it is seen by different generations or co-opted into new
purposes."[66] An intriguing example of the revaluation of monumental space is
in Santo Domingo, where a monument that former dictator Raphael Trujillo
originally ordered to be built in his honor was repainted with the images of
the Mirabel sisters. Trujillo had ordered the murders of the three women in
1960; "the Butterflies," as they are known, became martyrs for democracy in
the Dominican Republic. In 1997, the monument was then rededicated to their
memory, turning El Obelisco del Malecón into the canvas for a painting titled
"A Song to Liberty."

Monuments, then, are never *only* mirrors; as agents of representation,
they reduce, expand, contort, deform, embellish or streamline what they
purport to reflect. At the same time, the multiple (and often contested) mean-

ings that monuments generate are never fully anticipated or controlled by their creators. Instead, the symbolic topography of citizenship is continually reinterpreted and renegotiated in ways that may subvert its original intentions. Monumental space, then, is paradoxical. On one hand, monuments can create a hegemonic landscape, where the dominant culture is legitimated, preserved, and transmitted. On the other hand, attempts to fix meaning and identity in any system of signification are always imperfect, and excesses of meaning generated through experience, interpretation, and history escape even the most rigid intentionality.

City Beautiful, Body Beautiful

For the makers of Washington, however, monuments were enduring testaments to heroism, their meanings transparent and their purposes obvious. This was serious work, and thus the production of symbolic unity through city beautification was also a gendered production; monument building, park planning, and landscaping was also the work of sexing the body politic. In fact, the word "beautiful" in the City Beautiful movement was a site of contention, as city planners repeatedly tried to emphasize that their project involved more than cosmetic changes or "feminine adornment."[67] As the advocates of the City Beautiful were eager to point out, "there is nothing effeminate and sentimental about it, like tying tidies on telegraph poles and putting doilies on the crosswalks"; rather, it is "vigorous, virile, sane."[68] In other words, the masculine endeavor of arranging and beautifying public space ("landscape architecture") had to be kept distinct from the traditional "feminine" tasks of arranging and beautifying private space ("housekeeping").[69] As we shall see, the symbolic unity of the body politic as exemplified in the National Mall was achieved in part through containing (feminine or feminized) elements of the citizen-body that threatened to overflow, subvert, or undo it.

In short, making the city beautiful in the case of Washington was an exercise in making the body beautiful: isolating and reifying the virtues associated with the proper citizen body so as to communicate a univocal representation of the body politic. Of course, as Moira Gatens points out, such a representation is by definition an impossibility, since "images of human bodies are images of men's bodies or women's bodies," not "human bodies" as such.[70] In a very explicit sense—from the "great white shaft of the Washington Monument . . . to the Capitol itself"[71]—the Mall was designed to be an expression of spectacular and masculine power, conferring on the nation an appropriately authoritative symbolic landscape. The plan advanced by the Senate Park Commission aimed to materialize and spatialize a symbolic national unity, and to make eminently visible the contours of a proper citizen body.

Acknowledging the symbolic power of monuments in shaping the contours of citizenship allows us to flesh out (so to speak) how differences are made material, and built into the everyday awareness of individuals. Though we may experience monuments differently, they remain the official markers by which we are oriented to our history and memory, both individual and collective. The National Mall is a normalizing, symbolic, and heterotopic space: set apart from the rest of the city while at the same time being integral to it, a real space full of mythic images, where larger-than-life figures signify a presumably universal history of American citizenship.

Such a space was crucial at a time when the "common destiny" based in national identity was becoming increasingly difficult to specify. New bodies—those of former slaves, recent immigrants, and politically active women—were challenging the singularity of this identity. Anxiety over these other bodies manifested itself across the country in compulsory civic education in classrooms, in more regular city censuses, and in social reforms aimed at improving the health, housing, and hygiene of recent immigrants.[72] Washington was not isolated from these new urban issues. In fact, in the decades immediately before and after the Civil War, Washington became an important destination for former slaves; whereas blacks represented about one-fourth of the city's population until 1850, they represented about one-third the total population by 1870. European immigrants were drawn to Washington as well; the white population in 1850 was around forty thousand but exceeded one hundred thousand in 1870.[73] Learning how to address the problems posed by these new populations was of paramount importance, because (as one reformer so aptly stated) "Washington should be a model for the nation—not a warning."[74] As one prominent newspaper front page implored, "Let us make our city just as every true American would like to have it."[75] Beautifying the city would allow it to serve as a built expression of national identity, a body politic not only ideational but material.

"Plague Spots": Inhabited Alleys and Abject Bodies

Thus Washington's rapid expansion in the nineteenth century gave rise to a second type of urban planning discourse: social reform. As part of his efforts to understand, "humanly speaking," the problems faced by the city's poorest residents, social reformer Charles Weller took up residence in the Washington alleys for a short time and describes his first encounter with alley life:

> It is with some misgiving that one leaves the well lighted outer streets with their impressive residences and turns into a narrow passageway where he must walk

by faith, not by sight. Noises which faintly recall those of the Midway Plaisance at the world's fair, grow faintly louder as the explorer approaches the wider inside alleys. Night with its dark shadows accentuates the strangeness of the scene. Near a gas light . . . a group of people are seen playing roughly together. A cheap phonograph near by rasps out a merry ditty. The shrill cries of children pierce the air as the ragged, dirty youngsters dart among their elders. . . . From the little mission in an alley parlor comes occasionally a wail of primitive, weird chanting. An uncouth black man lounges up to a buxom young woman and hugs her. On a doorstep nearby a young man is heard arguing with his mistress and begging her to "le' me ha' fi' cen's." . . . Pandemonium reigns. One sees no immediate cause for fear, but feels intuitively a suggestion of evil possibilities and latent danger.[76]

Here the world's fair imagery is turned on its head; this is not the White City but the Black City, not the harmless faux urbanism and domesticated exoticism of the Midway, but the threat of real violence, and the "primitive" sensuality of otherness itself. Violence, poverty, delinquency, illegitimacy, chaos, and even evil itself occupied those corners of the city hidden from view.

The citizen body expressed in the symbolic space of the Washington Mall found its antithesis in the bodies of the urban poor who populated the Washington alleys at the turn of the century. Although they are frequently treated as distinct (and often opposed) reform impulses in the history of Washington city planning, in many ways, alley and tenement reform paralleled city beautification and mirrored its logic. Despite its often altruistic attempts at improving the living conditions of the alley-dwelling population, alley and tenement reform also had as its goal a city made beautiful by establishing and policing the parameters of a proper citizen body.

The space of the National Mall as conceived in the McMillan Plan—a spectacular public space of vistas and vision—could not be more different from the rest of the District. L'Enfant's grand grillwork of cross-cutting streets and axial boulevards produced large city blocks, which he divided into deep building lots. The impressive streetside residences on these plots of land, L'Enfant reasoned, would be serviced through the intricate systems of back-alleys that provided rear entrances to them. As a result, Washington's tall, narrow rowhouses, built side by side around city blocks, enclosed alleyways and courts that were nearly inaccessible and invisible from main roads (see Figure 3.4).

Although these small back streets were not originally designed for housing, increases in Washington's population, especially after the Civil War, provided ample opportunities for landowners to build inexpensive, often substandard dwellings at the backs of streetside residences to house poor tenants.[77] Prior

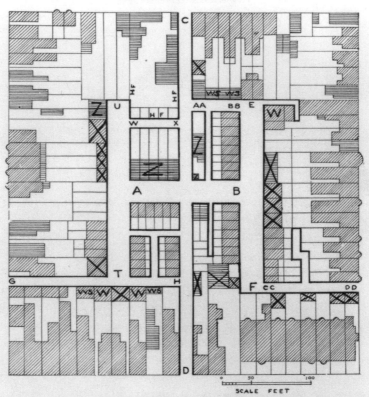

Exact Drawing of "Blagden's Alley" and Surrounding Square Between Ninth
and Tenth, M and N Streets, N. W.

[Drawing by Kemp, Stone and Craig]

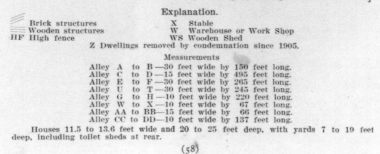

Explanation.

Brick structures	X	Stable
Wooden structures	W	Warehouse or Work Shop
HF High fence	WS	Wooden Shed
	Z Dwellings removed by condemnation since 1905.	

Measurements

Alley A to B —30 feet wide by 150 feet long.
Alley C to D —15 feet wide by 495 feet long.
Alley E to F —30 feet wide by 265 feet long.
Alley U to T —30 feet wide by 245 feet long.
Alley G to H —10 feet wide by 220 feet long.
Alley W to X —10 feet wide by 67 feet long.
Alley AA to BB—15 feet wide by 66 feet long.
Alley CC to DD—10 feet wide by 137 feet long.

Houses 11.5 to 13.6 feet wide and 20 to 25 feet wide, with yards 7 to 19 feet deep, including toilet sheds at rear.

(58)

Figure 3.4. A drawing of Blagden Alley from Charles Weller's *Neglected Neighbors.*
Reproduced courtesy of the Roosevelt Collection, The Harvard College Library.

to the development of mass transit, service providers and city workers needed to be close to their places of employment, and the deep lots provided room for the construction of a veritable second city of service workers, hidden behind the first.[78] Unlike "rear tenements" in other cities, alley buildings in Washington did not face the main street but looked inward, toward networks of small streets and buildings entirely closed off from the main avenues. In the 1880s, alley dwelling reached its peak. The alley population was estimated at twenty-five thousand, and the welfare of alley residents became an important issue in social reform.

The alleys posed a problem for the city for many reasons. The most straight-forward of these was that at the turn of the century, many of Washington's alleys housed the very poorest of the city's poor. The rates of illness and mortality in the alleys far surpassed the rates of disease and death for those residing on the main streets. Beginning in the last quarter of the nineteenth century, a number of studies focused public and political attention on the prevalence of disease and poverty in these areas and called for substantive improvements in the quality of life of the alley residents.[79]

Distress over overcrowding, inadequate or nonexistent sanitation, prevalent sickness, and the dearth of pure air pervade these early studies, which describe the deplorable alley conditions in great (and greatly repetitive) detail. For example, an 1874 report of the Board of Health notes that alley homes often had ". . . [l]eaky roofs, broken and filthy ceilings, dilapidated floors, overcrowded, below grade, having stagnant water underneath, no drainage, no pure water supply . . . having filthy yards, dilapidated, filthy privy and leaky privy box . . . [and were] unfit for human habitation."[80] And an investigator reported to Weller that when he visited the alleys ". . . there was a large pool of water in the roadway, covered with green slime. . . . [T]he roofs leak more or less and when plastering falls it is not replaced . . . the backyards are already damp; all sewage connections run under the house."[81] Both the inhabitants of the alleys and the spaces themselves were ripe contagions threatening the rest of the city, for ". . . such ill-conditioned hovels are culture beds of disease, the germs of which may be carried far and wide by the flies which feed on the rotting garbage and excreta."[82] Weller described a gruesome parade of condemned tenants who moved into (and were subsequently carried out of) contaminated homes, which he called "death traps, filled with tubercle bacilli of whose existence and deadliness the innocent new tenants are not informed."[83]

A variety of legislative initiatives at the turn of the century sought to bring the alley problem under control. As early as 1892, Congress passed significant legislation prohibiting the future construction of dwellings in Washington's alleys.[84] Ten years later, at the same time he chaired the Senate Park Commission, Senator McMillan helped the Senate Committee on the District of Columbia to create the Board for the Condemnation of Insanitary Buildings, permitting the city to destroy alley dwellings that did not meet contemporary standards of sanitation or structural safety.[85] Also during this time nationally recognized housing reformer Jacob Riis was brought to Washington to view the alleys, and his report convinced President Roosevelt to convene the President's Homes Commission, which produced a systematic study of the alleys and proposed possible legislative remedies. The purpose of the Homes Commission Report, its author pronounced, was "to map out and organize the city's future development in lines of civic social service, just as Major L'Enfant and the recent Park Commission planned the arrangement of her streets and parks."[86]

The result of these initiatives was a significant decrease in the alley dwelling population by 1910. No new dwellings were built in alleys after 1892, and several hundred of the houses, shacks, and huts in these alleys and courts were demolished under the direction of the Board for the Condemnation of Insanitary Dwellings. The number of inhabited alleys shrank, and the alley population was approximately halved.[87] What dwellings remained were, according to the Washington Board of Commissioners, structurally safe, not in themselves unsanitary, and had no reason to be shut down under the red light district laws of the time.[88] "We have accomplished all we can accomplish under the existing law," Commissioner Siddons concluded.[89]

Yet the alleys continued to vex reformers. Whether or not there were pockets of "decent folk" living in "decent homes" in the alleys seemed to make no difference. Furthermore, it seemed to make no difference that property owners were still making considerable profits from their alley-dwelling tenants, and by closing off the alleys, politicians and reformers would jeopardize these investments.[90] Finally, calculating crime rates in the alleys was more of an art than a science. "Moral delinquencies are hard to measure," one reformer admitted. "I have endeavored to get figures that would show something with respect to arrests of dwellers in alleys, but no records have ever been kept."[91] One social settlement reformer went so far as to assert that "we have not here a criminal population. The story is one simply of low standards . . . and a monotonous round of petty offenses."[92] Thus by 1914, policy makers could conclude that there were "a great many houses on alleys that are in pretty good condition and could not possibly be considered a nuisance."[93]

Regardless, then, of evidence to the contrary—regardless of the presence or absence of modern conveniences in alley houses, regardless of the profits extracted from the alley inhabitants, and regardless of the presence or absence of crime in the alleys—legislators and social reformers unequivocally contended that ". . . we should aim to *put an end* to the living of human beings in the alleys and courts of the National Capital. Even where you may find a house that is sanitary in and of itself, we still stand and urge . . . that legislation ought to be enacted by Congress that will forbid, in some reasonable way, the further habitation of the alleys."[94]

To accomplish this, Congress proposed in the Act of 1914 that "in the interest of public health, morals, and safety" the alleys should be declared unfit as places of human habitation.[95] Beginning on July 1, 1918, using any alley building as a place of residence would be considered unlawful, effectively emptying the alley spaces and rendering approximately twelve thousand people homeless.[96] Whereas previous legislative and reform activity had focused on broadly defined concerns for sanitation and public health, by 1914 alley dwelling *itself* was the problem; regardless of one's specific circumstances, living in the alleys, the Board of Commissioners argued, was "always productive of evil conditions."[97] And as Charles Weller concluded, this fact necessitated only one outcome: "alleys are evil [;] . . . their conversion into wholesome streets is quite essential to the common weal."[98]

What about alleys, specifically, was "evil"? (For that matter, why were the streets dubbed "wholesome"?) What about alley dwelling made reformers want not simply to improve alley conditions, but (as the magazine *Charities* put it) "to wipe Washington alleys off the map,"[99] to obliterate them from the space of the city? Foucault's account of the link between power and visibility manifest in disciplinary and biopower provides a starting point for analyzing the role of the Washington alleys in policy makers' discourse. However, as I argue next, the alleys also became *symbolically* important to the definition of both the city and citizenship. Washington alleys were heterotopic spaces, existing paradoxically both at the center and at the margins of political life.

Power and Vision

A partial interpretation of the excessive response toward the alleys might be found if we examine more closely the connection between visibility and social control—the connection Foucault elaborates in his analytics of disciplinary power and biopower. Washington's alleys were a social and political problem because they exemplified the invisibility and anonymity made possible by urban life. Quite simply, Washington alleys (appropriately often called "blind alleys") and their residents were hidden from the street; according to reformers at the time, they eluded the influence of a public morality both by not seeing (life outside the alleys) and by not being seen (by municipal authorities). Later called Washington's "secret city,"[100] the alleys were threatening in part because they were unknown territory in the very center of (what was supposed to be) civilization. One could be very familiar with the streets of Washington and have absolutely no knowledge of the city's impoverished interior.[101] As one housing reformer stated, "The Washington alley is peculiar, as it is in very many cases hidden from the view of the street, thus giving absolute seclusion to a class of people who are least likely to resist temptation."[102]

Charles Weller's oft-cited study of the area, aptly titled *Neglected Neighbors,* posits this problem in stark terms: "There is not the slightest relationship between the inside and outside set of homes. Longer acquaintance only strengthens the first impressions that the alley is a new and unfamiliar world. It is a case of Dr. Jekyl and Mr. Hyde in brick and wood, a dual nature incorporated in a prosaic city square."[103] It is not specific amenities (such as indoor plumbing) that are the problem, Weller argues; rather, "[t]he basic evil is the alley's ground plan."[104] The alleys were the monstrous alter ego of a seemingly respectable city, whose pleasant countenance was belied by deep disorder.

The horrible conditions of alleys, reformers reasoned, were perpetuated because alley dwellers could not see the outside world, and were not integrated into life beyond the alleys. "They have not bearing upon them the restraining influences of the daily observation of their better neighbors. They have no one to inspire them with any better ambition," one reformer argued.[105] The problems of the alleys, another continued, could not be solved by keeping these people "out of sight."[106] Instead, they needed to be "gathered in the full view of the public gaze."[107]

But bringing the alley population into public view was no easy feat. At the turn of the century, alleys were unmapped and, in many ways, unmappable sectors of the city. First, the definition of an alley itself was problematic. In more than one instance, public officials proposing legislation affecting the alleys could not articulate any standard definition of the term. Housing reformers and census takers often included small streets in their definitions of alleys.[108] Alleys were also called courts, streets, or cul-de-sacs, making any strict accounting of them impossible.[109] In one attempted clarification of the issue, Frederick Siddons (then Commissioner of the District of Columbia), said exasperatedly to his inquisitors, ". . . a minor street implies something *more than* an alley. A minor street implies a *street,* not an alley," but the Senate committee never agreed on an unequivocal definition.[110]

Furthermore, alley names were unusual and were changed frequently, even capriciously. They often were named by the census takers, the current residents, or according to the landowner of the block at the time.[111] Alleys that might be called M. Goat Alley, Pig Alley, Louse Alley, Quaker Alley, and Willow Tree Alley one year might disappear from city street maps the next.

(Weller notes that "suggestive" names such as these often indicate the low regard even residents had for these places.) One charitable group sought to remedy this problem by publishing a comprehensive Directory of Alleys, to map out the "hidden communities . . . menacing the city."[112] The invisibility of alleys, their illogical names and ambiguous status, disturbed both social reformers and the city police, who had no way to monitor or control alley residents.

In short, alleys posed a problem because their inhabitants eluded the gaze of social reformers and of the state. In the logic of what Mary Poovey calls a specular morality, what is invisible is suspect and potentially threatening.[113] In his *Theory of Moral Sentiments,* Poovey writes that Adam Smith reasoned that individuals are able to remain moral so long as they live in country villages, where their behavior both can be monitored and influenced by their neighbors. However, when a country dweller moves to the city, Smith claimed, he is thereafter "sunk in obscurity and darkness. His conduct is observed and attended to by nobody, and he is therefore very likely to neglect it himself, and to abandon himself to every sort of low prodigality and vice."[114] The link between morality and visibility is concomitant with the rise of capitalism and urbanization, and has underwritten a great deal of political theory, from Rousseau's deep-seated suspicion of the "big city, full of scheming, idle people without religion or principle," to more recent exultations of the "community" (rather than the city) as the apotheosis of civic life.[115] Specular morality, then, is a matter of "seeing and being seen."[116]

Thus while the definition of an "alley" in Washington may have changed from report to report, the most important aspect of every definition was always its degree of visibility. An alley was that space that was invisible from the main road, whereas "a minor street will be . . . wide enough so that police can, as they pass corners, look through the whole length of it . . . and on these people who live on there."[117] The definition of "alley," then, was a sociopolitical—as well as a spatial—definition.

The invisibility or impenetrability of the Washington alleys allowed the alley population to evade what Michel Foucault describes as disciplinary power and biopower. Disciplinary power (occurring at the level of the individual human body) "center[s] on the body as a machine: its disciplining, the optimization of its capabilities, the extortion of its forces . . . its integrations into systems of efficient and economic controls," whereas biopower (organized at the level of the population, or the "species body") details "the body imbued with the mechanics of life and serving as the basis of biological processes: propagation, births and mortality, the level of health, life expectancy and longevity, with all the conditions that can cause these to vary."[118] Both are visually and spatially organized; according to Foucault, the normalizing gaze that combines visibility, record keeping, and social control is built into most of our modern institutions, including that of the state. Surveillance and sanitation (i.e., keeping the public counted and healthy), the two principle concerns of turn-of-the-century urban social reform, both find their expression in these modes of modern power.

Furthermore, as Foucault makes clear, these practices are never free from normative, and normalizing, implications. Indeed, the medical discourse of health and disease very often and very quickly segued from the alley residents' degenerative *physical* conditions and dilapidated surroundings to their degenerative *moral* conditions: "Our experience in dealing with filth, crowd-poison and disease among these people . . . has taught us that the greatest public economy, viz., the preservation of public health, is defeated by allowing these filthy, worthless, dependent classes of humanity to congregate in the alleys and by-ways out of sight . . . until direful epidemic, incubated and nourished among them, spreads its black wings over the homes of the whole city."[119]

Weller, too, intones solemnly that "the more one learns about Average Alley the more characteristic does immorality appear to be. While there must be many alley families whose conduct is commendable, one is constantly impressed by the large number of households in which at least one or two members are immoral."[120] The "plague spots" that Weller identifies in the city are both "physical and moral swamps," breeding both malaria and its ethical equivalents.[121] Thus, public discourse about alleys focused explicitly on overcrowding, sanitation, and disease (conditions threatening to the physical body), reformers were quick to associate these problems with "[t]he impairment of moral qualities, the degeneration that goes on in the moral nature of man, [and] the evil things that men and women do in darkness and in filth,"[122] (conditions threatening to the sociopolitical body).

Using a Foucauldian lens, then, we might argue that the spaces of the Washington alleys baffled the technologies of disciplinary power and subverted the expansive thrust of biopower. The deviant bodies of the urban poor had to be brought under control, and the labyrinthian quality of alley space impeded this process. Instead of spatially (and therefore demographically) distinct individuals, reformers saw in the alleys anarchic sectors of the city that housed a chaotic, unspecifiable populace, made unmanageable and ungovernable through its invisibility. For this reason, we might postulate, it was imperative that alley residents be made visible, be brought out into the space of the main streets, be brought under the full view of the public gaze.

The difficulty with relying only on the Foucauldian interpretation, however, is that it does not adequately capture the horror with which the Washington alleys were regarded. Recall Charles Weller's description of his initial foray into the alleys quoted at the beginning of this section. Weller's assessment of alley life is not only a rational-cognitive one, based only on the power of a normalizing gaze, masked in the neutrality of scientific reason and progress. His response to his encounter with the alley "others" is also physiological, visceral; we can very well imagine his apprehension in inching down that first, dark alley entrance, and the onslaught of strange behaviors and noises he witnessed in his first few moments on the scene. Simply chalking this up as an instance of disciplinary power is not sufficient.[123]

Let us return, then, to the question of why it was necessary for reformers not to improve alley conditions, but to "wipe Washington alleys off the map." What about the alleys produced these excessive, unreasonable responses? What about the alleys evoked not reform but revulsion?

Lives Linked by Laundry Lines

In part this question can be answered by looking at *who* resided in the alleys and what they did there. Alley dwellers were often black (though some alleys were mixed, and several alleys had all-white populations), and many times disabled, sickly, or elderly.[124] In her house-to-house study of four Washington alleys over the course of a year, Edith Elmer Wood describes the alley population: "There are a large number of old people who are unable to do a full day's work and have no savings laid by for their old age . . . There are a large number of the victims of industrial accidents and industrial diseases. There are a large number of families in which the father is a victim of tuberculosis."[125]

As Iris Young describes, processes of normalization, segregation, and hierarchicalization make certain bodies the (white, male, heterosexual, able-bodied) standard against which all others are measured and found defective. This physical standard is often equated with mental competence and moral goodness, whereas deviations from this norm are thought to be degeneracies made manifest in flesh. Thus whereas a "normal" white, male body is equated with reason, health, beauty, intellect, and moral integrity, other bodies are more readily identified with emotion, frailty, weakness, ugliness, and promiscuity.[126]

In social reformers' accounts of Washington, these deficiencies were also spatialized; the alleys themselves became extensions of deformed or diseased bodies, and alley dwellers' bodies become synonymous with civic decrepitude: "The city might be compared to some great animal lying spread out on the plain, with the life blood not penetrating vigorously to all its parts . . . In short, the community's 'circulation is poor' and some of her extremities,

although not far extended, are partly atrophied."[127] The imperfect materiality of the alley dwellers' bodies, moreover, were often contrasted with the
idealized city they inhabited: "[The alley], with its crowded lodging houses
for Italian laboring men standing close beside the bawdy houses of colored
women, is in striking contrast to the white dome of the Capitol which is
always seen towering above alley hovels and only three blocks away."[128]

Many of the alley-dwellers were single women raising children. Wood
states that the "typical" alley population has ". . . very much more than their
normal proportion of families in which there is no male breadwinner. There
are a large number of widows and deserted wives."[129] In the alleys, "normal"
family relations (a married couple with "legitimate" offspring and a male
breadwinner) and economic relations were often, according to reformers,
"inverted." Because of overcrowding, "alley houses lack privacy, lack provisions for making the family life distinct and sacred. Instead there is discord,
disorder, and a constant, seething 'mixup' of the population."[130] Distant rela-
tives and friends occupied spaces together usually reserved for close family
members: bedrooms, kitchens, bathrooms, or outhouses. Even more striking
to reformers was the fact that ". . . among people whose marital standards are
not developed . . . woman sometimes becomes the more important member of the family. An inquirer at number 27 asks, 'Does Laura Keefe live
here?' Her husband Henry is less important. Alley folks speak usually of
the 'lady who has the room upstairs,' ignoring her male companion. They
refer to Alice Weaver's house instead of Henry Weaver's."[131] "Abnormal" or
"inverted" family relations result in the built environment (rooms, houses,
entire sections) of the alleys (and even the alleys themselves) being gendered
as feminine spaces.

The reason for this inversion, as Weller himself notes, is often economic,
because "[i]n many poor families of all descriptions," he writes, "the woman
is the treasurer and financial manager, but this is carried a long step farther
in typical alley houses where the woman becomes the more certain . . . wage
earner."[132] In fact, alley dwellers were not as isolated from the "main streets"
as many reformers (including Weller himself) initially indicate; rather, the
primary links to life outside the alleys were the various services alley women
performed to earn income for their families. Alley women frequently took
in washing, provided childcare, and worked as servants for more prosperous
families who lived in the streetside dwellings nearby.[133] Sometimes these connections to the outside world were with those of dubious moral character; as
Weller concludes, "The only influences which the Sammons family receive
from the world outside the alley come from the degraded but prosperous
women of 'the division' who pay fancy prices for their laundry work."[134]

But often this service work was performed for very "legitimate" customers. As Jacob Riis reported, "When I argued my case against the Washington slums . . . one smooth-shaven Senator was quite indifferent even to the unheard of contagious-disease record in Willow Tree Alley till I said that clothes lines full of towels hung across the alley. They were from the Senate barber shop which has its washing done there."[135] Weller also confirms this: ". . . [I]n one of the hidden alleys . . . the towels of the Senate barbershop were found to be regularly washed and dried . . . They [the Senators] employ servants who return nightly to these unwholesome hovels. Their nurse girls take the babies home for occasional visits to the alley homes."[136]

In one particularly telling photograph in Weller's book, these connections between alleys and streets along axes of class, race, and gender are made visible and tangible: laundry lines are shown stretched across the alleys and yards of alley homes, literally linking the alley community to streetside residences.[137] (See Figure 3.5.) Thus it was not *all* alley dwellers who were isolated from "wholesome" outside influences, but mainly alley men; women apparently traversed these boundaries regularly, "world" traveling (to use Maria Lugones' evocative phrase)—crossing the boundaries between alley life and street life, between dominant and subordinate cultures—every time they went to work.[138]

That women were the primary points of contact between alley life and the outside world had significant consequences for the social status of alley men, who often become known as "lovers" (rather than husbands, fathers, breadwinners, or providers): "Next door to the Keefe house the young woman in the lower front room is often asked for money by the young man whom she really 'keeps.' Some men are supported almost entirely by women who give them money earned in housework or even drawn from other men."[139] Such men were viewed by reformers like Weller as emasculated, and contributed to a larger culture of chronic weakness and dependency in the alleys. Whether by virtue of "inverted" sexual relations, illness, disability, or illegitimacy, alley dwellers were seen as morally weak and wrongfully dependent, "an idle class, and . . . living in those alleys under those conditions produces just that class," as Commissioner Siddons argued.[140] Another reformer reported that "[t]he class of people who live in alleys are peculiarly susceptible to the suggestion of example, especially unable to resist the temptation that seeks them out . . . [they are] well-meaning but weak persons . . . removed from the tonic action of public opinion and cut off from the general life of the community."[141]

Recent feminist scholarship has demonstrated how "dependency" became feminized and stigmatized over the course of the nineteenth and twentieth centuries.[142] As Young argues, "independence" is the principle virtue of the (male)

Figure 3-5. Laundry lines in the alleys. Reproduced courtesy of the Library of Congress, LCUSF33T01-171-M2.

citizen and property owner in a modern democratic republic.[143] Independence allows individuals to participate in economic transactions and political discussions, and the result of any agreement made by independent (freely contracting, equal) agents can then legitimately be called "just." If one does not possess the resources or abilities presumed by the virtue of independence—if one is judged to be "dependent"—then one is deemed incapable of participating fully in either economic or political life. A dependent person is feminized in the eyes of the state, as one who cannot make choices for herself, and so requires others to make choices for her. The results of "normatively privileging independence in this sense," Young continues, "implies judging a huge number of people in liberal societies as less than full citizens."[144]

The ideals of citizenship extolled by the Senate Park Commission and materialized in the National Mall stood opposed to the feminized masses embodied in the alleys. Indeed, building the body politic has always been an act of "man's creative power, that is *art(ifice)*" that defines itself against dependence and unreason.[145] Yet the alleys also served a heterotopic function by acting to mirror and invert dominant cultural values, thus undermining the binary logic that claimed that the "street" and the "alley" were distinct and opposed.

Symbolic Power and Abjection

Certainly alley dwellers were exemplars of a public feminized in this way. But alley residents were not only rendered dependent sub-citizens but also sub-*human* in their association with tuberculosis, malaria, promiscuity, high birth rates, high death rates, and leaky privy boxes. Reports like Weller's appeal to reactions more visceral than visual—reactions to filth, disease, waste, contagion, and infection—fearful, disgusted reactions to smell and taste and touch. Although alley dwellings were certainly subject to intrusive inspection, this was an inspection that often produced aversion, repulsion, and avoidance rather than the need for medical or political intervention. Alley dwellers were not to be treated, or assisted, or cured, but *expelled;* their homes were not to be improved but *destroyed.* Reports like these did not only trigger rational/cognitive responses (concerns about crime and health) but also physiological/affective ones (fear and disgust).

Alleys were inhabited not only by Foucault's docile bodies but also by repulsive bodies. They were populated by single mothers (that is, illegitimately birthing bodies), old bodies, disfigured bodies, and disabled bodies. Alley residents were neither soldiers nor workers nor patients nor students; they were untrainable, unmanageable, marginal, extra-disciplinary. The body of the alley resident was at once excessive and deficient, inadequately productive while also being immoderately reproductive. These abject, feminized alley bodies mirrored and contributed to abject, feminized alley spaces and the countless reports of "leaky" plumbing, "swampy" environs, and "marshy" surroundings that appear in official reports, "open sewer[s] of civic inanition."[146] Both of these "physical and moral swamps" represent not simply the risk of infection but the threat of social order dissolving under the pressure of an unreasonable, unruly—and yet hopelessly dependent—public.

All of these conditions threatening to individual bodies and to the social body are reported on (and/or invoked as symbols) for something different than disciplinary power. Viewing the Washington alleys through the theoretical lenses provided by Kristeva, we can see that alleys were problematic at least in part because they were sites of permeability and vulnerability in the social body. The ontological integrity of the body politic depended on a unified symbolic space (the National Mall). But like any representational system, the body politic derives its meanings only through repressing excessive identities or subsuming differences. Coherence, unity, and sameness in the representational space of the nation are achieved only by setting out parameters for the citizen body/body politic and displacing elements of the social body that fall outside of those parameters, by establishing a space for the abject and keeping it at bay.

Alley Space and Civic Atrophy

The "plague spots" in the alleys described by Weller ravaged the physical and moral constitution of both alley residents and the body politic writ large; it was a plague that attacked, ultimately, the ideal and practices of citizenship. At the same time, the discourse of alley reform helped to reproduce and reify those ideals and practices by providing the symbolic figure of the citizen with his other. Given the "immoral" or "amoral" behaviors he and his investigators witnessed as daily occurrences in alley life, Weller must ask: "Into what molds of citizenship are alley children being pressed?"[147] Weller suggests that the alleys are a "region of atrophied civic life" around the borders of the national capital.[148] Attending to these troubles, much like a careful physician, would benefit not just the alley residents but "the general commonwealth . . . Such an expenditure of public funds would be a direct investment in good citizenship."[149]

In the end, then, it was neither the health nor the criminality of the alley dwellers that required intervention from policy makers; instead, it was also their potential to un-make the city beautiful by fundamentally challenging the symbolic unity of the body politic. Collapsing the distinctions between geographic, corporeal, and moral topographies allowed citizen-planners to define the health and vigor of the proper public sphere (the National Mall, the monumental city) against the "civic atrophy" and repulsive spaces of the alleys. What is important, one reformer reminded the Senate Committee, is not only the specific complaints lodged against alley residents but rather ". . . the necessity for the proper development of the city, for its beautification, for the unification of its plan, all of which comes from the making of the minor streets in the place of alleys, which are bound to be more or less of a disfigurement from any point of view we may look at it."[150]

As heterotopic spaces, the Washington alleys were paradoxical. They continually threatened the symbolic unity of the city (and the nation), yet were integral to its functioning; alley dwellers were positioned at the borders or margins of subjectivity, while at the same time, helped to define the contours of legitimate citizenship. Whereas Weller compared the alleys to the atrophied "extremities" of a body, other accounts more frequently stress their centrality to city life. Alleys were not absolutely "other from" the city; on the contrary, they were a part of it, a structural necessity in so far as they served "*alley* purposes . . . necessary for the removal of garbage and ashes and bringing in food supplies and other things," as Commissioner Siddons asserted.[151] When cities are figured as social bodies, as "spatial systems of waste production and elimination,"[152] alleys are their intestines, processing and expelling actual and moral waste, while keeping the rest of the city clean and orderly.

As abject spaces, though, the alleys also constantly threatened to exceed or overflow their limits, to seep out into the city proper. These particular alleys became a problem when they exceeded the bounds of what the social body could bear. Policy makers argued that alley dwellers had ". . . got into . . . the heart of the city squares."[153] Instead of serving their original purposes ("*alley* purposes") they acquired new purposes over time. They were for working, raising children, and sleeping—for living. In contrast to the segregated, functional spaces planned for a White City utopia, the alleys complicated spaces, collapsed meanings.

As I have suggested, Foucault's account of modern power alone does not give us adequate theoretical leverage for understanding the expulsion of alley residents from their homes. The bodies of the Washington's alley residents fell outside the institutional parameters that Foucault's disciplinary power presumes. Alley bodies were repulsive bodies—disabled, dependent, illegitimate bodies—the feminine/feminized excess whose very existence undermined the symbolic unity of the body politic. Kristeva's account of abjection helps us to understand how the symbolic aspects of the body politic and the socio-political aspects of city building and nation building are linked in discourses of urban planning. Recognizing the limits of a Foucauldian spatial logic has important ideational and material effects, because whereas docile bodies can be corrected, cured, or treated, repulsive bodies require (in Grosz's words) "[r]ituals and practices designed to cleanse or purify the body."[154] Inhabited alleys—with their grotesque bodies and feminized spaces—were repulsive, requiring nothing less than decontamination. Accordingly, policy makers did not recommend institutional intervention in the lives of the alley dwellers; instead their discursive strategies might be seen as a kind of figurative purging, a reassertion of the appropriate lines between spaces of (in Mary Douglas' words) purity and danger.

Just as Foucault's Panopticon and Ship of Fools are potent figurative geographies that mediate between the real and the imaginary, the metaphorical and the material, so too are the alley and the Mall in Washington, D.C. The Mall (a clean, rational, orderly, open civic space) found its political antithesis in the alleys (disease-ridden, immoral spaces where "pandemonium" reigned). The National Mall was not simply a "park" (characterized by the presence or absence of monuments, memorials, and green space) just as the alley was not simply a "poor neighborhood" (characterized by certain conditions of disease, mortality, criminality, and illegitimacy that varied across different groups of people). The Mall and the alley were also sociosymbolic spaces, sites that helped policy makers define the requirements for citizenship and its others.

Modeling Washington after the White City, then, was a conscious use of spatial practices to produce both aesthetic and political results. Drawing on the lessons of the Columbian Exposition, the Park Commission's plan sought to impose a spatial and moral order on the chaos of urban life. At the same time, because Washington was not just "any city", this was to be a spatial and moral order writ large: an ordering of no less than the body politic itself. To make the city beautiful, wrote Daniel Burnham in an article promoting the McMillan Plan, also meant ". . . to remove and forever keep from view the ugly, the unsightly and even the commonplace."[155] In this case, the "ugly, the unsightly, and even the commonplace" were the ambiguous, indeterminate spaces and repulsive bodies of the Washington alleys. Rebuilding the Mall and reforming the alleys were not opposed but complementary processes of establishing and policing the parameters of a proper citizen body.

4. Remaking Washington at Midcentury

In our haste we have built our cities thoughtlessly and badly.
Let us destroy them completely—mercifully and methodically—
instead of allowing them to destroy themselves through decay
and disintegration.
—Louis Justement, Chairman, Urban Planning Committee of the
American Institute of Architects, 1946

If those who govern the District of Columbia decide that the
Nation's capital should be beautiful as well as sanitary, there is
nothing in the Fifth Amendment that stands in their way.
—Chief Justice Douglas, *Berman v. Parker,* Supreme Court of
the United States, 1954

We'll plan this city with gasoline.
—Anonymous, 1968

On an April day in 1968, then Governor of California Ronald Reagan addressed a Women's National Press Club luncheon in Washington, D.C. Reagan joked about movie stars and governors and had the crowd at the Hilton
laughing just minutes into his speech. While Reagan was warming up his
audience, riot police with helmets and rifles stood at the ready in Prince
George's County, tensely anticipating the need to subdue an unruly mob.
Montgomery County declared a state of emergency for the first time in its
history.[1] Later that afternoon, Mayor Walter E. Washington imposed a curfew
on the District of Columbia, as "marauding bands of Negroes" roamed the
city, many burning and looting as they went.[2] Entire streets in Washington
were covered with shattered glass and littered with debris from the homes
and businesses that had been destroyed. A smoky haze hung over much of
the city.

It was the day after the assassination of Dr. Martin Luther King Jr., and
cities across the nation were erupting in violence. The riots followed a decade
illuminated by vibrant civil rights activity. They also came in the wake of the
most intense period of urban rebuilding in the nation's history; by the time

of Dr. King's murder, urban redevelopment agencies in cities from Boston to San Francisco had acquired thirty-four square miles of land, displaced at least 400,000 families, and demolished 129,000 structures.[3] The civil disturbances in Washington were in many ways a referendum on these reconfigured spatial dimensions of citizenship, and a mapping of what Ernest Wohlenberg has called the "geography of civility."[4]

In this chapter, I examine a second moment in the history of urban planning discourse in Washington. In the 1950s and 1960s, the discourse from turn-of-the-century Washington (grounded in bodily otherness and radical abjection, of difference marked by class, race, and physical disease) was married to a discourse of economic rationality, where bodies and differences were metaphorically and literally erased from urban space. In its midcentury iteration, citizenship became defined by a rationalized aesthetic that sought to inscribe a new spatial order on the "other Washington," the city outside the space of the National Mall.

New Cities for Old

Despite the ambitious language of earlier legislation,[5] the law had a negligible impact on the actual lives of the alley-dwelling population. Although thousands of alley residents had been displaced prior to 1914 through the condemnation and demolition of their homes, efforts to wipe alleys off the map after the act's passage were thwarted by the onset of World War I and the housing shortages in the capital that ensued. Postwar enforcement was interrupted by later amendments to the law designed to prevent a "great number of poor persons . . . [from prowling] about the city in search of humble shelter," and finally by a lawsuit filed by alley property owners to keep the District commissioners from executing the act.[6] During the next decade, city planning and, more specifically, the elimination of alley housing received only sporadic and incomplete attention from policy makers.

In 1929 the National Capital Parks and Planning Commission (NCPPC; later known as the National Capital Parks Commission, or NCPC)[7] submitted a bill to Congress once again denouncing the Washington alleys and calling for the elimination of substandard housing therein. In what would be passed in 1934 as the District of Columbia Alley Dwelling Act, Congress approved the creation of the Alley Dwelling Authority (ADA; in 1943 it became the National Capital Housing Authority, or NCHA) to manage the reclamation of Washington's alleys and their inhabitants' relocation.

This law had much in common with its predecessors. First, it focused on the Washington alleys as the principal sites for government intervention and set time limits for their elimination; specifically, the act mandated the "discontinuance of the use as dwellings of the buildings situated in alleys" and ambitiously required the total elimination of alley dwellings by 1944.[8] Also like previous legislation, the Alley Dwelling Act continued to invoke "public health, comfort, morals, safety, and welfare" as the main reasons for undertaking reform,[9] which was interrupted by a second world war. Finally, like laws before it, its effects were rather limited: after its inception, the NCPPC had identified 2,400 alley dwellings (or 182 squares, housing about 2.5 percent of the city's population) in use in Washington. By 1945, the Authority was able to rehabilitate only about 8 percent of these. (Significantly, only 3 percent—or five squares—were rehabilitated as low-income housing.) Whereas supporters of the agency cited insufficient funds and the necessity of constructing wartime, temporary housing as the reasons for its slow progress, its detractors argued that the reason for the delay was the government's inefficiency in taking on what should be the tasks of private developers. By 1946 the NCPPC reported that the city had "an unprecedented number of unfit dwellings," twice as many substandard dwellings as it did before the war.[10]

Washington, like virtually every city across the country, was facing other challenges as well. As early as 1940, census figures indicated significant population emigration to the suburbs, resulting in shrinking retail sales and a diminished urban tax base. Between 1940 and 1950, suburbs surrounding thirty-two U.S. metropolitan areas grew three and a half times faster than central cities; in Washington suburbs grew nearly six times as fast as the city itself.[11] The conclusions drawn by politicians and policy makers from these results were unanimous: the city needed to be saved.[12] Clearly the rate at which the NCHA could reclaim and rehabilitate the city's spaces was outpaced by the rate at which these spaces could further decay. The comprehensive plans developed heretofore by the NCPPC, planners concluded, simply were not comprehensive enough; everyone interested in the future of cities agreed that a more thorough and aggressive approach to city building was in order. The outcome of these sentiments was unparalleled enthusiasm for ever more sweeping planning efforts.

The need for more comprehensive planning led to an improbable convergence of interests: real estate developers, construction firms, and public housing advocates all lobbied for a federal program that would somehow ameliorate the effects of the slums on American cities. This alliance culminated at the local level in the District of Columbia Redevelopment Act of 1945, and then in the national urban renewal program articulated in the Housing Act of 1949 and the amending act of 1954.[13] Although supporters of public housing were deeply opposed to the objectives of the real estate lobby, they acquiesced to the legislation in the hopes that some good could come from federal involvement in urban redevelopment.[14]

Because poor housing affected the totality of urban life, policy makers reasoned, its solutions also needed to be totalizing. Without systematic and coordinated effort, attempts to solve the city's problems would fail, a sentiment that was reflected in planning discourse nationwide: "City planning, planners, maps, plans, pictures, legislation, belief, good will and initiative," pronounced the publication *American City*, "are of little value unless combined in a united, aggressive, and enlightened community movement."[15] Thus the Redevelopment Act expanded the powers of the NCPPC by authorizing it to identify areas for redevelopment based on its master plan for the city, while the newly created Redevelopment Land Agency (RLA) was able to acquire the property in these areas for sale to public and private developers. The legislation vested in the commission the authority to rebuild "all of Washington's slum-ridden areas, to lay out a vast new highway system, to purchase land for additional parks and playgrounds, and to specify the sites for new public buildings."[16] In addition, the legislation instructed its agents to use "all means necessary and appropriate to [its] purpose."[17]

The District of Columbia Redevelopment Act, then, was the legislative manifestation of a new, comprehensive approach to urban planning. Not only the monumental core of the Mall but rather all living, working, and recreational urban spaces would be rethought in their relationship to the totality of the city. Influenced by Le Corbusier and the modernist desire for the city to be "a blank piece of paper," or a "clean tablecloth," this approach presumed that the wholesale clearance of existing cities should make way for new, modern urban spaces.[18]

Moreover, urban renewal enthusiasts across the country often took Washington, D.C., as their model city for redevelopment.[19] With its history of celebrated "master plans," Washington seemed the perfect place to attempt such sweeping reforms, and the legacies of L'Enfant's original design for the city and the Senate Park Commission's plan for the Mall were invoked by numerous commentators to garner support for these extensive changes.[20] "For the big slum areas of Washington the bulldozer and wrecking cranes are necessary," journalist Chalmers Roberts stated, "Whole blocks must be cleared."[21] In one typically ambitious midcentury program for Washington titled *No Slums in Ten Years*, James Rouse and Nathaniel Keith described this philosophy to the D.C. commissioners:

> . . . [U]nintegrated piecemeal attacks on the slum problem will not work. [Urban renewal] is intended to cover the total of municipal actions required to remove

blight and establish sound neighborhoods. Public housing, redevelopment, and code enforcement programs operating as separate and largely uncoordinated thrusts at slums will neither cure the city's slums nor prevent their future growth. These and all other available methods must be tied together into a carefully planned, well administered campaign.[22]

Or, as the *Washington Post* put it, "The way to do [urban renewal] is by a bold, imaginative and vigorously conducted redevelopment program."[23]

Whereas individual developers previously had to piece together different parcels of land over a period of many years, the new urban renewal agencies such as the RLA could "clear huge tracts of land in one stroke."[24] The result was, as Alison Ravetz suggests, a nationwide "'clean sweep' philosophy of planning to which all the parties that were in any way concerned about the built environment subscribed."[25] That is, rather than rely on partial commitments or gradual changes, the new logic of urban space required immediate action and forceful redirection, what Lewis Mumford called "a bulldozing habit of mind: one that sought to clear the ground of encumbrances, so as to make a clean beginning on its own inflexible mathematical lines."[26] Instead of the patchwork approach attempted in earlier (more primitive) efforts at the turn of the century, new legislation—like urban space itself—must be brought up-to-date. "[I]t is necessary to modernize the planning and development of . . . the District," the Redevelopment Act declared.[27] Efforts to redevelop areas (that is, to wipe the slate clean and start again), rather than to rehabilitate existing structures or neighborhoods, would be given priority.

Louis Justement's 1946 book *New Cities for Old* articulates a sensibility in urban planning that would drive Washington's midcentury redevelopment efforts. In his text, Justement, a Washington architect and influential member of the American Institute of Architects, used Washington as a case study for bringing rational and orderly growth to a city that (as he observed) was decaying before his eyes. The first step in creating a city that was not thrown together "hastily and carelessly," Justement argued, was to stop relying on the narrow opinions of "experts" whose vision was limited to their own particular areas of "authority." "Before we become absorbed in the intricacies of the details," Justement instructed, "we must begin with a broad, over-all view of the complete picture and grasp the relative importance of the various factors as well as the relationships which exist between them."[28]

For Justement, then, what was needed was a God's-eye view of the city, something that was impossible for "experts" encumbered by their partial visions. For Justement, the chance to redevelop cities was a chance for mastery, for "a degree of control [over them] never before attained."[29] Invoking Daniel

Burnham's famous direction for the architects of the City Beautiful, Justement calls on his readership to "[m]ake no little plans; they have no magic to stir men's blood."[30]

A New Spatial Vocabulary

Thus urban planning discourse in Washington and across the country began to take on a tone distinct from turn-of-the-century reform. Politicians and city planners began to discuss the problem of inadequate housing in the cities in markedly different language; treating the cities' problems at midcentury, it seemed, necessitated an entirely new spatial vocabulary. The Redevelopment Act of 1945 called for "the replanning and rebuilding of slum, blighted, and other areas of the District of Columbia and the assembly, by purchase or condemnation, of real property in such areas . . . for the redevelopment of such areas in accordance with said plan."[31] The national Housing Act of 1949 used similar language; one of the stipulations of the law held that urban renewal funds could only be used for "a slum area, or a blighted, deteriorated, or deteriorating area . . . which the [federal] Administrator approves as appropriate for an urban renewal project."[32] In legislation that defines a great number of terms ("housing," "project area," "low-rent housing," among others), it is curious that no definition is given for either "blight" or "slums." This shift in terminology, however, can tell us a great deal about transformations in planning discourse and planning practices over time.

The Problem of Blight

At midcentury, the urban planning magazine the American City defined blight[33] as a

> . . . municipal disease resulting from civic lethargy, political irresponsibility, lack of good city planning, and related causes. Blight attacks and destroys industrial and commercial areas as well as residential areas. Blight is a cancerous disease that afflicts and destroys cities and the property and investments in them. Even more important, it takes its toll on the people within those cities. The effect of the disease on the people in turn reinfects the property, business, and investments . . . That the disease of blight is transmitted from people to property and from property to people at an accelerating rate . . . is an acknowledged fact.[34]

Consider the implications of this redefinition of urban space. Blight, according to the Oxford English Dictionary, originated in the seventeenth century as an agricultural term, and meant "[a]ny baleful influence of atmospheric or invisible origin, that suddenly blasts, nips, or destroys plants, affects them with disease, arrests their growth, or prevents their blossom from 'setting.'" Later, the term came to mean "[a]ny malignant influence of obscure or mysterious origin; anything which withers hopes or prospects, or checks prosperity."

Describing urban poverty in terms of blight accomplishes several things that together constitute a significant transformation in the way we talk about cities. First, it likens the phenomenon of urban decay to a natural disaster, rendering it as inevitable as it is tragic. Blight, as it is manifested in run-down, aesthetically unpleasing property and a negligent population, is of "invisible" or "mysterious" origins, striking out of nowhere; it is unpredictable and therefore to some extent unpreventable. Blight jumps erratically from square to square, block to block. Second, and related to this first point, this definition obscures human choices as a cause of blight. The language of "blight" masks both individual and collective responsibility for the condition of American cities: capital flight, chronic un- or underemployment, inadequate schools and under-funded public transit, de jure and de facto segregation, and government-subsidized discrimination, for example, can remain unacknowledged as specific reasons for cities' decline.[35] When human causes for blight are acknowledged, they are *attitudinal*; blight is a disease of the spirit (exactly whose spirit is left open to interpretation), resulting from "lethargy" and "political irresponsibility" which somehow seep into the city, infecting urban space itself.

Furthermore, from its first connotations, blight is primarily an economic disease; these are not just any plants that are overtaken by blight but cash crops, and it is specifically the city's "prosperity" that is at stake in failing to combat the problem. Indeed, central business districts in urban areas were the principal beneficiaries of urban renewal funding, as rejuvenating downtown businesses and bringing back the consumer class from the suburbs soon became more important than building affordable housing.[36] Urban planning (as housing advocate John Ihlder remarked critically) thus became a matter of converting spatial liabilities into spatial assets, essentially a "business proposition."[37] Whereas reform at the turn of the century had focused (at least ostensibly) on the health of the population (alley dwellers' propensity to inculcate and spread actual as well as moral disease), by 1940 the "health" of the city had entirely different (that is, economic) connotations.

This more pervasive economic rationality changes the ways subjects are produced within and through urban planning discourses. As we saw in Chapter 3, at the heart of turn-of-the-century urban social reform was the body of the alley dweller: the single woman with children, the un- or underemployed middle-aged man, the victim of industrial disease, the tubercular child, and the elderly couple. The bodies of alley residents were the (often unwilling) subjects of the medical, managerial, and moral gazes of reformers and politicians; alley dwellers in fact became homologous with the spaces in which they resided.

At midcentury, however, individual bodies (with their peculiar maladies and tragic afflictions) and particular places (with their leaky plumbing and crumbling plaster) disappear entirely from planners' view. They are replaced by accounts of tenants, clients, low-income families, households, taxpayers, and builders, occupying or vying for sites, properties, vacancies, lots, dwelling units, census tracts, and land values. Each term in this series is an indicator of economic productivity or inefficiency, a term that represents a net gain, a net loss, or an economic opportunity. In these discussions, the inefficiency of certain spaces results in a net loss for the District:

> . . . [A study made in 1938] showed that there was an average of 53 1/2 persons to each net residential acre, in these tracts; that that compared to the average of 13.4 persons per acre for the city as a whole . . .; that 13 1/2 percent of the populations of Washington resided in this area; that 13.6 percent of all the persons arrested for other than traffic violations . . . came from that area; that 27.3 percent of the arrests of persons under 17 years of age in 1937 were from that area; that 20.2 percent of the delinquent children committed to institutions or placed on probation were from that area; that 31.3 percent of the persons receiving public assistance were from that area, in other words, that 13 1/2 percent of the population of Washington produced very high percentages of criminals and people requiring public assistance.[38]

Or in even starker terms, "This area produces 1.2 cents of every District of Columbia tax dollar, but it consumes 9 cents of every dollar spent for welfare services; 6 cents of every dollar for health services; 12.5 cents of every dollar for mental patients; and 6.4 cents of every dollar for incarceration of criminals . . . for slums and blight areas, a general rule is that for every dollar you take out of these areas in taxes, you put back $5 to $6 in city services."[39] The *Washington Post* put it more succinctly: "Slums mean extra policing, public assistance, unemployment compensation, all sorts of health and welfare expenditures."[40]

Note that in these last descriptions it is spaces, not people, which are consuming these resources, as blighted areas are transformed here from cesspools to money pits. Although commentators sometimes acknowledge that substandard housing does not *cause* these other maladies, their rhetoric often slides easily between structural problems and social problems, implying correlation if not causation. "The highest tuberculosis rate in the District . . . occurs in old Washington," states the *Post,* in an article titled

"Poor Health a Terrible Consequence of Blighted Areas in District." The article first acknowledges that redevelopment would not necessarily mean the end to poor public health, but then quickly moves past that issue to discuss the "inevitable link of housing and health."[41] In this way, it became possible for urban redevelopment enthusiasts to purport to remedy human and political problems through new configurations of buildings, roads, and retail. Making space differently became the solution to virtually every urban difficulty.

Alleys to Slums

Although alleys and their inhabitants were still a problem in the 1940s and 1950s (and still the source of the greatest concern in the District of Columbia), alleys were situated more frequently within the context of larger spaces, entire "run-down residential areas", or slums.[42] These distinctions are important, because they define both the problem and legitimize the legislative remedy. Although slums included alleys, they were not limited to alleys; slums were whole sections of the city marked by dilapidated buildings, unsanitary conditions, and (what would later be called) a culture of poverty.

Indeed, the new language of the city's slums or slum areas helped redefine the nature and scope of urban problems in several ways. First, whereas alleys (their trash, their diseases, their populations) threatened to overflow into the main streets, the slums threatened to overtake the entirety of urban life: ". . . the slums are spilling out into once respectable neighborhoods as the middle class leaves for suburbia," as one book (appropriately titled *The Exploding Metropolis*) warned. "They are eating away at the heart of the cities, especially their downtowns"[43] "An Encroaching Menace," *Life* magazine titled its article about the need for urban renewal. The "menacing" image accompanying the article showed two abandoned buildings in a lot full of rubble.[44] Slums had overtaken whole blocks, entire districts, and contiguous "deficient and defective" census tracts.[45] Thus although previous legislation which focused only on the alleys might have been sufficient at the time, it could no longer adequately combat urban problems: "It [is] obvious," reported John Ihlder, ". . . that the conditions which originated in the inhabited alleys [have] spread to streets and across the streets to other squares."[46] Instead of eliminating alley dwellings one substandard structure at a time, policy makers and city planners now talked in terms of generalized "slum clearance."

Furthermore, while turn-of-the-century alley life was troubling in part because of its insidious *invisibility,* slums were problematic because of their persistent *visibility,* the stark spectacle of poverty they offered to anyone entering city limits. A 1930 editorial in the *Evening Star* decried the display: "While tens of millions of dollars are being spent for magnificent public structures to make the model capital of the world, business and residential Washington· should not be permitted to present the aspect of the slums."[47] Slums were not only an economic and social problem but also an aesthetic one.

Casting the problem of urban poverty in the rationalized language of "blight" and "slums" allowed the subjects of discourse to disappear. It also allowed policy makers to erase the distinction between public and private space, so that all urban spaces were available for their appropriation. Alley dwellings, after all, were still just that: *dwellings,* homes, private spaces inhabited by private individuals, no matter how poorly either the space or the life was maintained. While interventions into these spaces were justified on the basis of "public health," policy makers and reformers were limited in how much or how often they could intrude. However, by designating the problem as "blight"—a city-wide, economic problem whose ravages affected commercial and residential spaces alike—policy makers elided the distinction between them. This was codified in law with the 1954 Supreme Court decision (*Berman v. Parker,* quoted previously) that upheld the right of Washington's National Capital Housing Authority to exercise eminent domain for urban redevelopment, the right to condemn and appropriate private property in the name of the public interest, broadly construed. In the District of Columbia, this conflation was especially pronounced as land was reclaimed for the broadest possible public, the "national" interest, so as to "set an example which will be followed in . . . cities across the Nation."[48]

The Production of Dead Space

Despite the new emphasis placed on homo economicus at midcentury, bodily metaphors of disease and cure also remained prevalent in planning discourses. Not only was blight characterized as disease, it was described as a *cancer:* no ordinary malady but one that required radical measures to eliminate; after all, the first and most effective remedy for a blighted area is to burn it, or to cut out the blighted parts of the remaining plants. Unlike their more contained alley predecessors, blighted areas threatened to choke the very life out of the city, and good city planning—by definition—would entail destruction and replanting. Rather than attempting rehabilitation, planners should remove immediately those buildings or blocks lost to blight. "[R]ehabilitation is no cure for the slums. It is no substitute for slum clearance," a *Washington Post* article declared.[49] Urban renewal is "like cutting out a little cancer," as one reformer put it.[50]

Louis Justement concluded that urban redevelopment was in fact a mercy killing: "Let us destroy [our cities] completely—mercifully and methodically," he wrote, "instead of allowing them to destroy themselves through decay and disintegration."[51] Or as Robert Moses said of New York at this time, "When you operate in an overbuilt metropolis, you have to hack your way through with a meat ax."[52] In short, the state of American cities at midcentury required—in fact, demanded—a violent response on the part of planners and policy makers. War had to be waged on behalf of—or against—dying cities; anything less would mean defeat.

Abjection and Abstraction

When blight attacks (mysteriously, perniciously, and totally), often those in the vicinity can only stand by and watch helplessly as their crops wither and their fields go to waste; blight produces *dead space*. The city's diagnosis, policy makers and planners concluded, was not good; central business districts in Washington and in other cities were frequently characterized as "dead," "dying," or "obsolete." Such language is a marked contrast to turn-of-the-century discourse, which attested to the relative "health" of various urban spaces, and as Alison Isenberg points out, the concept of obsolescence was "wielded as a weapon" by redevelopers to remake downtowns across the country.[53]

What is the significance, then, of figuring the city as "dead space?" For Julia Kristeva, death is the ultimate abject form, the most radical expression of alterity. Like all abjection, though, it is one in which we are intimately implicated. In the language of abjection, life and death commingle and imply, even as they oppose, one another. Dead space, by Kristeva's account, is the most other space, a space for those who are recognized as the most socially, psychically, and symbolically "other" in any given culture. Any beings found within this space are virtually unrecognizable; they are terrifying and/or superfluous, for they are either ghosts or corpses.

But in midcentury planning discourse, the "dead" city contained no ghosts and no corpses; in fact, it contained no subjects at all—neither the living nor the dead. The festering, abject ooze of the Washington alleys (decaying bodies, rotting food, sickly smells, and sinister sounds) documented so meticulously in previous decades was replaced by the antiseptic geometry of urban redevelopment, by the "rationalizing technologies of measurement, universalization, and monetary equivalence."[54] Dead cities, rather than being abject space, are depicted as what Henri Lefebvre calls *abstract* space—wholly rationalized space, where the totality of social life is shot through with exchange relations. Lefebvre describes abstract space as "formal and quantitative," it is space that "erases distinctions, as much those which derive from nature and (historical) time as those which originate in the body (age, sex, ethnicity)."[55] Abstract space erases embodied experience in favor of homogenization and sterilization; reduced to its price per acre, it is space to be planned, modified, torn down, built up, bought, sold, reconfigured, and remarketed. Following the trajectory of abstract space, urban planning at midcentury displaced people both discursively and materially from city space.

Justement expressed this frustration well: "The American city mocks at us," he wrote. "[T]he dead hand of the past baffles every effort that is made to reach even this limited objective [of arresting further urban decay]."[56] The rationalized space advocated in pursuit of the modern city, then, should not only seek to erase bodies, but also to eradicate evidence of the city's history from its enterprise. In so doing, Washington once again could become a tabula rasa for new development.

What Justement and others hoped for in Washington was the triumph of a purely rational space, whereby individuals might be reduced to equivalent economic units whose cost or value can be readily assessed through a series of calculations. These are truly the subjects envisioned by liberal political theory. Imagined to be unencumbered by the burdens of race, gender, history, or physical ability, they are abstract citizens endowed with interchangeable needs and manageable desires, whose behavior can be predicted and evaluated through the rational calculus of cost and benefit, profit and loss.[57]

However, when particular bodies *were* included in the plans for urban redevelopment projects, they illustrated how the abstract or universal citizens of liberalism are not, in fact, neutral or unencumbered, but reflect a very specific set of attributes and values that shore up particular political and economic systems. In a 1966 study of publicly funded downtown redevelopment plans, Edward Wood, Sidney Brower, and Margaret Latimer found that "planners' people" (the people who are depicted in planners' drawings, occupying a planned space) can be reduced to a "stock cast" of six types: the Gentleman with the Briefcase, the Fashionable Lady, the Mother and Child, the Young Lovers, the Viewer, and the Boulevardier. The authors wonder why all these planners' people are "young, clean, well-dressed, [and] white," when they are meant to illustrate a place "which in many parts of the United States is becoming increasingly elderly, low income, and Negro."[58]

The authors conclude that the illustrations of the planned spaces themselves communicate a set of assumptions about planners' people and their values: the spaces possess a "high degree of formal ordering . . . and [present] the image of a highly unified society;" there is a "high value placed on efficient and orderly operation;" and "a value placed on 'high' cultural and aesthetic tastes," as evidenced by the frequent depiction of "theatres, museums, fountains, sculpture, and exhibition planting."[59] The citizens that cities sought to produce through urban renewal were then, as James Q. Wilson put it, the "tax-paying, culture-loving, free-spending, middle class,"[60] and this meant that urban space had to be redefined and reorganized to meet their needs.

The elimination of "other" bodies from planners' discourse (or the desired repopulation of urban spaces with the middle-class, white consumers depicted in these plans) suggest that the sense of the city as an abject space (as described in Chapter 3) had not simply disappeared by midcentury. Instead, it undergirded and was given justification through planners' more explicit concerns about commerce and profitability.[61]

In summation, the discourses of urban planning during this period reflect several significant shifts in their accounts of urban space and consequently the construction of urban subjects. At the turn of the century, space was subject to intervention based on its "healthy/unhealthy" and "moral/immoral" character. At midcentury, however, urban space became either an asset or a liability, part of a calculus of profitability. Second, as the federal government enlisted the help of private developers to address the nation's housing problem (and as private developers enlisted the government's power of eminent domain to help assemble plots of land for redevelopment), the distinctions between "public" and "private" spaces became increasingly ambiguous, and the "private" subject and her "private" dwelling disappeared from public discourse. Third, urban centers were continually characterized at midcentury as "dead," "dying," or "obsolete," and the accounts of abject spaces and bodies found in earlier planning discourse were supplemented by a planning discourse characterized by uniform subjects in an increasingly rationalized, abstracted urban space.

With this redefinition of the city's spaces at midcentury now outlined, we address the next questions: How, then, did planners and policy makers agree to solve the problem of blight? Once they had eliminated blight from any given area, how would they prevent this disease (this infection of space) from recurring? How would they plan to bring dead cities back to life?

A Place from Which Men Turn

The impulse nested in Justement's and others' plans was not simply a question of comprehensiveness. Planning a city in toto was but a means to an end, and midcentury planners aspired to an aim not unfamiliar to turn-of-the-century reformers: *beauty*. A city's economic vitality and its citizens' well-being both depended on the satisfaction of aesthetic criteria. "The average citizen," Justement wrote, "may be satisfied with a program for the demolition of slum and blighted areas and the erection of efficient, modern buildings on the basis of a convenient city plan. It will be a pity if this is our ambition . . . On the contrary the thrill that comes from participating in a genuine aesthetic experience may be utilized as a powerful factor in inspiring us to overcome the obstacles that will confront us. The distinction we make between 'art' and the 'practical' phases of living is a pathetic commentary on modern civilization."[62] Prominent shopping mall developer Victor Gruen agreed. "The current condition of downtown repulses shoppers," he argued, and proceeded to revolutionize the shopping experience by putting ten acres and numerous stores under one roof, with a goldfish pond and skylight at its center.[63]

Quite simply, the language of beauty and ugliness pervades planning discourse at this time. As Justement queried, "Why does a civilization that is able to produce the beauty, efficiency, and order that we find displayed in a modern automobile or airplane produce the ugliness, chaos, and disorder that we find in the average city? Is it not because, in the first case, there is a conscious effort at creative design, whereas in the latter the growth is accidental rather than purposive?"[64] Reaffirming the sentiments of Daniel Burnham fifty years prior, the NCPPC added that what was "ordinary" (or "commonplace") was also not beautiful: "Washington is a beautiful city because of its Mall, its parks, and the river. Yet in spite of these, the bulk of the inner residential areas are quite ordinary and certainly not beautiful. One redeeming feature of these sections is that street trees hide the ugliness."[65]

"Drifting" (the word Justement disparagingly opposes to "planning" in his text) was ugly because it was irrational. Drifting was inefficient and lacked purpose and direction. "Shall we continue to drift," he asked rhetorically, "or shall we make the effort to create cities that satisfy our sense of order, efficiency, and beauty?"[66] "Shall downtown Washington . . . continue to drift into blight?" journalist Chalmers Roberts echoed, ". . . or shall Washington make that massive frontal attack necessary to stop deterioration?"[67] Planning itself, in fact, was beautiful, for it produced rational order out of an unseemly mess. The insistence on order and efficiency distinguish city planning from mere ornamentation; planning here is once again gendered as a masculine activity, counterposed as it is to irrationality, indecision, purposelessness, or mere decoration.

In fact, urban planners and architects often cast the city's physical decay in overtly gendered terms.[68] As Chief Justice Douglas reasoned in *Berman vs. Parker,* "[m]iserable and disreputable housing conditions may do more than spread disease and crime and immorality. . . . They may also be an ugly sore, a blight on the community which robs it of its charm, which makes it a place from which men turn. The misery of housing may despoil a community as an open sewer may ruin a river."[69] The city's problems (its "ugly sores") were, then, to a great extent, cosmetic; "men" "turned" away from the city, transferred their attentions elsewhere (to the rational, orderly landscapes of the suburbs?) for want of a better view. The city, in this figuration, is a woman who has lost her looks, and now requires the expertise of a (male) professional for an extreme, urban makeover. "[O]ne of the most dramatic pieces of plastic surgery ever undertaken on the face of an American city," the *New York Times* described urban renewal in Washington; the "face-lifting" would be performed by "skilled architectural surgeons."[70] The consequences of inaction were geographic infidelity.

In short, many of the same elements of turn-of-the-century aesthetic ideals were resurrected and redefined at midcentury: beauty was orderly and rational; ugliness was "drab, unorganized" sprawl and slums—but now was also "detrimental to social and economic values" rather than merely to citizens' moral and physical health.[71] Where one Washington (that planned by the McMillan Commission) was beautiful, the other Washington (almost everything else in the city) was not. Urban renewal at midcentury—either in the form of public housing or private investment—was an aesthetic endeavor, although the category of the beautiful now was significantly expanded and altered. For Justement (as for the other architects of Washington's urban renewal and redevelopment efforts), a beautiful Washington no longer meant the Beaux-Arts classicism that dominated the McMillan Plan at the turn of the century. Justement's beauty required clean, orderly modern lines without excessive ornamentation, and uniformity without strict repetition. Beauty was now modern, rational, and efficient (not classical or venerable), and these aesthetic criteria should be applied to all areas and activities of urban life: high-rise apartments, shopping plazas, highways, museums, and office buildings were legitimately subsumed under the mantle of the "beautiful."

In *New Cities for Old,* Justement includes several plates of drawings that depict his vision of a Washington made beautiful. In Plate 24, captioned "Order vs. Disorder," "disorder" is represented by a photograph of Georgia Avenue in Silver Spring, Maryland: a typical midcentury main street in a small town, lined with stores and cars parked along the street. "Order," on the other hand, is a strip mall on Massachusetts Avenue, which features uniform storefronts and a sizable surface parking lot.[72]

Another example of this midcentury ideal of beauty is found in an American Institute of Architects (AIA) publication titled *No Time for Ugliness.* Ugliness is a pressing problem, the AIA warns, but fortunately "[t]he architects of America have embarked on a continuing campaign to create community awareness. Magazines, newspapers, and the broadcast media are beginning to document our urban ugliness and examine its causes."[73] Photos and captions throughout the publication illustrate examples of beauty and ugliness. A highway overpass and the postredevelopment Southwest area in Washington are deemed beautiful. Slum housing (its location is not indicated) is shown as the ugly alternative to (beautiful) standardized public housing.[74]

One's appreciation of a beautiful Washington, these planners then concluded, should not have to stop at the borders of the Mall. The pursuit of beauty was orderly, and it should also be expansive (some might say predatory) in its range:

> We must extend the scope of order in planning and design to include larger areas; the entire view that meets the eye must be pleasing or, at least, inoffensive. If the architect sincerely tries to produce order in the chaos of our present cities, he will not be satisfied with his function as designer of individual buildings. He will become conscious of the relationships between buildings and between the buildings and the streets and the open spaces. He will, inevitably, be led to participate in city planning, unless he is willing to accept frustration and defeat in this vitally important phase of his work.[75]

By this account, urban planning and redevelopment was a natural outgrowth of an appreciation for aesthetic order, and would seek to cultivate and augment beauty in the world.

One might argue that the planners' aspirations toward (another version of) the city beautiful at midcentury constitute a legitimate desire to reclaim cities: to make over the spatial dimensions of our public life, to reinvent what the public sphere is and what good citizens are. Yet these seemingly innocent and even laudable ideals can often occlude our moral sensibilities, or our political responsibilities; in Kojin Karatani's phrase, they constitute a "will to architecture," or an "irrational choice to establish order and structure within a chaotic and manifold becoming."[76] Or as George Kateb writes, our "anxieties about beauty" often help us pursue "ideals that are untheorized but enacted . . . at large moral cost."[77] Aestheticism, Kateb eloquently argues, underwrites many of our best (and ostensibly nonaesthetic) intentions; in the myriad ways we strive to give order and meaning to our lives, we engage in "hungry perceptual and mental distortions of ruthless condensation, arbitrary displacement, forced representation, and opportunistic revision . . . which strain desperately to make the world come out right."[78]

In seeking to remake the cities at midcentury, the Park Commission's comprehensive plan for Washington made this ethos an imperative. "We must banish the ugliness which is almost as revolting as the squalor in our urban surroundings," Justement declared.[79] Or, as the commission itself recommended: "Beauty that exists must be preserved and enhanced. In the course of the improvement program . . . new beauty should be created."[80] The gaze of policy makers and planners turned out from the Washington Mall and onto the rest of the city.

Southwest Washington

What policy makers saw when they looked out from the Capitol (at least in one direction)[81] was Southwest Washington. Bounded by South Capitol Street (to the east), the Anacostia River and the Washington Channel (to the south and west), and the Mall (to the north), at midcentury, Southwest Washington was considered to be one of the worst housing areas in the United States. Not surprisingly, the 1950 Comprehensive Plan described the area as largely "obsolete," characterized not only by inadequate buildings but also by overcrowding and other threats to public health.[82] When the NCPPC examined the area in 1952, it described more than half of the area's dwellings as "substandard," where "more than 43 percent had outside toilets, more than 70 percent had no central heating, more than 44 percent had no baths, and more than 21 percent had no electricity."[83] That the spectacle of these Washington slums existed "but a stone's throw from the Capitol" made them nationally notorious and particularly offensive, as it interrupted the orderly ensemble of federal buildings and monumental space that bordered it to the north and east: "Because of its strategic location between the Potomac River and the Capitol Building," one commentator noted, "and because of the effort and talent which have gone into preparing a plan suitable for the national capital, Southwest Washington has become perhaps the most famous redevelopment project in the entire country."[84] In short, Southwest Washington—at least in the language used by policy makers—embodied all of the characteristics of an ugly, blighted area in need of radical renewal.[85]

Such was the opinion of the *Washington Post,* which in 1952 ran a series whose title put the choice in stark terms: "Progress or Decay? Washington Must Choose!" which chronicled the need for urban redevelopment and the various plans deliberated on by the Redevelopment Land Agency and the Planning Commission.[86] The *New York Times* also endorsed the "leveling of virtually the entire 500-acre quadrant that is drab, blighted Southwest Washington,"[87] and in 1958, the U.S. exhibit at the World's Fair in Brussels featured models of the area and the proposed redevelopment.

Drawing on the NCPPC Comprehensive Plan for Washington and the plan authored by Justement and Chloethiel Woodard Smith in 1952, the Southwest area was divided into three different project areas targeted for redevelopment, which together constituted approximately 560 acres.[88] The area was conceived of as a "city within a city," including new federal office buildings, a town center, a cultural/civic plaza, housing for more than five thousand families, and extensive waterfront redevelopment. The architects of the plan argued that it proposed "no sharp break with tradition, rather a regeneration of its best qualities" and to illustrate this point, they dubbed the centerpiece of their new plan "L'Enfant Plaza," once again invoking the first master plan for the city.[89]

By 1960, 99 percent of the buildings that had occupied the Southwest district—alley shanties and Victorian mansions, numerous small businesses, and the site of an extensive farmers' market—were razed, conforming to Le Corbusier's injunction that "WE MUST BUILD ON A CLEAR SITE! . . . *the existing centres must come down*."[90] "If we could climb to the top of the Capitol dome," one developer mused happily after the project had begun, "[W]e would see now the many acres, formerly dilapidated and degraded, now cleared and ready for rebuilding"[91] (see Figure 4.1). It was, to date, the largest urban redevelopment project undertaken in the United States, and was recognized as "a signpost and a symbol for the rest of the country."[92] Indeed, as Frieden and Sagalyn note, "These holdings were of a size not seen in American cities since the early land developers first laid out lot lines on the open countryside."[93] Such an area would be "a frontier for constructive achievement."[94]

By the time the Southwest redevelopment was complete, this urban "frontier" was transformed completely. The plan included an inner-loop freeway and the redevelopment of the area into a complex of offices, retail space, and housing that would stretch from the Smithsonian Institution to Fort McNair. Like other "frontiers" in American history, though, the Southwest's conversion into a civilized space required the forcible relocation of the unfortunates who had previously made their homes there. As Richard Slotkin persuasively argues, the myth of the American frontier—"the conception of America as a wide-open land of unlimited opportunity for the strong, ambitious, self-reliant individual to thrust his way to the top"—is at its heart a myth about regeneration through violence, and is the defining metaphor for capturing the American experience.[95] Indeed, the language of redemption is central to the discourse of urban renewal: the city must be destroyed so it can rise again. The Southwest project, as George Garrett told President Eisenhower, would become "a model . . . which could point the way for the salvation of obsolete city cores throughout the nation."[96]

At midcentury, the violence came in the form of the state's ability to relocate

Figure 4.1. Southwest Washington, "cleared and ready for rebuilding." Reproduced courtesy of the Library of Congress U.S. News and World Report Collection, LC-U9-2209-4.

families through the power of eminent domain; in Southwest Washington, about 23,500 people were relocated.[97] Although the difficulties involved in relocating such a large population was the source of much controversy in finalizing plans for the area, the conflict was resolved in favor of providing relatively little assistance to the displaced families. Less than 20 percent of the new structures built in the new Southwest could be considered "moderate-income" housing, and with the exception of the new Kober-Sternberg complex, there was no housing available for low-income families.[98] For Justement, these difficulties were outweighed by the need for rational and beautiful urban space. As he argued, "In extreme cases, residents of a community can and do move to another city when they are dissatisfied. This fact will, in itself, tend to curb any excessive interference with individual rights, while permitting a degree of wholesome experimentation."[99]

Truth and Beauty

It may seem clear to us that prioritizing a city's aesthetic well-being (at least as it had been defined by Washington's city planners) necessarily produces (or at least does not itself alleviate) social inequality. The title and theme of Gillette's compelling treatment of urban planning in Washington, *Between Justice and Beauty,* for example, posits these two concepts as opposites, where "beauty" has repeatedly, and wrongly, won the day in the capital city. But decisions about what constitutes justice often stem from affective or aesthetic, rather than cognitive, motivations, a result of the need to create order and beauty in an often chaotic and threatening world. This can result in injustice or oppression when these impulses remain unconscious, unacknowledged, unarticulated, and therefore *unpoliticized* in the ways we talk about and act in the world.

Recognizing how these affective and aesthetic motivations can undermine our attempts to work for justice is crucial for understanding the power that inheres in our spatiosymbolic order. What is less clear is how, if we are interested in social change, we combat these sorts of unconscious aesthetic and affective responses. How might we work to reshape the dominant spatial order? Can we (and should we) formulate an alternative, progressive aesthetics? To what criteria might we appeal?

Significantly, it was not only the moneyed interests or zealous reformers that appealed to aesthetic criteria for change in Southwest Washington, and this is the first tension we encounter in attempts to offer alternatives to Justement's vision of Washington. The series of photographs of Southwest Washington taken for the Farm Securities Administration (FSA) in the 1930s illustrates this point well. Beginning in 1935, Roy Stryker headed what was known as the Historical Section of the FSA, a unit intended to document the programs undertaken by that agency.[100] However, within a few years, Stryker's department was producing some of the most potent images in the history of photography in the United States. The photographs depicted the plights of farmers and immigrants, urban poverty, substandard housing, child labor, poor working conditions—all of the conditions which necessitated government intervention in the form of the New Deal. "Never before or since," the editor of *Life* magazine's New York News Bureau remarked, "has photography made so many people conscious of social problems . . ."[101] In fact, the FSA staff was the first group to have been (self-) described as "documentary" photographers; in the words of Stryker, this meant being a "realist rather than an escapist,"[102] being unwilling to shy away from the terrible conditions borne by individuals and families in the Depression years.

The photographs of Washington from 1935–42 are especially poignant. They show shabby, make-shift dwellings, back streets littered with trash and puddled with stagnant water, and small African American children sitting in the small, garbage-filled, dirt lots that constituted their "backyards." In several photographs, children appear as incidental to their decrepit surroundings; urban space in these photographs threatens to overwhelm them entirely (see Figure 4.2).

These bleak scenes were made especially affective by the fact that the outlines of "monumental Washington" (in particular, the Capitol Building or congressional office buildings) can be seen looming sadly and majestically in the background. Democracy, the pictures implied, was obviously (materially and symbolically) present and yet strikingly (materially and symbolically) absent in the lives of these people (see Figure 4.3). The photographs gave substance to the phrase "in the shadow of the Capitol," which appeared repeatedly in reporters' and planners' accounts of the city's problems to describe the Washington slums' proximity to and distance from the ideal of a working democracy.[103]

The FSA photographs achieved national and international attention in 1938 when they were shown at the International Photographic Exhibition in New York, and some were published in an annual edition of the magazine *U.S. Camera* in 1939.[104] Yet renewed interest in these areas (and the symbolic capital that inhered in these images) was double-edged. Like most well-intentioned reformers before them, I am sure, the photographers for the FSA series surely wanted to capture the "truths" of alley life to bring housing problems to the attention of the public and legislators. Especially in photographs taken by Godfrey Frankel, Carl Mydens, and Gordon Parks, the children of the South-

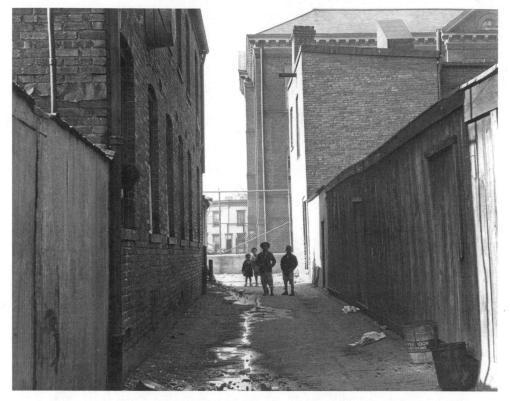

Figure 4.2. Boys in a Washington alley. Reproduced courtesy of the Library of Congress, FSA-OWI Collection, LC-USF34-000270-D.

west district are portrayed empathetically; they depict nothing if not terrific potential stunted by terrible circumstances.[105] However, the photographs also helped to construct their own reality regarding life in Southwest Washington, and helped to shape how legislators eventually would address the problem of urban poverty. Contrast the figures just described with the image of alley life depicted in Michael Gallagher's *Back Street*. In this print, done as part of a WPA series around the same time as these photographs were taken, the "back streets" are also sites of vibrant community life: a group of people gather in the street, conversing, and an onlooker (or participant) hangs out his window. A line of laundry (which in the aforementioned photographs often appears as a marker of poverty or slovenliness) waves as cheerfully as a flag. Billowing clouds (that is, open, airy space) are also part of this "street scene," an unmistakable contrast to narrow, dark spaces so often depicted in the FSA photos.

Figure 4.3. "In the shadow of the Capitol." Reproduced courtesy of the Library of Congress, Farm Securities Administration Collection, LC-USF34-015931-D.

Perhaps even more remarkably, what virtually never appear in the FSA photographs is the neighborhoods of which these alleys are a part. Even in the aerial view, the pre-redevelopment Southwest is shot from the backsides of its buildings, a sorry contrast to the glowing, white face of the Capitol perched above the scene. However, in a few photographs, what we see is perhaps an approximate ideal of urban life in that same Southwest community. In one photograph, the leaves on the trees and the light in the sky indicate it is perhaps a late spring or summer evening, and we witness a group of girls of various ages enjoying the spectacle of the street, and two or three men sitting on a stoop talking (see Figure 4.4). In another photo, neighbors gather in their front yards while a young girl sweeps the street in front of her house.[106] Retrospective accounts of urban renewal feature interviews with residents, who tell their interlocutors that the Southwest area was "the perfect place to have grown up, where the butcher, baker and banker were nearby and the faces

Figure 4.4. A neighborhood in Southwest Washington. Reproduced courtesy of the Library of Congress, FSA-OWI Collection, LC-USZ62-131660.

on the street were familiar."[107] These testimonies demonstrate that although the demographic profile of this area had changed over time, in the 1930s and 1940s, the old Southwest area was, for many, a living and livable space.[108]

My point is not to decide here which representation of "alley life" is true, because both images obviously tap into some portion of the truth of Southwest Washington at midcentury. Rather, I want merely to note that the set of images of Southwest Washington put into discursive circulation and into the legislative imagination (the majority of the FSA photos) offer only a narrow vision of this reality, and it is a vision that would shape the future of this Washington neighborhood. The photographs were incorporated into the discourse of urban renewal: a discourse that through its vocabulary of "blight" and "urban frontiers" emphasized economic viability and privileged wholesale clearance policies over rehabilitating existing properties and ensuring quality housing for the Southwest area's residents. By emphasizing the worst of the Southwest—in a genuine attempt to elicit sympathy and relief for its inhabitants—FSA photographers reinforced policy makers' ideas about the space being ugly, blighted, and dead—and not worth saving. Like all texts, these photographs are open to multiple readings and do not, in themselves, provide a clear "alternative" to the dominant spatial order.

How then might we work for change, work against the aesthetic imposed on low-income communities like that of Southwest Washington? One solution to the problem is what George Kateb calls "democratic aestheticism." Kateb argues that a democratic aestheticism would engender "receptivity or responsiveness to as much of the world as possible—its persons, its events and situations, its conditions, its patterns and sequences," to "make the unpromising world worthy of attention."[109] According to Kateb, such an attitude is found in the works of authors such as Emerson, Whitman, and Thoreau; it is an aestheticism conscious and attentive to the conflation of justice and beauty, and it will always interrogate its own, possibly crypto-aesthetic intentions. Democratic aestheticism seeks beauty in "the world as it is, not the world made over," and will thus find "beauty" in "the impure, the incomplete, the hybrid . . . the disorderly, the out of place."[110]

Cultivating a more democratic aesthetic is certainly a worthy project, but is itself fraught with difficulty. If we can upon Kateb's recommendation begin to appreciate "the world as it is," why would we be inspired to change anything about that world? Although Kateb acknowledges the possibility of passivity that might arise out of such an aesthetics,[111] he does not draw out the implications of this charge. More importantly, he does not recognize the possibly harmful effects of even a "democratic" objectification. Once again, the FSA photographs help illustrate this second tension well. After all, the photographs received national and international attention not only because they documented startling social problems or even because they tapped into a national mood; rather, they were recognized because at some level they are themselves beautiful objects. The photographs are effective (affective?) in part because they are, simply, *art*. Their lighting and composition, the photographer's choice of one angle and not another, of one subject and not another, make for pieces that are beautiful to look at: objects to hang in a museum (as these were) or to mass-produce in coffee-table books on documentary photography (as these are). Walter Benjamin might describe these photographs as an example whereby "poverty becomes an object of consumption."[112] By Kateb's account, beauty might now lie in the eye of the beholder, but there is nothing to ensure that the "beholder" is anyone other than who he has always been: a member of a dominant class or privileged social group. In this case, the results may be more benign but nonetheless unequal, a re-creation of the dominant self's vision of the subordinate other.

This is all to say that aestheticism, whatever its form, requires distance. Aestheticism helps to produce—or, in some instances, even widen—the space between self and other, without imposing any obligation on us to engage, inquire of, or interact with the object(s) of our admiration. Aestheticism privileges sight over sound; when we privilege vision in our public life, we diminish the necessity for, and the efficacy of, political voice. Democratic theorists have devoted considerable attention to the importance of political voice, often in the form of deliberative and participatory democracy. Nancy Love elucidates this distinction well. "Whereas vision marks differences with fixed boundaries," she writes, "voice establishes connections across space. Sound is a more interactive, relational sense. It involves two subjects, speaker and listener, instead of a subject and object. Speech occurs in an ongoing relationship . . . For this reason, voice can also undermine hierarchy and comparison. In contrast, visual imagery lends itself to stages, steps, positions, and levels."[113]

Any truly democratic aestheticism, then, needs to be attentive to how geographies predicated on vision affect the tone and timbre of political voice. In the modes of spatial practice discussed earlier, it is very apparent that visibility and invisibility are linked to both what is discussed and who may speak. Although a democratic aestheticism, as Kateb defines it, might act to curtail some of aestheticism's more vicious crimes, it is not truly democratic, as its subjects (objects) still remain voiceless and powerless against, for example, the will to architecture. In this way, the dominant spatial order remains largely unchallenged.

Losing Your Place

Between urban renewal and federally funded urban highway programs, over 700,000 people across the United States had been displaced by the mid-1960s. The relative success or failure of these programs was difficult to evaluate, and official information about them was notoriously unreliable; redevelopers had good reasons to overstate the successes and underreport the negative impact of these initiatives.[114] Some smaller-scale studies, however, did attempt to provide more balanced accounts of the results of redevelopment projects. In 1966, Daniel Thursz undertook a study of the impact of relocation on former residents of Southwest Washington. Thursz's inquiry into the matter, he relates, stemmed from a personal interest:

> I have often walked amidst the new, modernistic buildings of New Southwest and admired the careful planning that is evident in every part of this new glamorous neighborhood. Southwest is a source of pride to most Washingtonians and we rarely exclude it from the list of 'musts' for visitors to the Nation's Capital. In shepherding friends through the area, I would mention that this was once the shame of the Capital—an overcrowded and incredibly primitive slum. Sometimes, the visitors would ask, 'Well, where did all the slum dwellers go?' . . . My reply would leave them—and me—vaguely dissatisfied.[115]

The study resulting from this "vague dissatisfaction," *Where Are They Now?*, was published by the Health and Welfare Council of the National Capital Area five years after the area's redevelopment. Thursz and his team of volunteer researchers (operating with, as he reminds his readers, very modest funding) interviewed people displaced by Southwest redevelopment efforts to ascertain what impact urban renewal had on their lives. For the most part (and in keeping with the majority of accounts during that time), Thursz's conclusions emphasized the positive effects of urban renewal. Prior to relocation, Thursz reported, nearly half of the families in the Southwest area lived in dwellings that needed "major repairs" or were "unfit for use." After relocation, however, no families were located in such poor housing, and the "cleanliness and orderliness of the dwellings" had improved immensely. "If one measures the impact of relocation solely in terms of physical rehabilitation the urban renewal program is a huge success," he concluded.[116] That is, if one measures success in terms of abstract space—dead space emptied of its lived content, assessed in terms of new appliances, structural safety, and aesthetic order—then the program had fulfilled its aims.

Yet even Thursz acknowledged that the "huge success" had come with significant social costs, and he attempted to assess these through interviews with people displaced by redevelopment. One way he and his research team sought to tap into the social effects of displacement was through the Anomie Scale. Developed in 1950, the Anomie Scale was "designed to measure the degree of hopelessness and social dysfunction or disorganization in a selected population."[117] Based on the high scores accorded to displaced people on this scale, "[t]here is little doubt that the respondents in this study suffer from a high level of anomie."[118] Thursz also records displaced persons' more personal responses to their situation:

> Many of the respondents who lived in public housing had specific gripes, and most dealt with the rules established by the National Capital Housing Author-ity which administers public housing in Washington, or the project manager's interpretation of these rules. Several had global comments like "We've got to conform to the Capital Housing ideas . . ." or "They've got all sorts of project restrictions . . ." Others were much more specific, like the two women who complained that they could not plant their own flower seeds as they used to do in the Southwest.[119]

Twenty percent of his respondents told him that they would have preferred to have remained in the Southwest "without any improvement at all in . . . their environment" and under 30 percent were happy that they had to move, even though the respondents often liked their new homes better than their homes in the Southwest.[120] Fully a fourth of those surveyed reported "they had not made a single friend" since leaving their Southwest homes.[121] Mark Fried's earlier study of people forced to leave their close-knit Italian com-munity in the wake of urban renewal in Boston's West End came to similar conclusions: what displaced people experience is often "grief," or "feelings of painful loss, the continued longing, the general depressive tone, frequent symptoms of psychological or somatic distress, the active work required in adapting to the altered situation, the sense of helplessness, the occasional expressions of both direct and displaced anger, the tendencies to idealize the lost place."[122] That is, being forced to leave one's home is a profoundly emotional experience; losing one's place is also a loss of identity or sense of self, much like losing a loved one or losing a limb.

Thursz's and Fried's studies resonate with what social psychiatrist Mindy Fullilove describes as "root shock," or "the traumatic stress reaction to the destruction of all or part of one's emotional ecosystem." Between 1995 and 2003, Fullilove interviewed survivors of urban renewal in Pittsburgh, New-ark, and Roanoke, and found similar symptoms even in very different urban contexts: the sudden and staggering losses of one's sense of history, commu-nity, security, and social support. The reason for these extreme reactions to displacement, Fullilove argues, is that buildings, streets, and neighborhoods help us orient ourselves in the world. They are not simply the empty containers in which we live our lives; rather, they are "insinuated into us by life," and we are intricately and vitally connected to them.[123] Moreover, Fullilove holds that root shock has ramifications far beyond directly affected individuals or communities; instead, she contends, root shock has a substantial and persistent ripple effect, whereby the destruction of seemingly remote communities eventually has consequences for us all.[124]

We'll Plan This City with Gasoline

On the evening of Thursday, April 4, 1968, the country learned that Dr. Martin Luther King Jr. had been assassinated. In Washington, a small group of protesters gathered at the intersection of Fourteenth and U Street, then the central black business district in the District. Three days and an estimated twenty thousand participants later, the civil disturbances in Washington had claimed over twelve hundred buildings, caused more than $27 million dollars in property damage, resulted in over seven thousand arrests, and cost thirteen lives.[125] Over fifteen thousand troops were brought into the city over a week-long period to establish and maintain order (see Figure 4.5).

It would be a mistake to say that the riots that occurred in Washington, D.C.—or in any other city in the 1960s—were the *result of* slum clearance policies.[126] Yet there is certainly a relationship between displacement and disturbance: because central business districts were typically the oldest areas in cities, the poorest (or the most recent immigrants) were likely to be housed there, and thus also the most likely to be affected directly by urban renewal efforts. In fact, three-fourths of those displaced by urban redevelopment programs across the nation were black or Puerto Rican.[127] When President Johnson's Advisory Commission on Civil Disorders studied the issue, the commission found urban renewal evictions as a common complaint. The staff investigated Detroit, New Haven, and Newark, three cities which had been at the forefront of urban renewal effort, amassing millions of dollars in federal funds between them. The commission found that in all three cities there were significant discrepancies between the amount of low-income housing destroyed by urban redevelopment and the number of low-income dwellings built to house those displaced. In Detroit, 8,000 low-income housing units were destroyed, and 758 were built. In New Haven, 6,500 houses were destroyed, and 951 built. In Newark, 12,000 families were displaced, and 3,760 houses were built.[128] These three cities were also the sites of tremendous urban upheaval in the 1960s. Urban redevelopment projects, then, may not

Figure 4.5. Policing the geography of (in)civility. Reproduced courtesy of the Library of Congress U.S. News and World Report Collection, LC-U9-18946-5A.

have been the *only* cause of the riots in Washington or anywhere else in the country, but they did contribute to a larger geography of injustice; they were material evidence that these communities did not matter to the life of the city, and were reason for grief in the face of losing one's history, losing one's place.[129]

Indeed, although the disturbances would be characterized by most as chaotic, disorganized, random acts of violence (thankfully not the work of a "conspiracy," according to the U.S. Riot Commission Report), some of the protesters saw themselves involved in very specific forms of resistance. As one participant in the disturbances noted, the word "revolution" more adequately describes the events, since "riot" itself is a loaded word. "Riot is spontaneous. Revolution is planned. It's as simple as that."[130] Activist Stokely Carmichael called the violence "guerrilla warfare."[131]

I do not wish to speculate as to whether the disturbances were in fact "planned" or were "spontaneous" actions. Rather, I want to suggest that the spatial practices engaged in by the protesters might be characterized as what Orville Lee describes as "symbolic disobedience," or "the disruption of established patterns of symbolic interaction [which] enables ordinary citizens to raise a critical perspective on the legitimacy of the symbolic order."[132] Lee seems to limit the category by reserving it for transgressive art (e.g., Karen Finley and Robert Mapplethorpe), music (e.g., punk), and performative political protest (e.g., ACT UP), but tactics that challenge spatial practices (dominant modes of architecture, planning practices, and zoning ordinances, for example) are a logical and necessary extension of this concept. Symbolic disobedience in this sense might be regarded as any strategies that seek to subvert dominant (and dominating) spatial arrangements through the radical (re)claiming of space.

To claim that the riots are examples of symbolic disobedience is neither to endorse nor romanticize that particularly painful moment in the city's history. The seemingly "disorganized" practices of the Washington protesters are neither the only possible nor the most effective responses to spatiosymbolic injustices; arguably, many of the cities that endured riots in the 1960s are still recovering from them.[133] Other, nonviolent forms of such disobedience might include marches or parades, sit-ins, graffiti, and public murals, all of which introduce moments of reversal, contestation, and conflict into a hegemonic spatial order. Yet many of these options were unavailable, or would likely be deemed ineffective, by populations whose political interests and desires were systematically ignored when they were expressed in "legitimate" ways.[134]

The civil disturbances in Washington created what James C. Scott calls an "insurrectionary space,"[135] whereby the insurgents used the space of the city in publicly subversive ways. As we have seen, since (at least) the turn of the century, underprivileged parts of the city (its alleys and slums) have been regarded with suspicion; its nooks and crannies potentially shielding dangerous persons, hiding unthinkable and unspeakable horrors. In 1968, the spatial practices of nearly two hundred years (L'Enfant's boulevards inspired by Haussmann's postrevolutionary Paris, legislative initiatives designed to rout out disease and death from city spaces, and increasingly rationalized and segregated urban areas) were inverted, and the defensible space of the city was turned inside out. Participants used spatial resources to combat the imposition of visibility, order, and control. As one participant told a reporter from the *Washington Post* later that year, white flight and persistent racial segregation worked to disadvantage law enforcement officials trying to control the streets:

> Another thing, too, it's a disadvantage of these honkie cops that move out to the suburbs, 'cause nobody knows the city better than city-dwellers. There are alleys that the cops don't know about. And rooftops can take you plenty of places. . . . we are finding that the city is really a jungle in more respects than . . . in the past . . . This is really like a real jungle, man, a jungle where you have forts. Each block is like a fort in some areas. And, you can survive within those blocks . . . for a long time without the man ever finding you.[136]

The long, wide streets of the city, so carefully laid out by L'Enfant, so carefully preserved and enhanced by other planners, were overtaken. The imperative of movement, the necessary and carefully coordinated flows of vehicles and commerce, were interrupted. "White flight" in this context took on a whole new meaning; on the second day of the riots, massive numbers of white-collar workers attempting to leave early to begin their commutes to the suburbs caused the city's worst traffic jam. Warren Freeman, then a new member of the District of Columbia National Guard recalled: "You could see the traffic jams. . . . You could see groups of whites traveling home together through black neighborhoods to try to get home from work safely. That was the start of fires blocks long in lower Northwest . . . The road networks were just totally wiped out. There were people in the streets, vehicles damaged and stalled out in roads, fires going and firemen trying to pull them out, streets blocked off . . ."[137] Journalists' accounts at the time had the character of wartime coverage; a *Washington Post* reporter, for example, described Prince George's County as "the most vulnerable . . . because of its long border with the predominantly Negro Far Northeast and Southeast sections of the city."[138] One man stalled at a traffic light told a reporter that it would be all right once he got to Virginia.[139]

Such descriptions—of jungles, forts, groups huddled together seeking safety, and vehicular traffic brought to a halt—rendered the city both dis-cursively and materially an undeveloped frontier again. In the decade fol-lowing Washington's "modernization," "renewal," and "redevelopment," the riots were a spatial and temporal interruption in the march of progress, a reversal or a refusal of the way that class and race had been made material in the built environment. The time and the space of the city were altered in a matter of hours. One might say the Washington "riot" was a radical act of spatial disobedience that countered the ruthless logic of a century of urban planning.

5. Millennial Space: Securing History and Commemorating Threat

On a chilly March day in the nation's capital I was at the top of the Washington Monument, looking down. Through one of the narrow rectangular windows I observed a flurry of miniature activity below me: cranes, bulldozers, and workers crisscrossed a sunken, bowl-shaped construction site, engaged in an elaborate mechanical ballet. The view from the Washington Monument was my first experience of the newest structure to occupy the National Mall: the World War II Memorial. Since its location on the main east-west axis of the mall was dedicated in 1995 (it is the first monument to be placed in this central location since the Lincoln Memorial), the World War II Memorial has been a source of tremendous, often vitriolic, controversy. Supporters of the Memorial have lauded its neoclassical style, especially the intricately sculpted bronze eagles that sit atop its granite columns, gripping laurel wreaths in their beaks. Detractors have denounced architect Friedrich St. Florian's design as either *too* "monumental" (describing it as "imperialist kitsch," harkening back to the designs of Albert Speer)[1] or not monumental *enough* (an unfortunate victim of architectural political correctness).[2] Both the Memorial's fans and its critics agree that monument building is in crisis, and that this crisis is being played out in the space of the National Mall.

Getting to the top of the Washington Monument, of course, hadn't been easy. Even from some blocks away earlier that morning, I couldn't help but notice the concrete barricades forming an irregular and unsightly circle around the structure. Once I had purchased my ticket at the Fifteenth Street kiosk, my fellow tourists and I stood in line as our bags, cameras, water bottles and purses were searched. We walked through a metal detector, as courteous but serious-looking men from the U.S. Park Police appraised our threat potential. One young boy was stopped and his pocket knife was con-fiscated, to be returned later when his tour was finished. This is the second crisis now facing the capital city: how the symbolic spaces of democracy can remain open for business while at the same time acknowledge the pos-sibility of very real threats.

Millennial Washington is thus situated at the center of two crucial, and not unrelated, discourses about space and citizenship. The first concerns the proliferation of commemorative (that is, monumental and historic) spaces, the burgeoning number of memorial and museum sites in Washington that one historian has termed Washington's "monument glut."[3] Far from being unique to Washington, though, this "glut" is part of a national trend: the hyper-production of commemorative spaces, from simple memorial markers to entire historic districts. Although at first blush this might indicate a democ-ratization of identity and memory, I will argue that this crisis of monument making is in fact a result of the tension between the ethical commitments of a pluralist democracy and monumentality as a mode of making public space.

The second debate involves the extensive use of surveillance to monitor citizens' actions. Many commentators have described this tendency to be a result of the privatization of public space. Public space, however, is not any less monitored. In fact, especially in cities like Washington, and particu-larly in the wake of September 11, 2001, public space is now overwhelmingly surveilled and defensible space. In addition to more barricades and metal detectors and greater security force presence in public spaces, the District of Columbia's Metropolitan Police Department is making use of a vast new network of cameras to keep tabs on the city.

Both the discourses of hyper-memorialization and the expansion of disci-plinary technologies, I argue, reflect new anxieties about building the body politic. How best to represent and protect that body are concerns that un-derwrite plans for the twenty-first-century capital city. Through initiatives to create landscapes that are both commemorative and secure, portions of the city are increasingly made visible, while many of the socioeconomic realities of the city—as well as the persons behind the cameras—are simultaneously removed from sight.

These new ways of talking about and making space comprise a very dif-ferent public sphere from the places envisioned by writers such as Richard Sennett and Iris Marion Young, whose ideas about democratic space I ex-plore next. Rather, these new discourses support the infrastructure for an intensely scopophilic politics. As indicated previously, by *scopophilic politics* I mean a politics where citizens are those who are willing to watch and be watched, where persons not conforming to these new requirements of this new citizenship are excluded from the demos altogether. Citizens become targets as panoptic and state power become increasingly intertwined. Like all forms of power, however, scopophilic politics contains within it the possibilities for resistance. In the last section of the chapter, I examine several strategies that attempt to respond politically to these eviscerations of public space and political life.

Theorizing the Public Sphere

"The public sphere," as the phrase has been articulated within contemporary political theory, is an excellent example of an interstitial space: it is a space that is neither wholly metaphorical nor exactly material. When we talk about the public sphere, we may be signifying either an actual place or places, or indicating a loosely defined ethos of democratic interaction—or both at once. This tension in the concept, its definitive in-betweenness, is present even in its first formulations; in his book *The Structural Transformation of the Public Sphere,* Jürgen Habermas describes both a set of communicative ideals (discussion, debate, and consensus building) and an array of concrete places (the journals, cafés, literary salons, pubs, and meeting halls) that together comprised the network of social and political life in Britain, France, and Germany in the late eighteenth and nineteenth centuries. The bourgeois public sphere, as Habermas describes it, is neither an abstract ideal nor simply a set of particular institutions; rather, it is the means by which public opinion is formed and transformed in the course of communicative interaction.[4] The transformation of the public sphere that Habermas documents, though, is not only its genesis but also its deterioration, as democratic civil society buckles under the weight of the culture industry, state capitalism, and increasingly powerful corporations. In this way, "the public sphere" also becomes a normative benchmark against which to evaluate contemporary political life by gauging how close to, or removed from, the halcyon days of democratic engagement we might be.

Although Habermas's particular version of the public sphere has been modified, augmented, and critiqued by innumerable interlocutors in the decades since it was first introduced, the idea of the public sphere—as a set of democratic practices linked to, and to an extent dependent on, some version of public space—remains one of the central themes in contemporary political theory. In her influential book *Justice and the Politics of Difference* (1990), Iris Young argues that a robust, pluralist politics is best modeled on the democratic ethos she sees as inherent in city life. The public space of the city, she claims, necessitates a kind of "being together with strangers," which requires "an openness to unassimilated otherness."[5] The way of being facilitated by the city's variety, publicity, and anonymity, Young argues, is a much more auspicious model for political life than the Rousseauian desires for homogeneity, intimacy, and transparency, desires recast in many communitarian discourses of the 1980s and 1990s.

In many ways, Young's work complements Richard Sennett's (1974) thesis in *The Fall of Public Man:* that city life serves as a stage for public action.[6] Like Young, Sennett argues that urban life creates the anonymity necessary for specific kinds of interactions: "In a milieu of strangers, the people who witness one's actions, declarations and professions usually have no knowledge of one's history, and no experience of similar actions, declarations, and professions in one's past . . ."[7] It is in the absence of intimate knowledge of public actors, Sennett contends, that "a public geography is born."[8] Such a geography both presupposes and cultivates political imagination, by encouraging citizens to think, believe, and act in ways that transcend their particular experiences.

Also like Young, Sennett contrasts this vision of cosmopolitan, urban life with the suffocating and exclusionary confines of the community. The "tyranny of intimacy" fostered in a community predisposes its members to police each other's actions; as he writes, "community has a surveillance function in which people are attempting at once to be emotionally open with each other and to control each other." For Sennett as for Young, the stifling demands of community require "emotional withdrawal from society."[9] By contrast, urban space, when properly configured, constructs and requires boundaries between public and private life, and thus serves as "the forum in which it becomes meaningful to join with other persons without the compulsion to know them as persons."[10] Without these boundaries, public life (and the democratic politics that follow from it) is impossible.

For some, however, the idea of a cosmopolitan, urban public sphere is both hopelessly nostalgic and ultimately unworkable. For Jodi Dean, the very idea of "the public" itself is beholden to an unrealizable ideal of social unity, the hope that "we are all part of the same thing, members of the same public."[11] Instead of being bound together as a national public by a vigilant, governmental Big Brother, Dean claims, we are instead besieged by countless, fractal "little brothers" who "trade in information" rather than military might.[12] Moreover, what often markets itself as communicative democracy, Dean contends, is really communicative capitalism; these are new social and cultural formations forged in the name of—and that work to sustain the fiction of—the "public," but serve specific economic interests: twenty-four-hour cable news channels, the Internet, and the World Wide Web. Dean argues that focusing on conceptions like law, constitutionality, and the nation-state (as in Habermas's most recent work)—focusing, in other words, on the "Big Brother" or sovereign aspects of political power—risks abandoning the possibility of democracy altogether.

I agree with Dean that critical theorists need to be attentive to the possibilities advanced by new technologies, and that overly simplistic theses (i.e., that these technologies are either liberating, or the harbingers of a new totalitarianism) are unhelpful. However, Dean's assumption that technoculture and state power are mutually exclusive is highly problematic. As I describe here, millennial urban spaces generally—and capital cities specifically—are sites where sovereign power and disciplinary power intersect, creating a spectacle of state surveillance. Rather than an either/or scenario, we need topographies of democracy that explore questions of publicity, power, and justice where we live: in places thoroughly mediated but not yet wholly colonized by (among other social forces) technology, capital, and the sovereign power of the state.

Our Monuments, Our Selves[13]

> The Mall speaks. Day after day, workers and tourists in Washington, D.C., are drawn from the offices and great museums to hear its silent language.
> —Robert Ivy, FAIA

If the Mall speaks, then many argue that it is crying out for help; this is the conclusion one must draw if one reads any of the numerous commentaries on the state of monument building on the National Mall. The body politic, according to many journalists, architects, and planners, is in crisis. As they see it, the central dilemma that animates Washington at this new fin de siècle is the problem that historian James Reston Jr. has named "monument glut," or what journalist Elaine Sciolino terms the "sprawl on the Mall."[14]

Simply put, the "sprawl on the Mall" refers to the rapid rate at which monuments and memorials are proliferating in the symbolic heart of the nation. The National Capital Planning Commission (NCPC) estimates that between 1900 and 2000, an average of one memorial each year was dedicated in Washington.[15] Moreover, the number of people, groups, and events in need of commemoration, as well as the number of relics to be housed and contributions to be exalted, appear to be increasing exponentially. Aware of the potential ramifications of this development, Congress passed the Commemorative Works Act in 1986, which set stricter standards for the design and implementation of monuments in the nation's capital.[16] Apparently, however, the new law has done little to quell the proliferation of things we need to remember. By June 2001, there were 155 memorials and 74 museums in Washington, the vast majority of which are located on or along the Mall and its immediate environs.[17] At present, many others are in various stages of development, and will soon be ready to take their places in Washington. "If past trends continue," the NCPC has recently warned, "there could be more than 50 additional memorials in the heart of the Nation's Capital by 2050."[18]

Monument glut poses several problems, as architects and planners see it. One concern, of course, is that the prime real estate for monuments, the National Mall, is a finite space, and it simply may not be large enough to house the artifacts of our ever expanding collective memory. If we fill the Mall to capacity by 2050, architects, planners, and historians wonder, what space will remain for the monuments of future centuries? Assuming our republic enjoys longevity and prosperity, where will our heroes of the twenty-first or twenty-fourth centuries be remembered?[19]

This worry stems from the concern that the Mall itself is a "sacred space," "hallowed ground," the sanctity and integrity of which need to be vigilantly secured. Through monument glut, many planners worry, the sacred space of the Washington Mall will become profaned. Monuments, rather than inciting awe, solemnity, or patriotism, will be reduced to so much clutter on the nation's front lawn. As architect Roger Lewis contends, "[A]n excess of memorials built on or around the Mall will detract from and devalue those that are most sacred, the few that truly deserve to occupy the pantheon."[20] With such abundant monumentality, the "currency of collective memory will be debased."[21] In large numbers, apparently, monuments lose their powers to instruct and impel contemplation, and are demoted from art to kitsch. As one commentator summed up, "Washington may emerge as a giant historical theme park, with its stock of dignity diluted by too many memorials, each competing for the visitor's emotions for a brief span before the guidebook says, 'move on.'"[22] Or, as Reston argues, soon visiting the Lincoln Memorial, the Korean War and Vietnam Veterans Memorials will become "the walking-around equivalent of changing channels on the television."[23]

This anxiety about "diluting" the power and dignity of the National Mall coincides with the trend of what we might call monumental pluralism: the push to include previously marginalized groups into the pantheon of national memory. Recent additions to the Mall include the National Japanese American Memorial (honoring both Japanese American soldiers and those interned in camps during World War II), the Women in Military Service Memorial (located in the Arlington National Cemetery), and the National Museum of the American Indian. Monuments to Black Revolutionary War Patriots, Dr. Martin Luther King Jr., and an African American History Museum are in various stages of development. Each of these initiatives is premised on the belief that the version of "American-ness" originally imagined, depicted, and reified through the landscape of the National Mall is (as we saw in Chapter 3) exclusionary, and that a twenty-first-century Mall needs to speak to, and for, more people.

Visually expressing the reality of American diversity challenges the unanimity of the body politic and exposes as particular of a set representations that imply their own universality. Casting other identities and histories in stone gives them the permanence and seriousness previously reserved for master narratives. Not surprisingly, the plurality of bodies vying for commemorative space in the capital city are frequently cast as unruly minority groups or "specialist lobbies" that revel in their diversity, rather than being appropriately monumental and "ris[ing] above difference."[24] "Soon the National Mall may grow so cluttered as to resemble a graveyard full of stone edifices to special interests," an editorial in a national newspaper complained.[25]

The battles over *who* can represent the body politic are also battles over *how* that body is represented. One of the most vivid examples of this is the controversy over how to depict the president in the Franklin Delano Roosevelt Memorial that opened in 1997. This parklike memorial, located next to the Tidal Basin, features four "rooms," each dedicated to one of FDR's terms in office. Lawrence Halprin's design includes granite walls, waterfalls, and bronze sculptures, taking the visitor on "an experiential history lesson" through the Great Depression and World War II.[26] The memorial's size (seven and a half acres of the Mall) and its expense ($48 million), however, were far less controversial than the single statue of FDR that was initially placed there.

The original statue features the president seated in a wheelchair, but the wheelchair is obscured by a large bronze cape that is draped around Roosevelt's shoulders; only a small castor at the foot of one of the chairs indicates its function. Disability rights activists protested vociferously, arguing that the image of FDR included in the monument was a damaging distortion that reinforces the notion that disability is something shameful, and something to keep hidden. By contrast the new sculptural addition to the monument, paid for by the National Organization on Disability, is located at the entrance to the memorial; it clearly shows Roosevelt as physically challenged and using a wheelchair. The decision to include the second statue was met with hostility by some, who claimed that the FDR Memorial had become a case study in political correctness.[27] Conservative art critic Catesby Leigh, for example, scathingly remarked that, "A visit to the Roosevelt Memorial is less a rendezvous with destiny than a rendezvous with disability."[28]

The controversy over which statue "most accurately" represents FDR specifically, and the presidency generally, is not simply a case of "special interest groups" having their way (or not) with commemorative design. Rather, it is the result of our tendency to conflate what Michael Rogin called "the king's two bodies": the president's mortal, physical body and the body politic. If we depict the president as old, weak, or ailing—if we depict the president as anything other than totally self-reliant—then in our perpetual confusion over person, power, office, and nation we are also making a statement about our history and our future as a country.[29] Roosevelt's disability becomes an injury to the body politic, his weakened limbs a metonym for the end of "the American century." By confronting the history of Roosevelt's own body, we are forced to acknowledge the particularity and materiality of the body politic.

The newly constructed World War II Memorial might be read as another answer to the problem of embodying national identity. Catesby Leigh also weighed in on this debate, noting that in a war that claimed over 400,000 American lives, human figures are conspicuously absent from the memorial's design; no statues or other depictions of the human form, he notes, "whether allegorical, or realist, or both," represent Americanness in this place. Leigh speculates that this is no oversight, but may indicate either "Washington's official phobia of making too bold a statement on the Mall" or a fear of simply reiterating the figures found at the U.S. Marine Corps and Korean War memorials.[30] I would argue, however, that the no-body problem in the World War II Memorial is a symptom of the larger crisis of representation, a recognition that the "universal" figure used to designate a member of the armed forces (a white male) is now understood by many to be both specific and inaccurate. For Leigh, the multiplicity of bod*ies* politic is deeply unsettling; if the Mall is speaking, he complains, it is speaking in tongues, and, in his words, "we are left with babble."[31] Clearly, which bodies may count as presidents, as soldiers, and as citizens is once again—or still—a central question in planning the public spaces of democracy.

Democratic Monumentality or,
All Monuments Are Not Created Equal

Responding to the impending "glut" of monuments, the Joint Task Force on Memorials (JTFM) released the Memorials and Museums Master Plan in December 2000.[32] The plan aims for the dispersal of monuments, memorials, and museums throughout Washington, D.C., so that national spaces of celebration and remembrance are not limited to Washington's monumental core. Rather, most new monuments and memorials would be directed to other areas of the District, serving to dignify the "everyday" spaces of the greater urban area. The JFTM designates one hundred potential future sites for memorials and museums, creating out of the city "a new landscape of commemoration."[33]

The plan adopted by the task force divides Washington into three precincts. First, it establishes an area called the Reserve, or "no-build zone," which refers to the central Mall area. The White House, the Washington Monument, and the Jefferson Memorial form the north-south axis of the Reserve, and the Capitol Building, the Washington Monument, and the Lincoln Memorial mark out its east-west path. The policy prohibits any new building—memorial or museum—in this area.[34] Instead, the task force recommends that any new commemorative works be located in Areas I and II, areas that fan out from the Mall along "a lattice of Monumental Corridors" and are connected through "symbolic prominence, visual linkages, and aesthetic quality."[35] Nineteen of the proposed sites are considered "prime sites" for significant structures; the remaining eighty-three sites are located in areas that do not typically attract tourist traffic. The Memorials and Museums Master Plan proffered by the task force self-consciously harkens back to L'Enfant's original vision for the city, where monuments serve to build coherence and continuity between the city's symbolic and functional purposes and act as both the backdrop and catalysts for meaning-full public life.

Is this new commitment to public art and public memory an indication of an increasingly democratic sensibility in urban planning? On one hand, this dispersal of monumental spaces might be regarded as highly democratic, as the National Mall is asked to "share the wealth" of national identity and memory with surrounding communities, some of which have never had any sort of monumental architecture to speak of. As the JTFM specifically argues, "The plan promotes the idea that the cultural and historic diversity of our Nation's Capital can become a focus for a broader commemorative experience, par-ticularly within such historic locales as Anacostia, Brookland, Georgetown, Marshall Heights, and Shaw"[36]—with the exception of Georgetown, these are historically poor and racially diverse areas of the city. Simply by diversifying potential commemorative sites, the Memorials and Museums Master Plan might contribute to an ideal of national identity that is more plural, decentered, and complex than the version currently on display on the Mall.

There are a number of troubling implications of the plan, however. First, through its designation of a Reserve area, the new comprehensive plan further consolidates, rather than disperses, the authoritarianism inherent in the very project of monumentality. As Steven Johnston eloquently argues, the very idea of sacred space being compatible with democratic politics is deeply problematic: "That which is sacred, honoring the eternal and the unchanging, symbolic of truth and fidelity, eliciting reverence and awe, demanding deference and devotion, committed to unity and consensus," he writes, "runs counter to a vibrant democratic ethos featuring plurality and contestation."[37]

What is implicit in Johnston's reading of this space is a fundamental opposition in this democratic space: between life and death. In an obvious—and profound—sense, much monumental space is "dead" space: space devoted to those whose lives have been lost in war or heroes whose passing we honor with built tributes. The Mall and its immediate environs (the broad expanse of Arlington National Cemetery, the Holocaust Memorial Museum, and even the Capitol Building with Washington's intended crypt in the basement) is an enormous, elaborate diorama of death.[38] But the new plan attempts to make it dead space in the political sense as well; by putting a moratorium on future building projects in the Reserve area, the plan further rarifies the idea of the Mall as a sacred space, and teaches us that history is something timeless, unchanging, and not open to question.

With the creation of the Reserve, the agonism inherent in meaningful, democratic public life—its messiness, ambiguity, and continual negotiation—is sacrificed at the altar of symbolic order. The new plan insulates the Mall from future argument or contestation, essentially extracting politics from the very place that we hope to be the tumultuous epicenter of democracy. "[The Reserve] is essentially a completed work of art," said the chair of the Joint Task Force on Memorials.[39] At this juncture, we might do well to remember Jane Jacobs's warning: "A city cannot be a work of art." To approach a city as if it were simply an architectural problem, Jacobs argued, "is to make the mistake of attempting to substitute art for life. The results of such profound confusion between art and life are neither life nor art. They are taxidermy."[40] For this reason, as Johnston suggests, in "a democracy . . . both committed and ultimately unfaithful to its own affirmations as it pursues the commemorative enterprise," we might best save monuments by destroying them.[41]

In addition to reifying particular and uncontestable versions of identity and history, though, monuments serve other, less-than-democratic functions as well. Much of the literature on monumentality ignores the economic imperatives that undergird most attempts to build history into urban landscapes, such as those clearly spelled out in the JTFM recommendations. The monumental glut in Washington is a particularly nationalist variant of larger trends in cities across the United States, trends that have broad implications for imagining the shape of democracy. In the past thirty years, American cities and communities have spawned countless commemorative spaces, from simple memorial markers to entire historic districts. Not coincidentally, the origins of the historic preservation movement—the various initiatives to preserve the unique and precious character of many urban spaces—are concomitant with when the United States began to feel the homogenizing effects of suburbanization.

In Washington, D.C., as in many other cities, the suburbs of the 1940s and 1950s quickly morphed into what Joel Garreau calls "edge cities."[42] Despite garnering the collective scorn of the cultural elite, edge cities and suburbs continue to attract new residents, and consequently older urban centers are faced with the prospect of irrelevance: what can they offer that can't be done faster, better, and cheaper in these other places? The answer—in Washington, D.C., and in other cities—is *history:* it is the one good that these newer communities surely cannot provide. In an inversion of the planning rationale deployed at midcentury (that, as Justement so memorably put it, cities are places where the "dead hand of the past" mocks at us), urban planning at the millennium intends to resuscitate historical places, rather than methodically eliminate them. As a result, cities are increasingly in the position of needing to peddle their histories to survive, a situation evidenced in the countless redevelopment investments in large-scale renovations of historic market-places, boardwalks, theaters, and concert halls.[43]

Washington, D.C., has found economic success in marketing its history, and the new Master Plan reflects the economic imperatives of further success. A member of the NCPC described the new plan in this way: "A basic premise of [the plan] is that well designed and strategically located museums and memorials can spark investments in stores, hotels, office buildings and can contribute to community renewal and economic revitalization."[44] In addition to serving as transmitters of civic pride and virtue, memorials and museums today, the task force argues, must "work for a living;" they "can be powerful tools for bolstering economic development," specifically by bringing tourists off the beaten path and into economically depressed areas.[45] Rather than simply enhancing civic spaces, memorials and museums—and the entire industry of national history and collective—are engines of economic growth, put into service to rescue the city from its uneven development.

The focus of the plan, then, is to create a series of vantage points and vistas that communicate citizenship while encouraging consumerism—to produce images of Americanness, in other words, that are also commodities. This strategy represents Washington, D.C., not as a lived in and livable city, but as a series of tourist destinations, an artificial map which, as Christine

Boyer argues, "suppresses the continuous order of reality, the connecting in-between places, and imposes instead an imaginary order of things."[46] In so doing, the plan subjects the urban public sphere indefinitely to the aesthetic demands of a very particular public: tourists. Public space, then, is planned for spectators rather than participants; tourism is conflated with citizenship (or vice versa). By creating a series of "commemorative landscapes" in Washington, planners render the public tourists and voyeurs—rather than citizens and actors—in their own cities. Put another way, the spaces intended as allegories of democracy reify a version of citizenship predicated on consumerism, promoting a version of citizenship that is defined solely through purchasing power. In this way, the ideals of city making that were made manifest in the Columbian Exposition's White City are resuscitated for the twenty-first century in Washington, D.C.

Finally, although this is a plan for future monuments—monuments yet to be conceived, let alone built—we can speculate how this hierarchical ordering of monumental space might play out in future decades. For example, one might reasonably infer that the monuments planned for the most prominent sites—the monuments deemed "preeminently significant"—will represent those who have been traditionally represented by commemorative architecture, under the auspices of universality. Those planned for areas like Anacostia and Brookland (monuments of only "lasting significance"), on the other hand, may very well be those that represent "other" versions of history and heroes (perhaps those commemorative ideas advanced by "specialist lobbies"), or that trouble the very notion of monumentality. In this way, the centers of power (and the spatial narratives of nationalism and progress that accompany them) might be further separated materially and ideologically from the periphery.

This outcome would be the materialization of a resolutely liberal account of power, national identity, and difference. As William Connolly describes it, "A liberal nation [is] one in which the national majority extends tolerance to an assortment of minorities clustered around the vital center. Such an image is compatible, then, with variety and diversity and difference. It is how diversity and difference are imagined in relation to a constitutive cultural center that is definitive."[47] What is problematic about this version of public space and public history is that the center, both ideologically and materially, still holds. By contrast, true pluralism would mean either multiple, overlapping "centers," or a center that is continually transformed in light of alternate accounts and perspectives. The Museums and Memorials Master Plan for Washington, however, may very well cast a singular and unchanging center, quite literally, in stone.

Someone to Watch over Me

> What in fact was the Rousseauist dream . . .? It was the dream of
> a transparent society, visible and legible in each of its parts, the
> dream of there no longer existing any zones of darkness . . . The
> new aspect of the problem of justice . . . was not so much to punish
> wrongdoing as to prevent even the possibility of wrongdoing, by
> immersing people in a field of total visibility.
> —Michel Foucault, "The Eye of Power"

At the same time that the Joint Task Force on Memorials was unveiling the latest master plan for the monumentalization of Washington, the District of Columbia's Metropolitan Police Department (MPD) was testing its newest contribution to the urban landscape: the most comprehensive surveillance system in the United States.[48] More than a dozen police cameras currently survey downtown Washington locations such as the White House, the Capitol, and Union Station, and there are several other video feeds from cameras attached to police helicopters. The U.S. Park Police survey the monuments on the Mall. In an emergency, public schools, the Washington Metro, and the Department of Transportation can link hundreds of cameras into the system, and the network has a seemingly infinite capacity for expansion. From its Joint Operations Command Center in police headquarters, the MPD can monitor activity at forty different video stations; the FBI and the Secret Service have their own stations within the center. As Paul Virilio argues, this "new market of vision is characterized by rendering to sight whatever is happening in the world in the present moment—the new 'tele-present,'" or "omnivoyance."[49]

All the World Is a Stage

Extensive surveillance systems like the one in Washington raise important questions about the political possibilities now available to people in public spaces, and impel us to consider the new constraints such systems place on the practices of citizenship. Many commentators have described this trend towards surveillance to be a result of increasingly privatized spaces. For example, surveillance cameras are employed more and more frequently in gated communities (which have replaced traditional and more "open" housing developments), and in suburban shopping malls and downtown galleries (which have replaced main streets in small towns and big cities alike).[50] But the D.C. system, at the present time, monitors mainly *public* spaces, where, as several Supreme Court decisions have held, individuals do not have a reasonable expectation of privacy. What is more, as we transfer our previously public activities (walking, shopping, and entertainment) into private arenas such as shopping malls, and as technologies grow increasingly sophisticated (the cameras in Washington can peer into individual backyards or onto rooftops) our ideas about what constitutes public and private space become much more ambiguous.[51]

These systems create a very different kind of public sphere than the idealized city space imagined by democratic urbanists such as Iris Young and Richard Sennett. For Young and Sennett, as discussed above, the city's democratic potential follows directly from its ability to provide its citizens with a measure of anonymity, rather than from the communitarian promise of transparent authenticity. As a place where we practice "being together with strangers" without trying to "deny or repress social difference,"[52] the city can serve as a "stage" for public action. These traits distinguish the ideal of a cosmopolitan city from the "Rousseauist dream" of a transparent community, where public life is made possible only through immediate and intimate knowledge of one's fellow citizens. The assurance of anonymity and performative character of urban life, these theorists argue, create the necessary conditions for a democratic public sphere.

The surveillance system in place in Washington—and the kind of surveillance being imagined and designed for this and future cities—disrupts these conditions of possibility, and may then diminish the city's democratic potential. The possibility of anonymous public action is eradicated as the lines between private and public spaces are blurred. External video feeds from potentially any number of sites—automatic teller machines, apartment complexes, shopping malls, and outlying communities—can be connected with the central system, which already monitors parks, streets, and schools. Although the MPD assures citizens that cameras may be utilized *only* in those residential areas experiencing crime occurring in public space, in New York City, this means that cameras are used to monitor activity in and around public housing projects. Consequently, some groups (overwhelmingly poor people of color) will be allowed less spatial freedom, and less anonymity, than others—even in the "privacy" of the areas around their homes. In this way, the new technologies weave together public and private spaces, creating a seamless, videotaped topography indifferent to these traditional boundaries.[53]

Video surveillance also compromises anonymity as it allows officials to zoom in on, record, and replay the smallest details of public conduct. Because it is silent surveillance, it is subject to none of the same Fourth Amendment restrictions as wiretap searches, which require warrants to record information. Nonetheless, potentially damning evidence for crimes (and would-be crimes) might be garnered from videotape, as police scan the monitors to observe park bench conversations, reading materials, or intimate encounters. Although the MPD has issued guidelines stating that officials "shall not target/observe individuals arbitrarily or based on race, gender, ethnicity, sexual orientation, disability or other classifications protected by law,"[54] it is not difficult to imagine the many different kinds of profiling that are enabled through this technology. At the very least, surveillance in shopping malls, for example, allows for what might be called consumer profiling: alerting private mall security companies to the presence of "undesirables" (i.e., those unable to make purchases) by flagging the poor, homeless, or groups of adolescents.[55] Spaces designed for consumers or tourists—and under the Museums and Memorials Master plan this encompasses increasingly more of the city—are thus aestheticized and purified, cleansed of any person or activity that might somehow detract from the consumptive experience.

Finally, facial recognition software is already being tested in public arenas, such as the well-publicized use of Visage's Face-Finder software at Superbowl XXXV. As Timothy Druckrey describes, "*Every* attendee entering the gates was captured (without notification or permission) by an array of cameras. Faces were isolated and entered into a database comparing facial features . . . and search[ed] for 'similar or matching' features with criminal data bases."[56] Although the MPD and other police departments state that they currently have no plans to integrate facial recognition software into the current system, biometric software is already standard issue in casinos and prisons, and is being tried at several airports. The creators of Face-Finder, moreover, see possibilities for its use at "ATMs, car rental agencies, DMV offices, and border crossings."[57] Assertions that the system will not be that intrusive, then, do little to dilute the force of Gaston Bachelard's prediction that "the destiny of every image is magnification."[58]

Interlinking technologies such as video surveillance and biometrics pin individuals at the center of a web of personal information that may be accessed by whomever is behind the monitor. The logical extension of these technologies, then, is the elimination of a "public self" (or, for that matter, a "private self"). As "private" information of all sorts—citizenship or immigration status, medical, financial, or criminal records—might be readily brought up on screen at any time, anonymity becomes an impossibility. In this Foucauldian dystopia, every person becomes a walking collection of data to be mined; she becomes the sum of her various histories, a case whose potential for normalization or deviance is something that risk managers, actuaries, and law enforcement officials can ponder. Rather than safety in collective and anonymous action, citizens are threatened with individuation and exposure when they now enter public space, and public space itself might come to mean "places under public scrutiny."[59]

Scopophilic Politics

The spatial practices of commemoration and surveillance are becoming increasingly intertwined and indistinguishable as they are materialized in contemporary urban life. Washington's commemorative spaces have also become surveilled spaces. As discussed previously, many of the cameras linked into Washington's new surveillance system are located in and around monuments and memorials on the National Mall. As the sites of public memory are dispersed throughout the District under the provisions of the new master plan, more and more of the city will be subject to surveillance. In a very real way, when we visit these historic spaces, our eyes are not only on democracy but also democracy's eyes are on us; Jane Jacob's famous condition for safe communities—"eyes upon the streets"—takes on a new meaning.[60]

And in its opposite formulation, surveillance has become, in its own way, something of a tourist attraction. Some of the cameras situated in public spaces are indeed "hidden cameras," and we can never be sure when we are being watched. For the most part, though, urban surveillance systems are not secret, guilty observation that makes law enforcement officials into peeping toms. Rather, much of the new surveillance equipment, and many of the aspects of the new homeland security state generally, are intended to be noticed: the elaborate metal-detection machinery in federal building lobbies and the armed guards and traffic checkpoints one periodically encounters, for example. Other tranformations are more subtle; the unsightly concrete barriers mentioned at the beginning of the chapter have been replaced by sleek granite walls surrounding the Washinton Monumnet that—despite their rather modest appearance—are designed to stop a two-ton, explosives-laden Humvee in its tracks.[61] These are part of a landscape of (in?)security—a spectacle of (in)security—where these are not only agents of surveillance but also of *assurance,* serving to assuage our collective nerves by giving us the appearance of control.

In this way, the urban panopticon is not simply a repository of disciplinary power. Instead, panopticism operates in the service of sovereign power, reasserting and reinscribing the territoriality of the state by creating the infrastructure for a relentlessly visible capital city, and engendering forms of behavior suited to an intensely *scopophilic politics.* This is a form of citizenship predicated on vision, where citizens are defined as those who are willing to watch and be watched, and where spaces and people not conforming to certain aims are considered deviant or criminal.[62] Although I am not particularly interested in appropriating its psychoanalytic origins, I do think the term is very useful in describing the new relationship between citizenship and visibility. First, scopophilia implies not only a "love of looking" (i.e., voyeuristic tendencies) but also a love of being looked *at*—the need to be the object of continuous and omniscient watchfulness. Indeed, the spectacle of security has its comforts; as one woman interviewed at the National Mall said, "That watchful eye. I feel more protected when someone is watching over my shoulder."[63] Being watched produces many different, and sometimes contradictory responses: it can make one feel taken care of, or worried, or (often needlessly) guilty.

Second, the term allows us to draw attention to the violence inherent in this circumstance; *scope,* of course, not only entails "vision," but also connotes the practices of pursuing, aiming at, and firing on someone. A scope in this sense serves to target individuals. Finally, the term also reflects the broader ambiguity inherent in millennial citizenship: does one feel safer, or more at risk, in her exclusive membership? Does being an American, or a Brit, or an Iraqi, make one feel more protected, or more vulnerable? Or both at once?

Scopophilic politics exacts significant transformations in our understanding of public space and the production of citizens. To be a citizen under this regime is also to be transparent; people who are not willing to be observed at any time, at all times, are assumed to have something to hide. Anonymity—or anything that helps to cloak, conceal, or disguise identity—is a threat. Thus while our urban spaces may not resemble Rousseauian communities in architecture, geography, or population density, they serve the same function ("immersing people in a field of total visibility") and feed the same fears. Today our scopophilic anxiety stems not from being watched, but rather from the possibility that there is someone out there who is *not* being watched, someone who has managed to slip under, over, or around the omnivoyant gaze. The citizen produced at the intersection of security and spectacle is a target: someone who willingly subjects herself to the gaze of the state.

Scopophilic Politics and Political Resistance

Although the MPD's command center is now promoted as an instrument to combat international terrorism after September 11, 2001, in fact, the technology's first use was to police precisely the kind of activity public space is supposed to encourage: the World Bank and IMF protests that took place in Washington in 2000. In many different cities, the protests were characterized by creative, playful political expressions, such as giant puppets, costumes, and marching bands. More recently, the surveillance system was used to monitor the activities of the antiwar demonstrators that convened in Washington in

January 2003. The majority of these protestors are the performative embodiment of what Holloway Sparks calls dissident citizenship: "marginalized
citizens who publicly contest prevailing arrangements of power by means of
oppositional democratic practices." As Sparks argues, such citizens are not
peripheral to, but rather are a constitutive feature of, a vibrant democracy.
If democratic citizenship means active, collective participation in making
decisions about their collective existence, then, in Sparks' words, "the marginalized dissident citizens who address the wider polity in order to change
minds, challenge practices, or even reconstitute the very boundaries of the
political itself engage in a form of democratic citizenship that is essential for
the continuing revitalization of democratic life."[64] The lack of anonymity and
perpetual visibility described previously can potentially have a chilling effect
on dissident, democratic practice.

The question any democratic theorist must ask next, then, is how to resist
the encroachment of vision, this new economy of visibility, in urban space.
As I see it, there are several possible strategies for resistance. The first is for
citizens to attempt to "turn off the scopes" and reclaim our right to privacy
through lawsuits and local initiatives to limit the use of police surveillance.[65]
This is the strategy employed by organizations such as the American Civil
Liberties Union (ACLU), which has devoted considerable resources to com-
bating the presence of the extensive D.C. surveillance system.[66] Although such
strategies are certainly necessary, they are not sufficient. First, they do not
seem to recognize the increasingly muddled geography of public and private.
Second, the ACLU's tactics are largely reactive and provide only temporary
obstructions against the relentless advance of intrusive technologies.

More creative and proactive tactics are available to citizens seeking to
protest the proliferation of surveilled space. These include *mapping, masking,* and *reversing* the direction of the gaze. *Mapping* includes the activities of
groups such as the New York Civil Liberties Union who detail the locations
of police and private cameras surveilling public, urban spaces, and post these
locations on the Internet.[67] The group has mapped nearly 2,400 cameras in
Manhattan, and plans to expand their maps to include all five New York
City boroughs. Another group, the New York Surveillance Camera Players,
has mapped publicly installed camera locations in Boston, New York, Chicago, New Haven, and Portland; the group also performs plays in front of
the cameras, using their own visibility to protest the state's requirements of
visibility.[68] The intent of these projects is to raise public awareness about the
proliferation of surveillance technologies and encourage public discourse
about their continued presence in our cities. In this way, the group's work

serves to document the changes in the shape of the public sphere, plotting the places where privacy becomes permeable and transparency is mandated.

Masking refers to the increasingly common practice of donning masks or costumes when engaging in political protest. These can be everything from simple bandanas to elaborate and often ironic disguises (for example, caricatures of political leaders). The costumes and puppets frequently employed in the World Bank, IMF, and G8 protests, for example, are not only creative and playful democratic performances but were also deeply subversive political tactics, in that they serve to protect protest participants from the scrutiny of surveillance. Demonstrations like these not only resist surveillance (a reactive function) but also create a kind of counter-spectacle to the spectacle of (in)security and sovereign power (a proactive strategy). In this way, costumed protestors resuscitate democratic politics by bringing dead space to life: by showing the Washington Mall, or downtown streets, as places where the performative and agonistic character of democracy is played out.[69]

Finally, and most radically, activists can turn surveillance back on those in power (i.e., *reversing* surveillance), using new technologies both to record abuses and to circulate these images widely. The Electronic Privacy Information Center's (EPIC) Observing Surveillance Project is one good example of this. The project's aim is to document and promote public debate about the presence of cameras in Washington. Observing Surveillance is a multimedia endeavor; some of the strategies employed by EPIC include the construction of a Web site, the publication of "travel postcards" (featuring pictures of cameras in the nation's capital), and the placement on hotel telephones of stickers that read "Suitable for government surveillance."[70] Another group turning information technology back on itself is Copwatch, whose express aim is to "turn police culture against itself."[71] Copwatch encourages protestors to use video and audio equipment to record encounters with law enforcement; Copwatch members post their accounts on the group's Web site. Finally, resistance is present in independent media activism, such as that employed during the 1999 WTO protests in Seattle compiled in the documentary *This Is What Democracy Looks Like*.[72] The footage of the Seattle police beating and gassing protestors is particularly disturbing (and effective) as it is contrasted in the documentary with mainstream media coverage, which talked incessantly about the "self control" and "restraint" being exercised by law enforcement. *This Is What Democracy Looks Like* is also particularly effective in showing the relationship between the construction of consumer-oriented public space and the deployment of police and disciplinary power to protect such spaces.[73]

Although I do not want to suggest these technologies somehow equalize the field of power relations, they do provide citizens with potentially subversive tools for challenging the parameters of this field. Cameras turned on the police state, or turned on those areas of the city unsuitable for tourists and shoppers, flip the switches on what or who is supposed to be visible or invisible, identifiable or anonymous. This is also not to suggest that all new technologies have equally emancipatory potential, or are liberating in and of themselves. The tactics described above have in common the fact that new technologies (which privilege vision and speed) are being used in combination with more traditional forms of political organizing and protest; that is to say, they are being employed with the intent of utilizing and amplifying dissident political voices.

Debates over the future shape of the public sphere, and what democracy looks like when it is embodied in a spatial form, are now more important than ever. Understanding the mechanisms and possibilities for social change requires us to understand the role of space in creating and sustaining power relations. Our sense of what is politically necessary, desirable, and possible may be either disabled or enhanced in the future spaces we are able to imagine for ourselves.

6. Building the Body Politic

Our ideas about ourselves and each other are often inextricably linked to the spaces we occupy. "Townie," "homeless man," "red-state recruit," "tourist group," "urban youth," "suburban housewife," and "Southern Democrat"—these are all spatialized subjectivities, given depth, texture, and meaning at the juncture of politics and geography. We understand *who* we are in part by understanding *where* we are; we recognize each other through and across the medium of the built environment. Said more succinctly, subject production is inextricably linked to spatial production.

As the place where subjectivity and space intersect, planning discourses not only offer descriptive accounts of cities and their residents but also perform constructive and prescriptive functions. The previous chapters have shown how cities and citizens are not already constituted entities, waiting to be discovered and described by urban planning specialists; rather, these spaces and subjects take shape and acquire significance through the very language that attempts to depict them. Planning discourses provide the lenses through which we see cities and subjects: as healthy or diseased, productive or inefficient, benign or menacing. The results of planning discourses—the buildings that are proposed, constructed, or razed, and the people that are lured into the city or displaced from its neighborhoods—then make material the effects of power. As economic, cultural, and political resources are consolidated and represented through the built environment, they simultaneously reflect and reify relationships of privilege and oppression.

These same discourses which help constitute urban space also inform who can claim legitimate access to this space. This becomes particularly true in the case of planning a capital city, where the product of planning discourses is nothing less than the spatial representation of the body politic itself. Here subjects are also citizens, and what is at stake is whether and to what degree our definitions of citizenship are fixed within specific limits, permitting (or disallowing) certain forms of political expression. It is important to recognize that in many cases, plans for "building the body politic" are motivated as much by a conscious desire to *enhance* the practices of citizenship (such as in the case of the National Mall) as they are from a (sometimes subterranean) need to expedite social control.

The task of normative social theory, then, is to provide the tools to recognize the effects of power, even—or especially—when they result from a genuine desire to improve our collective existence. Understanding how planning for citizenship can both make possible and constrain political action is crucial if we are interested in creating spaces for vibrant, democratic engagement. Moreover, whether or not we recognize ourselves as "citizens" has consequences far beyond whether or not we cast ballots or feel entitled to hold our representatives accountable. As William Connolly argues, our identities as citizens in a democracy (for example, the recognition that we possess various rights and liberties, are capable of making reasoned choices, and can contribute meaningfully to the public good) influence how we perform other social roles and make other kinds of commitments. Our self-identification as citizens shapes our understandings of our roles as parents, spouses, workers, students, and neighbors.[1] How we define citizenship in our planning practices, then, reverberates in realms other than the political, narrowly defined.

The purpose of this book has been to examine the citizen-subject at the point of its production within planning discourses, and to show how language builds certain assumptions into our understandings both of citizens and of the spaces they occupy. In Table 6.1, I have attempted to codify the different parameters of citizenship that have emerged in my analysis of Washington. The three moments in Washington's planning history documented in the previous chapters illuminate six different configurations that the spatial production of citizenship has taken over time. From the City Beautiful plan for the National Mall to the new security measures put in place to guard against terrorist threats, strategies for remaking the capital city have relied on normalizing definitions of citizenship that simultaneously legitimate some groups and interests while rendering others irrational, illegitimate, or (often quite literally) out of place.

Each row in the table represents one monothematic space of citizenship. Column A describes the problems perceived with particular existing spaces. Column B is a set of what might be called planning keywords, the various terms used to depict what spaces "should" look like. Column C asks which

Table 6.1. The spaces of citizenship.

	A	B	C	D
	Existing Space: How is the perceived problem with the current space described?	Discursive Space: What kind of language is used to describe/define the planned space?	Material Space: What kind of space will be planned and built?	Subject-Citizen: What kind of subject-citizen is assumed and produced?
1	common, unremarkable, unpatriotic	heroic, instructive in civic virtue	monumental, edifying	citizen–mimic
2	ugly, plain, disorderly, unplanned	beautiful, orderly	beautiful, planned, rational	citizen–aesthete
3	diseased, dirty, cancerous, infected	healthy, clean	sanitary, antiseptic	citizen–patient
4	unprofitable, wasteful, inefficient	profitable, valuable, conducive to economic development	prosperous, commercial, efficient	citizen–economic indicator
5	bland, unremarkable	unique, historic, entertaining	tourist friendly	citizen–tourist
6	dangerous, threatening, chaotic, hidden	secure, safe, manageable	open, transparent, visible, monitored	citizen–target

type of space is planned or built as a response to the needs identified in column A. Column D shows what type of citizen is anticipated and constituted by this configuration of discursive and material space (see Table 6.1).

A few caveats. First, this codification is not intended to produce a complete map of the territory; rather, it should be understood as a way of clarifying and making connections between various modes of making spaces and subjects. Second, these categories should not be understood to correspond exactly to a particular time period, although it is easy to see how certain discourses emerge as dominant at different points in history. Finally, although I treat these formulations as analytically distinct, none of these categories is exclusive; it is clear that there are many instances where various categories might overlap. Moreover, as the previous chapters have indicated, oftentimes several of these discursive threads are woven into a particular plan for making, and remaking, the city.

When we look at this table, it is important to note that none of these categories is, in itself, a "bad" way of thinking about public space. After all, don't we all want spaces that are beautiful, orderly, and safe? (Or, to ask the question in the negative: would we want spaces that are ugly, disorderly, and threatening?) Rather, my aim in tracking these discourses has been to show that our ways of thinking and talking about space have material consequences; they shape the field of the possible and the desirable—while at the same time they shut out those experiences and identities not conforming to these parameters.

Indeed, as I argued in Chapter 2, binaries such as those listed above (beautiful/ugly, orderly/disorderly, safe/threatening) are ultimately unhelpful in trying to understand lived space. Both Foucault and Lefebvre make clear that we should be suspicious of spaces that claim to be singular or absolute, and wary of planners that claim that spaces are either one thing (beautiful, orderly, safe) or another (ugly, disorderly, threatening). Instead of simplistic dualisms, we should produce accounts of the built environment that emphasize its interstitial and contradictory character.

The table helps us do this by illustrating (some of) the various ways spaces have been imagined or perceived, and how these perceptions contribute to the production of subjectivity. Each variant indicated in column D indicates a way of making—and normalizing—the category of citizen, by implicitly or explicitly defining whose concerns are recognized as legitimate and rational, whose desires should be taken into account in future planning efforts, and who should have access to public space. Through the label of "citizen," we designate what we view as our common problems, recognizable reference points, and shared understandings. Where we locate these constraints, then, and how much variation the signifier "citizen" can contain, can help us assess whether the spaces we are making are more or less democratic.

The table demonstrates that too often, the citizens anticipated and produced through planning discourses more closely resemble the one-dimensional sketches of "planners' people" we encountered in Chapter 4 (the Gentleman with a Briefcase, the Mother with Children, the Young Lovers, etc.) than the rich plurality of identities and experiences that make up any actually existing democracy. For example, in the first row, the subject of monumental space (the citizen-mimic) is assumed to model himself on the surrounding environs; he will uncritically absorb the message that the architects or planners of that space intend. In other words, the citizen-mimic posits an unrealistic (and undesirable), strict correspondence between the space and its intended message. The Arthur Ashe monument I discussed in Chapter 3 is a metacommentary on this way of making space: the statue features the African American tennis star flanked by small children, cast in bronze, looking up to their idol. That is, the statue itself models emulation. The ideal of the citizen-mimic does not account for the multiple experiences and readings spectators bring to any given space, no matter how didactic the space tries to be. In this way, the assumptions that make possible the citizen-mimic attempt to create "pure" spaces of nationalism or remembrance, and disregard or suppress the contestability and contingency inherent in political life.

The citizen-aesthete in the second row assumes that the subject for that space should be responsive to and judge the space according to a set of objective aesthetic criteria. Although we all might agree that "beautiful spaces" are desirable, what constitutes "beauty" has, of course, varied tremendously over time. However, the common denominator for beauty in Washington—despite the vastly different architectural sensibilities that animated the City Beautiful and modernist urban renewal—is order: a sense of things (and people) having their place, and staying in place. The urban redevelopment project in Southwest Washington, for example, made material what Jane Jacobs has described as "purely visual notions of order";[2] it prioritized "beauty" (as defined by clean lines, clearly defined spaces, and the absence of visible poverty) over viable communities. Thus the singular pursuit of beauty justified through the citizen-aesthete can—and does—often serve as a rationalization for other, less honorable interests, and may obstruct our ability to make just decisions about the uses and misuses of space.

The citizen-patient described in row 3 and exemplified in the initiatives to purge the Washington alleys is a citizen who is ready to "take her medicine"; that is, a person who is willing to be diagnosed and treated by the state. Through the production of the citizen-patient, the ailments of individual bodies are linked explicitly to the well-being of the social body. The good intentions of public health initiatives in this instance become problematic when physical illness often becomes implicated in, and synonymous with, moral degeneracy. In the case of the Washington alleys, the "plague spots" in need of remedy refer not only to sites of tuberculosis but also sites of improper sexual behavior and "inverted" gender roles; we saw the same sort of discursive production at work in the first decade of the AIDS epidemic.

In row 4 (citizen–economic indicator), citizenship is defined primarily by market measures, by consumption of or contribution to economic and cultural resources. This kind of citizenship is constrained by its reliance on the language of profit and loss. The result is space planned solely to attract middle- and upper-class consumers, and sustain a robust tax base. Although economic viability is a necessary and legitimate concern for cities (especially in the wake of the mass exodus to the suburbs), defining citizenship in this way makes other assessments of value (for example, keeping a neighborhood intact, encouraging racially and economically integrated neighborhoods, or preserving public green space) seem irrational, unless they can somehow contribute to the bottom line.

Space planned for the citizen-tourist (row 5) is also concerned about market measures, but here the focus is on the consumption of space itself. Space planned for the tourist gaze, as Elizabeth Wilson argues, is space that has been "cleansed, sanitized, and rearranged" to fulfill the expectations of those seeking a meaningful (and "authentic") experience.[3] Times Square in New York, Fanueil Hall Marketplace in Boston, and the Inner Harbor in Baltimore demonstrate how closely the citizen-tourist is allied with the citizen–economic indicator. Like the spaces created for the citizen-mimic, places planned for tourists are often one-dimensional and overly prescriptive, predicated on the idea that there *is* an authentic and singular experience to be had at a particular location.

Finally, in the case of the citizen-target, the rights seen as the mainstay of democratic citizenship are trumped by national security interests, broadly construed. As in the case of the citizen-patient, "good citizens" in this formulation willingly relinquish their autonomy and submit to the prerogatives of the state, or risk being the subject of surveillance and/or state-sponsored violence. If one does not conform to the role citizen-target, one risks not only exclusion from the ranks of citizens, but may in fact be cast as their opposite: a person rendered stateless and therefore stripped of the protections of citizenship (for example, through designation as an "enemy combatant").

Although it is helpful to treat each of these categories of citizenship in isolation, it is also useful to examine how they are often explicitly combined in planning discourses. For example, citizen–economic indicator and citizen-tourist frequently overlap. As a capital city, with an economy bolstered by countless tour buses and school field trips, these categories are especially intertwined in a city like Washington. In the recently devised Memorials and Museums Master Plan that we examined in Chapter 5, we can see that the initiative integrates the spaces of heroism, tourism, and economic development in its effort to distribute new monuments across the city. Or when we are planning cities in the interests of national security, "order" and "disorder" becomes not only the purview of the citizen-aesthete but the citizen-target: busy sidewalks and train stations become perceived as places to conceal bombs, or overcrowded immigrant neighborhoods may be regarded as terrorist safe-havens.

What the different varieties of "planned citizenship" sketched out here have in common is that all of them approximate Lefebvre's description of *dominated* space rather than *appropriated* space: they signify the "realization of a master's project," whose aim is continual reproduction and limitless commodification.[4] What makes these spaces problematic is that none of them engenders the traits necessary for participation in a heterogeneous democracy. A sample of these might include the capacity for exercising good judgment about political matters, the talent to engage others in reasoned deliberation, and the ability to negotiate—if not appreciate—the deep pluralism that characterizes most contemporary nation-states. Rows 1, 3 and 6 (mimic, patient, and target) posit a version of citizenship that is far more subject than citizen; in each case, citizenship is based on one's ability to conform to a particular identity endorsed by the state. In rows 2, 4 and 5 (aesthete, economic indicator, and tourist), emphasis is placed on the citizen's capacity for judgment, but these judgments are either aesthetic or pecuniary (or both). As Lefebvre's work implies, the qualities most useful for democratic practice are those cultivated in and through *appropriated* rather than dominated space: spaces that are claimed and shaped according to the shifting needs and desires of a group of people, where people are active agents of space making, instead of passive recipients of a pregenerated "master plan."

As I hope the previous chapters have shown, though, not even dominated spaces are absolute. By making explicit the assumptions inherent in these different modes of building the body politic, I have presumed that we are able to, and will, make better spaces. Democratic politics exists in its negotiation of a set of related, and perpetual, contradictions: between individual identity and social cohesion; between a need for authority and a deep suspicion of potential domination; and between the necessity of establishing a set of shared meanings and the impossibility of doing so with any kind of finality. Democracy, for better or worse, is always interrupting itself and its aspirations; if it is working well, it continually recreates itself through intense (though not crippling) deliberations and meaningful social (ex)change. Democracy is not, by definition, orderly. It is therefore not a mode of being conducive to master plans, if by "master plans" we mean blueprints that connote certainty, finality, and perfect control. Democracy is itself an interstitial space: a space of contestation, paradox, and reversal.

I do not mean to suggest here that democratic spaces should be unplanned, disorganized, or chaotic. In fact, in the absence of planning in a capitalist society, the interests of capital more often than not dictate how space is utilized. This is clearly the case in current development patterns commonly called "sprawl": land is sold to the highest bidder with little regard for what might be in the public interest. Indeed, many democratic spaces are the result of specific, intentional planning choices. Sometimes these might be as simple—and profound—as expanding our repository of what is worthy of emulation, or what counts as beautiful. Again, the Arthur Ashe statue is a case in point. By showing Arthur Ashe surrounded by admiring children, the monument does produce another variant of the citizen-mimic. At the same time, though, this statue's placement on Monument Avenue (previously occupied only by Confederate heroes) reconfigures that particular landscape of commemoration; Arthur Ashe's presence in this pantheon brings racial identity and racial segregation to the front and center of the discussion of building for citizenship, rather than keeping them as part of the often unspoken backdrop of U.S. history.

Kirk Savage makes a similar point in proposing a monument for Dr. Martin Luther King Jr. Savage suggests that the King monument should be located where King delivered his most famous speech: on the steps of the Lincoln Memorial. As it stands, the Lincoln Memorial does not explicitly discuss slavery or race; instead it conforms to the broader trend Savage identifies: memorializing slaves as beholden to whites for emancipation. Placing a life-size statue of King on the steps of the Lincoln Memorial, as Savage recommends, would amount to allowing (at least) two narratives about slavery, racial identity, and justice to exist at the same site.[5] In a much different example, Maya Lin's design for the Vietnam Veterans' Memorial described in Chapter 3 facilitates intimate interaction with the structure, and the culture that has developed since it was built encourages people to share their own personal histories and memories both of the conflict itself and of their visits to the wall.

What all three of these planned sites have in common is that they encourage critical thinking and acting on the part of citizens; they not only allow but to some extent require citizens to create their own meanings for these places. Planning discourses, then, should recognize, and embrace, the open-ended and contingent character of any democracy worthy of the name. Plans for democratic spaces—plans that aim to create democratic citizens—do not shy away from argument, antagonism, or contestation; they allow for multiple readings and uses of that space, cultivate an appreciation for the contestability of established meanings, and offer support for entering into public life and public conversation.

Building democratic spaces also means recognizing that lived space often undermines or supersedes our best intentions. After all, planning often produces unintentional effects; people's lived lives exceed, subvert, or re-code the spaces they inhabit, no matter how carefully designed. To use a linguistic metaphor, although planning discourse may represent the language (*langue,* or system) of the built environment, the patterns of its use—walking, shopping, working, socializing—connote its speech (*parole,* the act).[6] The works of both Jane Jacobs and William Whyte, for example, attest to the unforeseen consequences and contradictory meanings that emerge out of lived spaces when these spaces are used, reused, and misused.[7] City parks become havens for crime; sidewalks become street bazaars; industrial warehouses are transformed into loft apartments; alleys become places of residence and sites of community. The implications of this are that even the most seemingly dominated spaces are never only, or will never always be, that.

In the case of Washington, the National Mall—originally envisioned as a ceremonial boulevard by Pierre L'Enfant—has become the site of important political spectacles. Rather than being solely a solemn, commemorative site, or a site of unambiguous national hagiography, the Mall has also been a staging ground for political activity. The Mall's symbolic spaces have served to amplify a wide range of civic expression, from Martin Luther King Jr. to the AIDS quilt to the Million Mom March. The green space of the Mall enables but does not prescribe political action; in regarding citizenship as a realm of "unspecified possibility," the Mall offers a model of planned space that can also be liberating in its imprecision.[8]

When we plan to build for citizenship, we speak a language that links our geographic imagination to our political imagination. The spaces we create reflect, reify, and (in some cases) challenge the established order of things; in this way, mapmaking is indeed world making.[9] Our "noble diagrams" (to reinvoke Daniel Burnham's famous directive) for representing the body politic are a record of our utopian ambitions, our nostalgic longings, and our democratic energies. It is the last of these that has the potential to allow us to build better, more inclusive spaces, to reinvent and reinterpret the spaces we have built, and to continually challenge ourselves to push the limits of possibility.

Notes

Chapter 1: The Infrastructure of the Political

1. Sheldon Wolin, *Politics and Vision: Continuity and Innovation in Western Political Thought, Expanded Edition* (Princeton: Princeton University Press, 2004), 16.

2. One issue raised by both philosophers and geographers in their discussions of the subject is the difference between "space" and "place," the relative value of each of these terms, and the problems with assigning definitions to each. Both Massey and Casey argue that in conventional philosophic and geographic vocabularies, space/place is a gendered binary; that is, whereas "space" is often thought of as abstract, universal, timeless, and/or global (qualities also figured as masculine), place is considered specific, time-bound, concrete, and local (qualities associated with femininity). See, for example, Edward S. Casey, *The Fate of Place: A Philosophical History* (Berkeley: University of California Press, 1997) and Doreen Massey, *Space, Place, and Gender* (Minneapolis: University of Minnesota Press, 1994). For the purposes of this project, however, I will use "space" to mean specific material environments that human beings have organized for the purposes of work, family, leisure, commerce, and politics.

3. There are some notable exceptions, as recent work in political theory has begun to address the relationship between space and power. See, for example, Susan Bickford, "Constructing Inequality: City Spaces and the Architecture of Citizenship," *Political Theory* 28, no. 3 (June 2000): 355–76; Marcel Hénaff, and Tracy B. Strong, ed. *Public Space and Democracy* (Minneapolis: University of Minnesota Press, 2001); Steven Johnston, "Political Not Patriotic: Democracy, Civic Space, and the American Memorial/Monument Complex," *Theory & Event* 5, no. 2 (2001); Margaret Kohn, *Radical Space: Building the House of the People* (Ithaca: Cornell University Press, 2003); Margaret Kohn, *Brave New Neighborhoods: The Privatization of the Public Sphere* (New York: Routledge, 2004); and Michael J. Shapiro, "Constructing 'America': Architectural Thought-Worlds," *Theory & Event* 7, no. 4 (2004).

4. Neil Smith and Cindi Katz, "Grounding Metaphor: Towards a Spatialized Politics,"

in *Place and the Politics of Identity,* edited by Michael Keith and Steve Pile (New York and London: Routledge, 1993), 67. See also Ilana Friedrich Silber, "Space, Fields, Boundaries: The Rise of Spatial Metaphors in Contemporary Sociological Theory," *Social Research* 62, no. 2 (1995): 323–53. For a wonderful account of how subjectivity is defined through spatial metaphors, see Kathleen M. Kirby, *Indifferent Boundaries: Spatial Concepts of Human Subjectivity* (New York and London: The Guilford Press, 1996).

5. Manuel Castells, *The Informational City: Information Technology, Economic Restructuring, and the Urban-Regional Process* (Cambridge: Blackwell, 1989); David Harvey, *The Condition of Postmodernity: An Enquiry into the Origins of Cultural Change* (Cambridge: Blackwell, 1989); Fredric Jameson, *Postmodernism, or the Cultural Logic of Late Capitalism* (Durham: Duke University Press, 1991).

6. Jameson, *Postmodernism,* 48.

7. See Rosi Braidotti, *Nomadic Subjects: Embodiment and Sexual Difference in Contemporary Feminist Theory* (New York: Columbia University Press, 1994); Kathy Ferguson, *The Man Question: Visions of Subjectivity in Feminist Theory* (Berkeley: University of California Press, 1993); Donna J. Haraway, *Simians, Cyborgs, and Women: The Reinvention of Nature* (New York: Routledge, 1991), ch. 9; and Nancy C. M. Hartsock, *Money, Sex and Power: Toward a Feminist Historical Materialism* (Boston: Northeastern University Press, 1983).

8. Silber, "Space, Fields, Boundaries," 348.

9. Stephen K. White, *Sustaining Affirmation: The Strengths of Weak Ontology in Political Theory* (Princeton: Princeton University Press, 2000).

10. Quoted in Eugene F. Miller, "Metaphor and Political Knowledge," *American Political Science Review* 73, no. 1 (1979): 161.

11. Ibid., 158.

12. Henri Lefebvre, *The Production of Space* (Cambridge: Blackwell, 1991), 3.

13. Edward W. Soja, *Thirdspace: Journeys to Los Angeles and Other Real-And-Imagined Places* (Cambridge: Blackwell, 1996), 60.

14. Gillian Rose, *Feminism and Geography* (Cambridge: Polity Press, 1993), 58.

15. Lefebvre, *Production of Space,* 5.

16. Hubert L. Dreyfus and Paul Rabinow, *Michel Foucault: Beyond Structuralism and Hermeneutics* (Chicago: University of Chicago Press, 1983), 48.

17. James S. Duncan, *The City as Text: Interpretations in the Kandyan Kingdom* (New York: Cambridge University Press, 1990), 16.

18. See, for example, Lorraine Dowler, "'And They Think I'm Just a Nice Old Lady': Women and War in Belfast, Northern Ireland," *Gender Place and Culture* 5 (1998): 159–76; and Duncan, *City as Text.*

19. Wolin, *Politics and Vision,* 16–17.

20. Peter Bachrach and Morton S. Baratz, *Power and Poverty: Theory and Practice* (New York: Oxford University Press, 1970); Matthew A. Crenson, *The Un-Politics of Air Pollution: A Study of Non-decisionmaking in the Cities* (Baltimore: Johns Hopkins University Press, 1972); Robert A. Dahl, *Who Governs? Democracy and Power in an American City* (New Haven: Yale University Press, 1961); John Gaventa, *Power and Powerlessness: Quiescence and Rebellion in an Appalachian Valley* (Urbana and Chicago: University of Illinois Press, 1980).

21. Dahl defines the Social Notables as members of the community with the highest social standing, operationalized by those who receive an invitation to the annual assemblies held in the New Haven Lawn Club (*Who Governs?* 64). Economic Notables are the economic leaders in New Haven (for operationalization criteria see *Who Governs?* 67–68).

22. Ibid., 85.

23. Ibid., 101.

24. Ibid., 311.

25. For example, Dahl begins the book with a discussion of equality, asking his readers to "disregard for the moment the question on slavery" (*Who Governs?* 1), as if "the question of slavery" can be neatly extracted from any account of American history.

26. Ibid., 54.

27. Margaret Kohn, *Radical Space;* Susan Bickford, "Constructing Inequality;" and Clarissa Rile Hayward, "The Difference States Make: Democracy, Identity, and the American City," *American Political Science Review* 97, no. 4 (November 2003): 501–14.

28. Andy Merrifield, "Between Process and Individuation: Translating Metaphors and Narratives of Urban Space," *Antipode* 29, no. 4 (1997): 424.

29. This recent work in political theory is very much in concert with studies in architectural, geographic, and social theory, especially that done or influenced by Mike Davis, Dolores Hayden, David Harvey, Neil Smith, and Sharon Zukin. See Mike Davis, *City of Quartz: Excavating the Future in Los Angeles* (New York: Vintage, 1992) and *Magical Urbanism: Latinos Reinvent the US City* (New York: Verso Press, 2000); Dolores Hayden, *The Power of Place: Urban Landscapes as Public History* (Cambridge: MIT Press, 1997) and *Redesigning the American Dream: Gender, Housing, and Family Life* (1984, repr. New York: W. W. Norton, 2002); David Harvey, *Consciousness and the Urban Experience* (Baltimore: Johns Hopkins University Press, 1985) and *Spaces of Hope* (Berkeley: University of California Press, 2002); Neil Smith, "New City, New Frontier," in *Variations on a Theme Park,* edited by Michael Sorkin (New York: Hill and Wang, 1992); and Sharon Zukin, *Landscapes of Power: From Detroit to Disneyworld* (Berkeley: University of California Press, 1991).

30. Friedrich Nietzsche, *On the Genealogy of Morals,* translated by Walter Kaufmann (1967, repr. New York: Vintage Books, 1989), 61.

31. Michel Foucault, "Body/Power," in *Power/Knowledge: Selected Interviews and Other Writings 1972–1977,* edited by Colin Gordon (New York: Pantheon, 1980): 57–58.

32. When the U.S. Constitution was adopted, it provided for the establishment of a separate federal district and gave Congress the power ". . . to exercise exclusive legislation in all Cases whatsoever, over such District (not exceeding ten Miles square) as may, by Cession of particular States, and the acceptance of Congress, become the Seat of Government of the United States." From its inception, then, Washington's residents have had a peculiar relationship with the federal government. Most significantly, throughout its history, it has been primarily Congress who has governed the city, although the specific configurations of this relationship have varied. Thus, unlike every other American city, "federalism" is not a salient characteristic; in Washington, D.C., there is no state-level government to mediate between city and nation.

33. U.S. Senate, *DC Area Monuments and Memorials: Hearing before the Subcommittee*

on National Parks, Historic Preservation and Recreation of the Committee on Energy and National Resources (March 23, 2000), 7.

34. Howard Gillette, *Between Justice and Beauty: Race, Planning, and the Failure of Urban Policy in Washington, D.C.* (Baltimore: Johns Hopkins University Press, 1995), xi.

35. National Capital Park and Planning Commission (NCPPC), *Washington: Present and Future: A General Summary of the Comprehensive Plan for the National Capital and Its Environs* (Washington, D.C.: National Capital Park and Planning Commission, 1950), 41.

36. Lewis Mumford, *The Culture of Cities* (1938, repr. New York: Harcourt, Brace & World, 1970), 3.

37. Lauren Berlant, *The Anatomy of National Fantasy: Hawthorne, Utopia, and Everyday Life* (Chicago: University of Chicago Press, 1991), 34.

38. Judith N. Shklar, *American Citizenship: The Quest for Inclusion* (Cambridge : Harvard University Press, 1991), 14–17. See also Joel Olson, "The Democratic Problem of the White Citizen," *Constellations* 8, no. 2 (2001): 163–83.

39. Barbara Cruikshank, *The Will to Empower: Democratic Citizens and Other Subjects* (Ithaca: Cornell University Press, 1999), 5.

40. This point is made abundantly clear at the Web site for tourism information regarding Australia's capital city, Canberra: "What does it mean to be an Australian? To find out, come and see the one city designed to reflect an entire nation." The city's slogan is "See yourself in Canberra." From www.canberratourism.com.au. The phrase "technologies of citizenship" is from Cruikshank, *Will to Empower*, 2.

41. Here I am paraphrasing Engin Isin's idea that the city serves as a "difference machine," as citizens and others are constituted by and through their encounters in city space. See Engin F. Isin, *Being Political: Genealogies of Citizenship* (Minneapolis: University of Minnesota Press, 2002), 49–50.

42. Looking at the construction of subjects and spaces in a historical framework means that I utilize a wide range of materials. My sources include congressional hearings on the legislation in question and supporting documents and studies from various federal agencies; well-known texts written by reformers and planners (such as Charles Weller's *Neglected Neighbors* and Louis Justement's *New Cities for Old*); periodical sources, especially from the *New York Times*, the *Washington Post* and the *Evening Star*; and relevant national journals or magazines (such as *Charities, Municipal Affairs, American City,* and *Architectural Record*).

43. Michel Foucault, *Language, Counter-Memory, and Practice: Selected Essays and Interviews,* edited by Donald F. Bouchard (Ithaca: Cornell University Press, 1977), 139.

44. Lauren Berlant, *Anatomy of National Fantasy,* 20.

Chapter 2: Making Space for Power

1. Kojin Katarani, *Architecture as Metaphor: Language, Number, Money,* translated by Sabu Kohso, edited by Michael Speaks (Cambridge: MIT Press, 1995), 5.

2. David Harvey, *Justice, Nature & the Geography of Difference* (New York: Routledge, 1996), 5, italics removed.

3. Michel Foucault, "The Subject and Power," in *Michel Foucault: Beyond Structuralism and Hermeneutics,* edited by Hubert L. Dreyfus and Paul Rabinow (Chicago: University of Chicago Press, 1983), 208.

4. For two views of Foucault's contributions to understanding power, see Peter Digeser, "The Fourth Face of Power," *Journal of Politics* 54 (1992): 977–1006, and Clarissa Rile Hayward, *De-facing Power* (Cambridge: Cambridge University Press, 2000).

5. See, for example, Susan Bordo, *Unbearable Weight: Feminism, Western Culture, and the Body* (Berkeley: University of California Press, 1993); Judith Butler, *Gender Trouble: Feminism and the Subversion of Identity* (New York: Routledge, 1990); William E. Connolly, *The Ethos of Pluralization* (Minneapolis: University of Minnesota Press,1995); and Thomas Dumm, *united states* (Ithaca: Cornell University Press, 1994).

6. Michel Foucault, "Space, Knowledge, and Power," in *The Foucault Reader,* edited by Paul Rabinow (New York: Pantheon, 1984), 252.

7. Michel Foucault, "Questions on Geography," in *Power/Knowledge*, 69.

8. Michel Foucault, "Space, Knowledge, and Power," 246.

9. Dumm, *united states*, 106.

10. Michel Foucault, *The History of Sexuality, Vol. I* (New York: Random House, 1990), 31.

11. Dreyfus and Rabinow, *Michel Foucault,* 109.

12. Michel Foucault, "Of Other Spaces," *Diacritics* 16 (Spring 1986): 24. See also Thomas Dumm, *Michel Foucault and the Politics of Freedom* (Thousand Oaks: Sage Publications, 1996). Quoted in Dreyfus and Rabinow, *Michel Foucault,* 128.

13. For an excellent discussion of the Ship of Fools and its role in shaping our modern sensibility towards the spaces of reason, madness, and the imagination, see Dumm, *Michel Foucault and the Politics of Freedom,* 41–42.

14. Foucault, *Discipline and Punish: The Birth of the Prison* (New York: Vintage, 1977), 205.

15. Mike Davis, *City of Quartz: Excavating the Future in Los Angeles* (New York: Vintage, 1992), ch. 4.

16. Foucault, "Of Other Spaces," 24.

17. Foucault, *Discipline and Punish,* 27.

18. Foucault, "Space, Knowledge, and Power," 254.

19. It should be noted here that Foucault mentions heterotopias in only two places: in the introduction to *The Order of Things: An Archeology of the Human Sciences* (New York: Vintage, 1994), xviii, and in a lecture titled "Of Other Spaces," which was delivered in March 1967. "Of Other Spaces" was translated and printed in *Diacritics* in 1986, but as the editor's note points out, the article was never reviewed for publication by Foucault and is thus not part of the official corpus of his work (22). However, I would argue that the idea of "heterotopic" space (or at least a heterotopic sensibility) is present throughout many of Foucault's analyses, and the concept is therefore a suggestive one that need not be restricted to Foucault's own limited usage.

20. Foucault, "Of Other Spaces," 24.

21. Ibid., 25.

22. Ibid.

23. Ibid., 26.

24. Ibid., 26.

25. Ibid., 26.

26. Ibid., 27.

27. See Dumm, *Michel Foucault and the Politics of Freedom,* esp. ch. 2.

28. Foucault, "Space, Knowledge, and Power," 245.

29. Ibid.

30. Michel Foucault, "Questions of Method," in *The Foucault Effect: Studies in Governmentality,* edited by Graham Burchell, Colin Gordon, and Peter Miller (Chicago: University of Chicago Press, 1991), 73–86.

31. Jürgen Habermas, *The Philosophical Discourse of Modernity,* trans. Frederick G. Lawrence (Cambridge: MIT Press, 1987), 276.

32. Foucault, "Subject and Power," 221–22.

33. Michel Foucault, "Two Lectures," in *Power/Knowledge,* 98.

34. For an excellent account of the causes and effects of spatialized difference, see Peter Dreier, John Mollenkopf, and Todd Swanstrom, *Place Matters: Metropolitics for the Twenty-first Century, Second Edition* (Lawrence: University of Kansas Press, 2004), esp. chs. 1–3.

35. This is not to say that Foucault wholly ignores or is unsympathetic to these differences. For example, Foucault clearly asserts that "for the State to function the way it does, there must be, between male and female . . . quite specific relations of domination which have their own configurations and relative autonomy," Michel Foucault, "The History of Sexuality," in *Power/Knowledge,* 188. That is, nationalist discourses regarding the nuclear family (and subsequent discourses concerning illegitimate sexuality and prostitution) depend on gender dominance for their effective circulation. It is to say, however, that these differences are not always foregrounded in his work.

36. Lefebvre, *Production of Space,* 416–17.

37. Lefebvre quoted in Rob Shields, *Lefebvre, Love, and Struggle: Spatial Dialectics* (New York: Routledge, 1999), 76. Lefebvre's work parallels Foucault's in many respects, although his work has received little critical engagement when compared with the voluminous secondary literature that Foucault's oeuvre has spawned. It might well be argued that although both Lefebvre and Foucault work in the theoretical spaces opened up by (and between) Marx and Nietzsche, Lefebvre's work can be more easily allied with the former, whereas we would place Foucault much closer to the latter. Drawing their inspiration from these important sources, both Lefebvre and Foucault articulate the components of a complex materialism, a materialism that is characterized by its emplacement, its embodiment, and its historical specificity.

38. Lefebvre, *Production of Space,* 61.

39. Ibid., 135.

40. Elizabeth Grosz, *Volatile Bodies: Toward a Corporeal Feminism* (Bloomington: Indiana University Press, 1994), 191.

41. Foucault, "Space, Knowledge, and Power," 251–52.

42. Ibid., 252.

43. Iris Marion Young, *Justice and the Politics of Difference* (Princeton: Princeton University Press, 1990), 131.

44. Russell Jacoby and Naomi Glauberman, ed. *The Bell Curve Debate* (New York: Three Rivers Press, 1995).

45. It is important to note that these are things that a culture regards as dirty or impure; they are not dirty or impure in themselves. Freud points out that the medical concerns for hygiene, etc., were an ex post facto justification of the social taboos and mores already in place rather than their proximate cause. See Sigmund Freud, *Civilization and Its Discontents,* edited and translated by James Strachey (New York: W. W. Norton, 1961), 52.

46. Julia Kristeva, *The Powers of Horror: An Essay on Abjection* (New York: Columbia University Press, 1982), 3.

47. Kristeva makes the distinction between a threat to identity from without (symbolized by excrement, decay, infection, disease, and the corpse) and a threat to identity from within (symbolized by menstrual blood). See Kristeva, *Powers of Horror,* 71.

48. Ibid., 2.

49. Ibid., 72, emphasis in the original.

50. Mary Douglas, *Purity and Danger: An Analysis of Concepts of Pollution and Taboo* (New York: Frederick A. Praeger, 1966), 115.

51. Ibid., 4.

52. Ibid., 3–4.

53. Grosz, *Volatile Bodies,* 203.

54. Leslie Kanes Weisman, *Discrimination by Design: A Feminist Critique of the Man-Made Environment* (Urbana and Chicago: University of Illinois Press, 1992), 2.

55. Lefebvre, *Production of Space,* 57.

56. Ibid., 165. Interestingly, the examples Lefebvre cites as "dominated spaces" (military architecture, dams and irrigation systems, meshwork or grids imposed on the landscape) bear some resemblance to Foucault's disciplinary architecture.

57. Ibid.

58. Ibid.

59. Ibid., 166

60. Ibid.

61. Ibid.

62. Orville Lee, "Culture and Democratic Theory: Toward a Theory of Symbolic Democracy," *Constellations* 5 (1996), 443, italics removed.

63. Ibid., 448.

64. See O. H. Gandy, *The Panoptic Sort: A Political Economy of Personal Information* (Boulder: Westview, 1993).

65. See Weisman, *Discrimination by Design,* ch. 2, "Public Architecture and Social Status," for a brief account of the social symbolism inherent in the office tower, the department store, the shopping mall, and the maternity hospital. Ibid., 440, 443, italics removed.

66. For how public memorials can either consolidate or subvert state power, see Jenny Edkins, *Trauma and the Memory of Politics* (Cambridge: Cambridge University Press, 2003).

67. Davis, *City of Quartz,* 226.

Chapter 3: Nation Building and Body Building in Washington, D.C.

1. Foucault, "Of Other Spaces," 11.

2. Scott cited in Gillette, *Between Justice and Beauty,* 6–7.

3. L'Enfant cited in John W. Reps, *Monumental Washington: The Planning and Development of the Capital Center* (Princeton: Princeton University Press. 1967), 16–18.

4. Michael Carmona, *Haussmann: His Life and Times, and the Making of Modern Paris* (Chicago: Ivan R. Dee, 2002).

5. The Columbian Exposition, as the 1893 World's Fair in Chicago was called, ostensibly celebrated the four hundredth anniversary of Columbus's arrival in the New World.

The Senate Park Commission reconvened most of the luminaries from this World's Fair. The commission included Daniel Burnham (the Superintendent of Construction of the Columbian Exhibition, who later drew up plans for remaking the entire city of Chicago); Charles McKim (the neoclassical architect who designed the Columbian Exposition's Art Building), Augustus Saint-Gaudens (the sculptor responsible for overseeing the White City's patriotic municipal art), and Frederick Law Olmstead Jr., a landscape architect (his father was the celebrated creator of Central Park, and was also the landscape architect for the Columbian Exposition). Charles Moore, McMillan's secretary, coordinated much of the planning effort. See James Gilbert, *Perfect Cities: Chicago's Utopias of 1893* (Chicago: University of Chicago Press, 1991). For a colorful popular history of many of these larger-than-life personalities, the White City itself, and the tension between this "utopian" space and the violence that underpinned actual urbanization at the turn of the century, see Erik Larson, *The Devil in the White City: Murder, Magic and Madness at the Fair that Changed America* (New York: Vintage, 2003).

6. See Mona Domosh, "A 'Feminine' Building? An Inquiry into the Relations between Gender Ideology and Aesthetic Ideology in Turn-of-the-Century America," *Ecumene: A Journal of Environment, Culture and Meaning*, 3, no. 3 (1996): 305–24.

7. Gilbert, *Perfect Cities*, 81.

8. Robert W. Rydell, *All the World's a Fair: Visions of Empire at American International Exhibitions, 1876–1916* (Chicago: University of Chicago Press), 236.

9. John Coleman Adams, "What a Great City Might Be—A Lesson From the White City," *The New England Magazine* 14 (1896): 4.

10. Adams, "What a Great City Might Be," 9.

11. Charles Zueblin, "The White City and After," in *A Decade of Civic Development*, edited by Charles Zueblin (Chicago: University of Chicago Press, 1905), 65.

12. Zueblin, "White City and After," 62.

13. Although the Columbian Exhibition did not expressly discriminate against working-class patrons, Gilbert argues that the simple cost of a stay at the fair effectively made the experience inaccessible to all working-class visitors except those in Chicago. That is, although millions of Americans made pilgrimages across the country to experience the White City, the price of travel, lodging, and food for such a venture was quite steep. See Gilbert, *Perfect Cities*, 61, 121.

14. Zueblin, "White City and After," 62–63.

15. Adams, "What a Great City Might Be," 4–5.

16. Zueblin, "White City and After," 65.

17. Georg Simmel, "The Metropolis and Mental Life," in *On Individuality and Social Forms: Selected Writings*, edited by Donald Levine (1903, repr. Chicago: University of Chicago Press, 1971), 325.

18. Adams, "What a Great City Might Be," 6. See also Domosh, "'Feminine' Building?" 311.

19. Adams, "What a Great City Might Be," 3; Zueblin, "White City and After," 59.

20. George Kriehn, "The City Beautiful," *Municipal Affairs* 3 (1899): 598–99.

21. Quoted in Gilbert, *Perfect Cities*, 92.

22. Adams, "What a Great City Might Be," 10. It is interesting to note that Elias Disney, Walt's father, was one of the workmen who helped construct the White City. His

experience there was so meaningful to him that he considered naming one of his sons Columbus, after the exhibition. See Larson, *Devil in the White City*, 373.

23. Cited in Gilbert, *Perfect Cities*, 78.

24. And ushered in an era in which, as Elizabeth Wilson writes, "in the great cities of the world at least, but also certainly in any smaller cities that can capitalize on a historic past . . . not only is the tourist becoming perhaps the most important kind of inhabitant, but we all become tourists in our own cities." Elizabeth Wilson, *The Sphinx in the City: Urban Life, the Control of Disorder, and Women* (Berkeley: University of California Press, 1992), 157. Historic waterfronts, churches, markets, even sites of political conflict are resurrected or recycled into products in their own right, appearing on lists of things a tourist "must see" when visiting an area to get to know the "real" city.

25. Timothy W. Luke, *Museum Politics: Power Plays at the Exhibition* (Minneapolis: University of Minnesota Press, 2002), 4.

26. The Columbian Exposition is considered a turning point in American architecture. Architectural critics such as Louis Sullivan and Montgomery Schuyler would say it set American architecture back fifty years, whereas supporters of the City Beautiful movement, which emerged out of the architecture of the fair, would hail its new commitment to municipal art and civic spirit.

27. Gillette, *Between Justice and Beauty*, 90.

28. For an account of the political battles waged over who would control the planning process in Washington, see Jon A. Peterson, "The Nation's First Comprehensive City Plan: A Political Analysis of the McMillan Plan for Washington, D.C., 1900–1902," *Journal of the American Planning Association* 51 (Spring 1985): 134–50.

29. U. S. Senate Committee on the District of Columbia, *Report of the Senate Committee on the District of Columbia on the Improvement of the Park System of the District of Columbia*. Senate Report No. 166, 57th Cong., 1st Sess. (Washington: Government Printing Office, 1902).

30. Dietrich Schirmer, "Nation-building and Nation-Buildings: Washington Art and Architecture and the Symbols of American Nationalism," in *Identity and Intolerance: Nationalism, Racism, and Xenophobia in Germany and the United States*, edited by Nobert Finzsch and Dietrich Schirmer (Cambridge: Cambridge University Press, 1998), 150.

31. Gillette, *Between Justice and Beauty*, 90.

32. Cited in Schirmer, "Nation-building and Nation-Buildings," 150.

33. *The Century*, "Civic Improvement a Phase of Patriotism," 63 (1902): 793.

34. Daniel H. Burnham, "White City and Capital City," *The Century* 63 (February 1902): 619.

35. In the summer of 1901, the Senate Park Commission made a tour of several European cities to trace European influences on L'Enfant and to generate inspiration for their changes to his original design. In his account of the urban reconstruction of fin-de-siecle Vienna, Carl Schorske amusingly describes the imitative impulses of the city's planners by noting that "Where historical tradition was lacking, historical education had thus to fill the void." Carl E. Schorske, *Fin-de-Siècle Vienna: Politics and Culture* (1961 repr. New York: Vintage Books, 1981), 43.

36. Charles Moore, "The Improvement of Washington City, Second Paper," *The Century* 63 (1902): 751.

37. Charles Moore, *The Life and Times of Charles McKim* (Cambridge: Riverside Press, 1929), 916.

38. Luke, *Museum Politics*, 12.

39. Charles Mulford Robinson, *Modern Civic Art or, The City Made Beautiful* (1903 repr. New York: Arno Press, 1970), 12. Robinson's book is considered a foundational text of the City Beautiful movement. It went through four editions between 1903 and 1918. In it, Robinson wholeheartedly endorses the Senate Park Commission Plan for Washington as a successful experiment in City Beautiful ideals.

40. Quoted in Gillette, *Between Justice and Beauty*, 90.

41. H. K. Bush-Brown, "New York City Monuments," *Municipal Affairs* 3 (1899): 602.

42. Kriehn, "City Beautiful," 599–600.

43. Bush-Brown, "New York City Monuments," 602.

44. Lefebvre, *Production of Space*, 220.

45. Judith Butler quoted in Joanne P. Sharp, "Gendering Nationhood: A Feminist Engagement with National Identity," in *Bodyspace: Destabilizing Geographies of Gender and Sexuality*, edited by Nancy Duncan (New York: Routledge, 1996), 98.

46. Schirmer, "Nation-building and Nation-Buildings," 128.

47. In 2005, Congress announced the creation of a task force to study and commemorate the contributions made by African American slaves in the building of the Capitol. According to historians, "Slaves cut trees on the hill where the Capitol would stand, cleared stumps from the new streets, worked in the stone quarries where sandstone was cut and assisted the masons laying stone for the walls of the new homes of Congress and the president. They also were involved in the expansion of the Capitol in the late 1850s." See Associated Press, "Capitol Slave Labor Studied," *Washington Times* (June 1, 2005), http://washingtontimes.com/national/20050531-110046-7574r.htm.

48. "The Architect of the Capitol," *Frieze of American History*, www.aoc.gov/cc/art/rotunda/frieze/frieze.htm

49. "The Architect of the Capitol," *Apotheosis of Washington*, www.aoc.gov/cc/art/rotunda/apotheosis/apotheosis.htm

50. Sharp, "Gendering Nationhood," 100.

51. Quoted in Olson, "Democratic Problem of the White Citizen," 175–76. The phrase "the wages of whiteness" is from David R. Roediger, *The Wages of Whiteness: Race and the Making of the American Working Class* (New York: Verso Press, 1991).

52. See James W. Loewen, *Lies Across America: What Our Historic Sites Get Wrong* (New York: The New Press, 1999), especially 327–32.

53. Edkins, *Trauma and the Memory of Politics*, 54.

54. Quoted in Hayden, *The Power of Place*, 67.

55. Steve Pile, *The Body and the City: Psychoanalysis, Space, and Subjectivity* (New York: Routledge, 1996), 212–13.

56. Schirmer, "Nation-building and Nation-Buildings," 122.

57. The controversy that exploded in Richmond, Virginia, over the inclusion of a statue of Arthur Ashe on Monument Avenue after his death in 1993 is one example of how monuments serve as lightning rods in the politics of memory.

Monument Avenue is well known for the statues of Southern Civil War heroes placed along the tree-lined boulevard, including a sixty-one-foot statue of Robert E. Lee. The proposal to add a statue of African American tennis star Arthur Ashe to a place long regarded as a Pantheon to the Confederacy resulted in feelings of anger, confusion, and betrayal from many citizens, both white and black. Whereas many, including the former Virginia Governor L. Douglas Wilder, thought the statue's placement was a "symbol of racial healing," and that it was only appropriate that Ashe's statue be placed in the city's "symbolic heart," others thought it would be insulting to the memory of the dead—either to the Confederate heroes or to Ashe himself—to have the statues in such close proximity to one another. Some felt the monument would have more symbolic significance if it was located in Byrd Park, where as a young boy Ashe was refused entry because of his race. The controversy was resolved in 1996, in favor of placing the statue of Ashe on Monument Avenue, where it has become a major tourist attraction. See Donald P. Baker, "Controversy Aside, Ashe Statue Is a Hit," *Washington Post* (April 19, 1996): D2.

58. Berlant, *Anatomy of National Fantasy*, 2.

59. For an insightful comparison of the VVM and the World War II Memorial that recently took its place on the Mall, see Johnston, "Political Not Patriotic," available online at http://muse.jhu.edu/journals/theory_and_event/toc/archive.html#5.

60. Maya Lin, *Boundaries* (New York: Simon and Schuster, 1999), 4:15.

61. Ibid., 4:16.

62. Ibid., 2:03.

63. Ibid., 4:10.

64. Ibid., 2:03.

65. Some of the objects appeared in an exhibition at the Smithsonian Museum of Natural History, thus becoming part of the "official" collective memory of the war. A similar "monument" was erected at the Federal Building in Oklahoma City immediately after the bombing there. Wreaths, flowers, pictures, baby shoes, stuffed animals, letters, and cards were attached by visitors to the fence that surrounded the building, creating a very personal space of reflection and remembrance at this site of collective tragedy.

66. Edkins, *Trauma and the Memory of Politics*, 109.

67. Alison Isenberg, *Downtown America: A History of the Place and the People Who Made It* (Chicago: Chicago University Press, 2004), 37–39.

68. Robinson, *Modern Civic Art*, 28.

69. The creation of public spaces such as the Washington Mall marks an interesting place between the terms "building" and "dwelling" (originally Heidegger's). As Young (1997) describes this distinction, building allows human beings to establish a world and their place in it; it is a foundational act in creating subjectivity and is typically a masculine endeavor (136–37). In contrast, dwelling allows us to create and renew meaning in the spaces we have built; it is typically feminine work associated with the tasks of preservation. Young uses the example of house building and housekeeping to represent these two aspects of human experience, and calls on feminist theorists to positively revalue the important work associated with the latter. The construction of memorials, monuments, and other civic spaces does not seem to fit neatly into either category of meaning making, however; perhaps this is the reason City Beautiful adherents were so anxious about its "virility." See Iris Marion Young, *Intersecting Voices: Dilemmas of Gender, Political Philosophy, and Policy* (Princeton: Princeton University Press, 1997), ch. 7.

70. Moira Gatens, "Corporeal Representation in/and the Body Politic," in *Cartographies: Poststructuralism and the Mapping of Bodies and Spaces*, edited by Rosalyn Diprose and Robyn Ferrell (North Sydney: Allen & Unwin, 1991), 82.

71. *The Century,* "Civic Improvement," 63 (1902): 793.

72. For an excellent account of these various initiatives, see Paul S. Boyer, *Urban Masses and Moral Order in America, 1820–1920* (Cambridge: Harvard University Press, 1978).

73. Reps, *Monumental Washington,*, 53.

74. Edith Elmer Wood, "Four Washington Alleys," *Survey* 31 (1913): 46.

75. *The Evening Star,* "The Future Capital," (February 23, 1900).

76. Weller, *Neglected Neighbors,* 17.

77. James Borchert, *Alley Life in Washington: Family, Community, Religion, and Folklore* (Urbana and Chicago: University of Illinois Press, 1980), 17.

78. Borchert, *Alley Life,* 224.

79. In Washington, the first studies of the alleys were conducted by the Board of Health of the District of Columbia in the 1870s. After the Board was replaced by a less powerful Health Officer in 1878, other reports on health and housing were generated by the Civic Center and the Women's Anthropological Society (1894), the Committee on Housing (1897), and the President's Homes Commission (1908). See Marion Ratigan, *A Sociological Study of Disease in Four Alleys in the National Capital* (Washington, D.C.: Catholic University of America Press, 1946), 8–10.

80. Quoted in George M. Sternberg, *Report of Committee on Building of Model Homes* (Washington, D.C.: The President's Homes Commission, 1908), 12.

81. Quoted in Weller, *Neglected Neighbors,* 238.

82. Quoted in Sternberg, *Report of Committee,* 14.

83. Weller, *Neglected Neighbors,* 25.

84. "That no dwelling house hereafter erected or placed in an alley shall in any case be located less than twenty feet back, clear of the center line of such alley, so as to give at least a thirty-foot roadway and five feet on each side of such roadway for a walk or footway, and that it shall be unlawful to erect or place a dwelling house on or along any alley which does not run straight to, and open at right angles upon one of the public squares bordering the square in which the alley is located, with at least one exit fifteen feet in the clear," quoted in Sternberg, *Report of Committee,* 11. Another section of the act allowed the commissioners to widen, open, or straighten alleys "when necessary to the preservation of public morals, good order and peace" or for the preservation of public health. This act was amended in 1894, 1901, and 1905. Ratigan, *Sociological Survey of Disease,* 14–15.

85. Borchert reports that "[f]rom 1873 until its abolition in 1877, the Board of Health condemned 985 alley shanties, of which nearly 300 were demolished." The Board for the Condemnation of Insanitary Buildings, created in 1906, condemned and destroyed 375 alley houses between 1906 and 1911. Borchert, *Alley Life,* 45–46.

86. Sternberg, *Report of Committee,* 10.

87. In 1873, the Board of Health reported that there were five hundred inhabited alleys in Washington, while in 1914 the Committee on the District of Columbia reported that there were 267 or 268. However, the number of alley inhabitants was a continually contested issue among city officials and social reformers. City officials and members of the Senate Committee on the District of Columbia cite numbers from the police census at the time to describe the number of alley residents displaced during the first decade of the twentieth century. These figures had the alley dwelling population at around twenty-five thousand in 1892 and eleven thousand in 1914, with approximately ten thousand blacks

and a thousand whites. However, Rev, J. Milton Waldron, President of the Alley Improvement, who addressed the Committee in 1914 (". . . at the request of the colored Baptist, Methodist, and Congregational ministers of the District of Columbia"), argued that these census figures significantly underestimated the number of people living in alleys. Waldron stated that there were actually about twenty-five hundred whites and sixteen thousand people total living in the Washington alleys. U.S. House of Representatives, *Certain Alleys in the District of Columbia, Hearing before House Committee on the District of Columbia* (March 13–14, 1914), 47.

The Committee dismissed his concerns, although as early as 1896, social reformers noted that "'[C]rowding goes on to an extent not acknowledged to the canvasser by the tenants. At night, these poor roofs shelter many more people than are here reported,'" (quoted in Sternberg, Report of Committee). James Borchert makes a similar claim, citing two important reasons why the police census was inaccurate and underrepresented the alley dwelling population: (1) the police who conducted the census were often afraid to venture into the alleys; (2) alley dwellers were concerned that their houses would be judged "overcrowded" by city officials (and then condemned), so they did not give accurate information to bureaucrats or police officers. See Borchert, *Alley Life*, 42–44.

88. U.S. House of Representatives, *Certain Alleys*, 13, 27.

89. Ibid., 18. Speaking as a health expert for the District of Columbia Board of Commissioners, one doctor argued that ". . . it is not that the individual buildings are insanitary, not so much that the paving is bad or that there is an absence of water and sewer connections, because defects with respect to these matters have been and can be corrected; but it is the fact that people are living together in an isolated court, you might term it, without the general sweep of open air, without the restraining influence of association with other people, and without the presence of other people to give better ideals of living." U.S. Senate, *Inhabited Alleys in the District of Columbia: Hearing of the United States Senate Subcommittee on the District of Columbia* (1914), 17.

90. Ratigan states that there was 12 to 40 percent interest on investments in alley property (10). The estimates used by the Senate Committee in 1914 were also high; Siddons said that he "heard as high as 14, 15, 16, and 18 percent was received net from those buildings." U.S. House of Representatives, *Certain Alleys*, 18.

91. U.S. Senate, *Inhabited Alleys*, 18.

92. Quoted in Weller, *Neglected Neighbors*, 56.

93. U.S. House of Representatives, *Certain Alleys*, 17.

94. Ibid., 5–6, emphasis added.

95. Ratigan, *Sociological Survey of Disease*, 16.

96. Ibid. U.S. House of Representatives, *Certain Alleys*, 8.

97. U.S. Senate, *Inhabited Alleys*, 6. One of the members of the Senate Committee was unique in speaking out against the Committee's collective mindset, arguing that it would look like ". . . an abuse of power to simply say arbitrarily, 'You shall not use this,' irrespective of the goodness or badness of the particular place; irrespective of the particular sanitary conditions which might prevail there. It would look to me like an abuse of power which would result in a very great public evil." U.S. House of Representatives, *Certain Alleys*, 27.

98. Weller, *Neglected Neighbors*, 117.

99. *Charities,* "To Wipe Washington Alleys off the Map," 13 (1905): 960.

100. Constance McLaughlin Green, *The Secret City: A History of Race Relations in the Nation's Capital* (Princeton: Princeton University Press, 1967).

101. A fact that is discussed repeatedly in the various studies of alley life. One notable case is the alleys in the Northwest area of the District, home to lavish embassies and exquisite townhouses that ringed some of the most horrible alley conditions in the city.

102. U.S. Senate, *Inhabited Alleys*, 22.

103. Weller, *Neglected Neighbors*, 11.

104. Ibid., 15.

105. U.S. Senate, *Inhabited Alleys*, 19.

106. Ibid., 22.

107. Ibid., 19.

108. See Borchert, *Alley Life*, and Weller, *Neglected Neighbors*.

109. See Weller, *Neglected Neighbors*.

110. U.S. House of Representatives, *Certain Alleys*, 20, emphasis added.

111. Borchert, *Alley Life*, 27; Ratigan, *Sociological Survey of Disease*, 10.

112. Quoted in Borchert, *Alley Life*, 45.

113. Mary Poovey, "The Production of Abstract Space," in *Making Worlds: Gender, Metaphor, and Materiality*, edited by Susan Hardy Aiken, Sallie A. Marston, and Penny Waterstone (Tuscon: University of Arizona Press, 1998), 72.

114. Quoted in Poovey, "Production of Abstract Space," 73.

115. Rousseau quoted in Richard Sennett, *The Conscience of the Eye: The Design and Social Life of Cities* (New York: W. W. Norton, 1992), 118. For "community" and civic life, see Young, *Justice and the Politics of Difference*, ch. 8.

116. Poovey, "Production of Abstract Space," 76.

117. U.S. House of Representatives, *Certain Alleys*, 22.

118. Foucault, *History of Sexuality, Vol. I*, 139.

119. Quoted in Sternberg, *Report on Committee*, 13.

120. Weller, *Neglected Neighbors*, 27.

121. Ibid., 234.

122. U.S. Senate, *Inhabited Alleys*, 12.

123. It also does not explain why the same sort of (il)logic of revulsion and expulsion can guide current debates over welfare reform and public housing when (as Young points out) many of the explicit scientific/medical discourses of race and sex superiority have been discredited. See Young, *Justice and the Politics of Difference*, 132–33.

124. Interestingly, although many of the reforms at this time are now considered racist, directed at the normalization of either African Americans or new immigrants, Weller saved some of his most pointed criticisms for native-born whites: "Immigration is also needed as a leaven in this [alley] community of native white people. The native-born population clearly tends to degenerate when left without stimulus from the outside. . . . [L]ocal communities of native whites, whose ancestors have had considerable opportunity in America and have failed to make the most of it, are notably lacking in ambition and energy, in the consciousness of any need for improvement, and in high moral standards." *Neglected Neighbors*, 285.

125. U.S. Senate, *Inhabited Alleys*, 24. See also Wood, "Four Washington Alleys," 44–46.

126. Young, *Justice and the Politics of Difference*, 124–30.

127. Weller, *Neglected Neighbors*, 242.

128. Ibid., 73.

129. Wood, "Four Washington Alleys," 6.

130. Weller, *Neglected Neighbors,* 69.

131. Ibid., 28.

132. Ibid.

133. Borchert, *Alley Life,* 113.

134. Weller, *Neglected Neighbors,* 23.

135. Quoted in U.S. Senate, *Investigation of the Program of the National Housing Authority: Hearings before a Subcommittee of the Committee on the District of Columbia* (October 5, 1943, and January 24, 1944), 135.

136. Weller, Neglected Neighbors, 73.

137. Ibid., 119.

138. See also Nancie Caraway, *Segregated Sisterhood: Racism and the Politics of American Feminism* (Knoxville: University of Tennessee Press, 1991), 100–109.

139. Weller, *Neglected Neighbors,* 29.

140. U.S. Senate, *Inhabited Alleys,* 11.

141. Wood, "Four Washington Alleys," 45.

142. See Nancy Fraser and Linda Gordon, "Decoding Dependency: Inscriptions of Power in a Keyword of the U.S. Welfare State," in *Reconstructing Political Theory: Feminist Perspectives,* edited by Mary Lyndon Shanley and Uma Narayan (University Park: Pennsylvania State University Press, 1997), 25–47.

143. Young, "Intersecting Voices," 123.

144. Ibid., 125.

145. Gatens, "Corporeal Representation," 79.

146. Weller, *Neglected Neighbors,* 243.

147. Ibid., 29.

148. Ibid.

149. Ibid., 120.

150. U.S. House of Representatives, *Certain Alleys,* 26.

151. Ibid., 13, emphasis added.

152. Poovey, "Production of Abstract Space," 75.

153. U.S. Senate, *Inhabited Alleys,* 12.

154. Grosz, *Volatile Bodies,* 193.

155. Burnham, "White City and Capital City," 620.

Chapter 4: Remaking Washington at Midcentury

1. Ward Just, "The City Besieged: A Study in Ironies," *Washington Post* (April 6, 1968): A14.

2. William Clopton, "Four Thousand Troops Move into District after Day of Looting and Arson," *Washington Post* (April 6, 1968): A1.

3. Bernard J. Frieden and Lynne B. Sagalyn, *Downtown, Inc.: How America Rebuilds Cities* (1989 repr. Cambridge: MIT Press, 1994), 29; Isenberg, *Downtown America,* 173.

4. Ernest H. Wohlenberg, "The 'Geography of Civility' Revisited: New York Blackout Looting, 1977," *Economic Geography* 58, no. 1 (January 1982): 29–44.

5. That alley dwellings were "hereby declared injurious to life, to public health, morals, safety and welfare" and that "such use or occupation of any such building . . . from, and after the first day of July, nineteen hundred and eighteen, shall be unlawful." Quoted in Ratigan, *Sociological Survey of Disease,* 16.

6. Ratigan, *Sociological Survey of Disease,* 17–18. The Alley Dwelling Act of 1914 was eventually declared unconstitutional.

7. In many ways a successor to the McMillan Commission, this group was charged with preparing a "comprehensive, consistent, and coordinated plan for the National Capital" which would include recommendations for "transportation, plots and subdivisions, highways, parks, parkways, schools, library sites, playgrounds . . . housing, building and zoning regulations, public and private buildings, and so forth." By entrusting a single group of experts with the creation of a comprehensive plan, Congress hoped to replicate the success of the McMillan Commission throughout the District.

8. Later amendments postponed the alley closing dates to July 1, 1945, and then to July 1, 1946.

9. 73 P.L. 307; 73 Cong. Ch. 465; 48 Stat. 930.

10. *The Evening Star,* "NCHA Reports on Number of Unfit D.C. Dwellings to Congress" (April 16, 1946): B1.

11. Chalmers M. Roberts, "Progress or Decay?", *Washington Post* (January 27, 1952): B1. In another article in the same series, Roberts reports that the population of "old Washington" dropped 13,211 people between 1940 and 1950, while suburbs in Maryland and Virginia more than doubled their total populations. Chalmers M. Roberts, "Capital's Problem Area Pronounced Ripe for Redevelopment," *Washington Post* (February 1, 1952): B1. For a thorough analysis of both the crises facing cities at midcentury and postwar urban renewal efforts in the Northeast and Midwest, see Jon C. Teaford, *The Rough Road to Renaissance: Urban Revitalization in America, 1940–1985* (Baltimore: Johns Hopkins University Press, 1990).

12. This is not to say that there were not significant differences of opinion on what a new Washington should look like, whom it should privilege, or how these changes should be enacted. Two important debates we find in the discourse at this time are (1) whether and to what degree the government should be involved in housing low-income people, and (2) to what degree city officials should have a voice in replanning the city (there was another push for District representation in Congress at this time). Although these issues are certainly important in the debate concerning housing in Washington, they do not affect the larger consensus I describe here: private developers, public housing advocates, city officials, and congressional committee members all agreed that what was needed was a sweeping, comprehensive plan to remake the city.

13. Certain elements of this new initiative and its turn-of-the-century counterparts remained the same. Both identified similar targets for rehabilitation (alleys remained the primary sources of concern) and both were suspicious of the government's role in building housing (although this discussion became much more explicit at midcentury and was linked more closely with the influence of socialism). One typical example of this association between public housing and socialism is found in the hearings on the effectiveness of the National Capital Housing Authority (NCHA): "We are fearful that if subsidized housing is accepted in this country, that subsidized medicine, subsidized

food production, and eventually completely subsidized industry will follow, destroying our unique American system, and gradually changing us into a socialistic state." See U.S. Senate, *Investigation of the Program of the National Housing Authority*, 143.

14. Peter Hall, *Cities of Tomorrow: An Intellectual History of Urban Planning and Design in the Twentieth Century* (Oxford: Basil Blackwell, 1988), 228.

15. Quoted in "Everyone Pays for Blight," *American City* (May 1947): 102. This power was initiated even in the Alley Dwelling Act (ADA) of 1934; in addition to setting a deadline of 1944 for the complete elimination of alley dwellings, the act also recommended ". . . the replatting and development of squares containing inhabited alleys." 73 P.L. 307; 73 Cong. Ch. 465; 48 Stat. 930. That is, the ADA not only had the power to demolish buildings, but also to rebuild the land on which the buildings stood, to "put the cleared land to an appropriate new use." See U.S. Senate, *Construction of Certain Government Buildings in the District of Columbia: Hearings before a Subcommittee of the Committee on Public Works*, 84 Cong. 1st sess. April 27, May 2, and May 16, 1955, 38. In performing this dual function, the ADA had—as an article in the *American City* noted at the time—the unprecedented power to "make over at will whole city blocks" (1934, 67). Quoted in Gillette, *Between Justice and Beauty*, 139.

16. Constance McLaughlin Green, *Washington: A History of the Capital, 1800–1950* (Princeton: Princeton University Press, 1962), 492.

17. Specifically, these purposes included the "replanning, clearance, redesign, and re-building of project areas, including open-space types of uses, such a streets, recreation, and other public grounds, and spaces around buildings, as well as buildings, structures, and improvements . . . '[R]edevelopment' also includes the replanning, redesign, and original development of undeveloped areas which, by reason of street lay-out, lot lay-out, or other causes, are backward and stagnant and therefore blighted." 79 P.L. 592; 79 Cong. Ch. 736; 60 Stat. 790.

18. Quoted in James C. Scott, *Seeing Like a State: How Certain Schemes to Improve the Human Condition Have Failed* (New Haven and London: Yale University Press), 117; Chalmers quote from Nigel Taylor, *Urban Planning Theory since 1945* (Thousand Oaks: Sage Publications, 1998), 23–24.

19. Frieden and Sagalyn report that at a 1957 conference on urban redevelopment sponsored by the Connecticut General Life Insurance Company, participants "pointed with approval" to the renewal efforts underway in Washington, D.C. *Downtown, Inc.*, 15–16.

20. For example, the comprehensive plan issued by the NCPPC invokes this history in its opening pages (NCPPC, *Washington: Present and Future*, 5). Louis Justement also grounds his plan in Washington's history. See *New Cities for Old: City Building in Terms of Space, Time, and Money* (New York: McGraw-Hill, 1946), 95–96. See also the *Evening Star* editorial "An Overdue Master Plan" (September 27, 1947).

21. Chalmers M. Roberts, "One 'Super-Block' Could Replace Four Blocks of D.C. Slums," *The Washington Post* (February 12, 1952): B1.

22. James W. Rouse and Nathaniel Keith, *No Slums in Ten Years: A Workable Program for Urban Renewal*, (Washington: Report to the Commissioners of the District of Columbia, 1955), 3. For a fascinating account of Rouse's influence in planning American cities, see Nicholas Dagen Bloom, *Merchant of Illusion: James Rouse, American's Salesman of the Businessman's Utopia* (Columbus: Ohio State University Press, 2004).

23. Roberts, "Progress or Decay?" B2.

24. Frieden and Sagalyn, *Downtown, Inc.*, 27.

25. Quoted in Taylor, *Urban Planning Theory since 1945*, 25.

26. Lewis Mumford, *The City in History: Its Origins, Its Transformations, and Its Prospects* (New York: Harcourt, Brace, & World, 1961), 387.

27. 79 P.L. 592; 79 Cong. Ch. 736; 60 Stat. 790.

28. Justement, *New Cities for Old*, 3.

29. Quoted in Gutheim, *Worthy of the Nation*, 234.

30. Justement, *New Cities for Old*, 6. The concern for comprehensive, orderly rebuilding was not limited to Washington, however. Louis Justement was also instrumental in creating a national committee dedicated to the "rebuilding and orderly future development of American cities." The group consisted of six major professional organizations: the American Institutes of Architects (AIA), the Society of Landscape Architects, American Society of Civil Engineers, American Society of Planning Officials, American Institute of Planners, and the International Congress of Modern Architecture ("Group Forms to Stimulate 'Orderly' City Rebuilding," *Evening Star*, November 22, 1946).

31. 79 P.L. 592; 79 Cong. Ch. 736; 60 Stat. 790.

32. Quoted in Frieden and Sagalyn, *Downtown, Inc.*, 23.

33. I can only speculate why a word with botanical or agricultural associations would be introduced in urban planning discourse at this time. It is interesting to note, though, that during the 1930s, cities were becoming important political centers for the first time in our history, and were also for the first time the beneficiaries of significant federal funds via New Deal programs. Identifying cities' problems in agricultural terms may have served to explain or legitimate federal programs in a language comprehensible to a non-urban population.

34. "Everyone Pays for Blight," *American City* (May 1947): 102.

35. As Constance Green notes, between 1930 and 1950 Washington saw a mass exodus of whites, while nonwhite areas of the District became increasingly concentrated and segregated, due in large part to racist lending practices. (Green, *Washington*, 398–401). See Hayward, "The Difference States Make," 501–14, for an account of how specific insurance, housing, and transportation policies shape our understandings of identity and difference.

36. Frieden and Sagalyn, *Downtown, Inc.*, 25.

37. U.S. Senate, *Low-Cost Housing in the District of Columbia: Hearings Before a Subcommittee of the Committee on the District of Columbia*, February 26, 27, 28, and March 1 and 7, 1945, 47. John Ihdler, then chairman of the NCPPC, wants to distinguish here the bills leading to the District of Columbia Redevelopment Act of 1945 from the Alley Dwelling Act of 1934 by claiming that the latter has a heart in its concern for the people displaced by redevelopment. However, this distinction is a bit overdrawn, for the Alley Dwelling Act certainly contained within it the possibilities for the later legislation by giving the ADA the power to replan and redevelop the squares in which the alleys were located—essentially (as *American City* noted and as I cite earlier) "the power to make over entire blocks at will."

38. U.S. Senate, *Investigation of the Program of the NCHA*, 37.

39. U.S. Senate, *Construction of Government Buildings*, 17, 18. In this particular exchange,

Senator McNamara responded to this assertion with the (reasonable) question: "You are not suggesting that this problem would be solved by moving these people out of this area into some other area, are you? The same people need welfare; the same people will be involved, even though this particular redevelopment would cause other healthier and better economically established people to live in the area. . . . These statistics may remain with the people wherever they are" (19). Although his objection was noted and commented on briefly, the overall logic of economic rationalization remained unchallenged throughout these hearings.

40. Chalmers M. Roberts, "It's Costly and Dangerous for District to Maintain Slum Area," *Washington Post* (January 30, 1952): B1.

41. Chalmers M. Roberts, "Poor Health a Terrible Consequence of Blighted Areas in District," *Washington Post* (January 29, 1952): B1.

42. *American City* (May 1947): 162.

43. Editors of *Fortune* Magazine, *The Exploding Metropolis* (Garden City, N.Y.: Doubleday Anchor Books, 1958), 92.

44. See Isenberg, *Downtown America*, 190.

45. U.S. Senate, *Investigation of the NCHA*, 90.

46. Ibid., 2.

47. Quoted in Gillette, *Between Justice and Beauty*, 137.

48. U.S. Senate, *Construction of Certain Government Buildings*, 12. Thus, *Berman v. Parker* was a clear precedent for the controversial 2005 decision in *Kelo v. the City of New London*, in which the Fifth Amendment's provision of "public use" was broadly interpreted by the Supreme Court to include a plan for the city's economic revitalization.

49. Roberts, "One 'Super-Block,'" B1.

50. U.S. Senate, *Investigation of the NCHA*, 19, 27.

51. Justement, *New Cities for Old*, 226.

52. Cited in Marshall Berman, *All That Is Solid Melts into Air: The Experience of Modernity* (New York: Penguin Books, 1988), 290.

53. Isenberg, *Downtown America*, 193

54. Poovey, "Production of Abstract Space," 71.

55. Lefebvre, *Production of Space*, 49.

56. Justement, *New Cities for Old*, 3.

57. Scott, *Seeing Like a State*, 345–46.

58. Edward M. Wood, Sidney N. Brower, and Margaret W. Latimer, "Planners' People," *Journal of the American Institute of Planners* 32 (July 1966): 232.

59. Ibid., 233.

60. Quoted in Frieden and Sagalyn, *Downtown, Inc.*, 39.

61. I would like to thank Clarissa Hayward for helping me to think through this issue.

62. Frieden and Sagalyn, *Downtown, Inc.*, 37.

63. Gruen quoted in Isenberg, *Downtown America*, 176; See M. Jeffrey Hartwick, *Mall Maker: Victor Gruen, Architect of an American Dream* (Philadelphia: University of Pennsylvania Press, 2003).

64. Justement, *New Cities for Old*, 226.

65. NCPPC, *Washington: Present and Future*, 41.

66. Justement, *New Cities for Old,* 3.

67. Roberts, "Progress or Decay?", B1.

68. Isenberg, *Downtown America,* 176.

69. *Berman v. Parker,* quoted in Rouse and Keith, *No Slums in Ten Years,* 2.

70. Russell Baker, "Capital Planning City within a City," *New York Times* (January 2, 1956): 23; *New York Times,* "Zeckendorf Acts on Capital Slums," (March 15, 1954): 14.

71. In contemplating the question "What is a monument?" the debate over the FDR memorial during this time is fascinating. "Decision on Slabs" in the *Evening Star* (September 23, 1966) tells us that the debate "may not precipitate the most significant debate of the session [b]ut it certainly should produce the most heated." The paper calls the design "awful," saying "it would be hard to imagine an architectural design more strikingly incongruous" in the context of the Mall. This design (called "the giant slabs" by the *Evening Star*) was eventually abandoned, but an equally "incongruous" design was approved in 1978 and ground was broken for it in 1991; quotes from NCPPC, *Washington: Present and Future,* 5

72. Justement, *New Cities for Old,* 142–43. In plate 22, Justement describes the necessity of competing with suburban shopping areas by designing downtown shopping districts "for the comfort, convenience, and pleasure of shoppers." Thus Justement's urban shopping center is for all intents and purposes a suburban mall relocated downtown: in contrast to a photograph of a traditional urban downtown (with the caption "Is this good enough for the Capital's main shopping street?"), Justement pictures acres of low, uniform buildings punctuated by larger department stores surrounding a street reserved for pedestrians and buses. Parking lots are adjacent to the shopping complex (138–39).

73. American Institute of Architects, *No Time for Ugliness: An appraisal of the American City by the American Institute of Architects* (Washington, D.C.: American Institute of Architects, 1966), 20.

74. Ibid., 10–12.

75. Justement, *New Cities for Old,* 92.

76. Karatani, *Architecture as Metaphor,* 17.

77. Kateb, "Aestheticism and Morality,", 11.

78. Ibid., 15. Kateb distinguishes between conscious and unconscious aestheticism and is mainly concerned about the latter as it is manifested in "innocent ideals": religion, the maintenance or advancement of a specific culture or group identity, politics as an end in itself, masculinity, the passion to live for symbols, and radical environmentalism (8–10). He argues (albeit tentatively) that a conscious aestheticism, in contrast, "may be either more self-limiting and hence less productive of immorality or, by being given a proper name, more easy to denounce and resist" (11). The history of urban policy making in Washington, however, is a history of both conscious aestheticism (L'Enfant, the Park Commission Plan and Southwest redevelopment) and unconscious aestheticism (that alley dwellers and Southwest inhabitants were problematic in part because they obscured the vision of a clear, orderly, and rational city).

79. Justement, *New Cities for Old,* 8.

80. NCPPC, *Washington: Present and Future,* 41.

81. It is important to note here that Southwest Washington was not the only choice for policy makers for redevelopment. In fact, much of "old Washington" was in need

of redevelopment, according to planners, and potential redevelopment sites were also proposed in the Northwest and Southeast sections of the central city. When the NCHA gave its report on the city in 1946, it noted that there were "the existence of twice as many substandard dwellings as the city had before the war" and "an unprecedented number of unfit dwellings." *Evening Star,* "NCHA Reports," (April 16, 1946).

82. NCPPC, *Washington: Present and Future,* 20–22.

83. Daniel Thursz, *Where Are They Now? A Study of the Impact of Relocation on Former Residents of Southwest Washington Who Served in an HWC Demonstration Project* (Washington, D.C.: Health and Welfare Council of the National Capital Area, 1966), 2.

84. U.S. Senate, *Construction of Government Buildings,* 49.

85. Because of the ambiguous definitions given for the word, however, blight often existed in the eye of the beholder, and both city officials and private developers had an incentive to stretch the definition to suit their purposes. For example, in New York, Robert Moses planned his New York Coliseum project around the Columbus Circle area, where, "only 10 percent of the tenements were substandard and only 2 percent of the entire area could be considered a slum. It became a slum when the city planning commission declared it blighted, and federal officials accepted this declaration." Frieden and Sagalyn, 23–24.

86. Positing the problem as a choice between "progress" (meaning slum clearance and central business district urban renewal) and "decay" (meaning the status quo, and succumbing to encroaching blight) was a typical formulation. Justement framed the issue in the same terms, as did many commentators across the country. For example, in 1950, the *St. Louis Post-Dispatch* published a series of similar articles, titled "Progress or Decay? St. Louis Must Choose!" See Teaford, *Rough Road to Renaissance,* 82.

87. Baker, "Capital Planning City within a City," 23.

88. Thursz, *Where Are They Now?,* 2–3. For an account of the various alternatives proposed for redeveloping this area, see Gutheim, 314–15. See also Gillette, *Between Justice and Beauty,* esp. ch. 8.

89. U.S. House of Representatives, *Public Buildings—Soutwest Redevelopment—D.C.: Hearings before the Subcommittee on Public Buildings and Grounds and the Committee on Public Works,* 4.

90. Gillette, *Between Justice and Beauty,* 163; Quoted in Hall, *Cities of Tomorrow,* 208–9, capitals and italics in the original.

91. U.S. Senate, *Construction of Certain Government Buildings,* 41.

92. *New York Times,* "Project to Erase Washington Slum," (January 8, 1957): 49.

93. Frieden and Sagalyn, *Downtown, Inc.,* 27.

94. Justement, *New Cities for Old,* 8.

95. Richard Slotkin, *Regeneration through Violence: The Mythology of the American Frontier, 1600–1860* (New York: HarperCollins, 1973), 5.

96. Quoted in *New York Times,* "Rebuilding Plans Gain in Capital," (June 8, 1956): 57.

97. Thurz, *Where Are They Now?,* 2. This pattern was repeated across the country in city after city.

98. Gillette, *Between Justice and Beauty,* 163–64.

99. Justement, *New Cities for Old,* 144.

100. The agency existed under a variety of names during its tenure: the Resettlement Administration (RA, 1935–37), the Farm Security Administration (FSA, 1937–42), and finally the Office of War Information (OWI, 1942–44).

101. Quoted in R. J. Doherty, *Social-Documentary Photography in the USA* (Garden City, N.Y.: American Photographic Book Publishing Company, 1976), 79.

102. Quoted in Doherty, *Social-Documentary Photography*, 9.

103. In the hearings on redevelopment in the Southwest, this sentiment is used repeatedly to describe the reality of a divided Washington in phrases like these: "Witnesses to living conditions in the southwest are appalled by the dilapidation, the inadequacy of the houses that lie a stone's throw from the Nation's Capitol" (U.S. House of Representatives, *Public Buildings*, 4). It is also used in later works, for example in Charles Suddarth Kelly, *Washington, D.C., Then and Now: 69 Sites Photographed in the Past and Present* (New York: Dover Publications, 1984), 10.

104. Doherty, *Social-Documentary Photography*, 81. Currently, the FSA-OWI collection is housed in the Library of Congress and contains the approximately seventy-seven thousand images made by photographers working for Stryker in the History Section as it existed in a succession of government agencies. It also includes images taken by other government agencies and also those acquired from nongovernmental sources.

105. See Godfrey Frankel and Laura Goldstein, *In the Alleys: Kids in the Shadow of the Capitol* (Washington, D.C.: Smithsonian, 1995).

106. See Gutheim, *Worthy of the Nation*, 232.

107. Linda Wheeler, "Broken Ground, Broken Hearts—Urban Renewal Cost Homes," *Washington Post* (June 21, 1999): 1.

108. According to Gillette, "[b]oth a survey by the Homebuilders' Association of Metropolitan Washington . . . and the 1950 census revealed large numbers of structurally sound homes in black as well as white portions of the areas designated for redevelopment" and "even the RLA's survey of the area noted a high level of residential stability" (*Between Justice and Beauty*, 161). For example, the population of Area C changed drastically as urban renewal progressed. The area began as an integrated area (blacks made up 68 percent of the population, and although low-income families were clearly the majority, the area also served as home to businessmen and government officials) but as urban renewal progressed, the families in higher socioeconomic classes moved away, and the result was "a large increase in the total percentage of socially and economically dependent families and a concomitant increase in the overall percentage of Negro families in the area" (Thursz, *Where Are They Now?*, 3).

109. Kateb, "Aestheticism and Morality," 31.

110. Ibid., 32–33.

111. Ibid., 34.

112. Walter Benjamin, *Reflections: Essays, Aphorisms, and Political Writings* (New York: Schocken Books, 1978), 231.

113. Nancy Love, "Politics and Voice(s): An Empowerment/Knowledge Regime," *differences* 3, no. 1 (1991): 96. Although I agree with Susan Bickford that many theorists often overstate the opposition between vision and voice, and that the former is not necessarily or only an instrument of oppression, in this context Love's analysis seems apt. See Susan Bickford, *The Dissonance of Democracy: Listening, Conflict, and Citizenship* (Ithaca: Cornell University Press, 1996), esp. 142–44.

114. Frieden and Sagalyn, *Downtown, Inc.*, 33

115. Thursz, *Where Are They Now?*, ix.

116. Ibid., 28.

117. Ibid., 71. The Anomie Scale consists of five statements to which individuals could agree or disagree:

(1) There is little use in writing to public officials because often they aren't interested in the problem of the average man.

(2) Nowadays, a person has to live pretty much for today and let tomorrow take care of itself.

(3) In spite of what some people say, the lot of the average man is getting worse, not better.

(4) It's hardly fair to bring children into the world with the way things look for the future.

(5) These days, a person doesn't really know whom he can count on.

". . . The individual, then, who is found agreeing with all five statements can be said to be anomic and to feel alienated from the community and its evolution." Thursz, *Where Are They Now?*, 71–72.

118. Ibid., 72.

119. Ibid., 65.

120. Ibid., 56–7.

121. Quoted in Frieden and Sagalyn, *Downtown, Inc.*, 34.

122. Quoted in Thursz, *Where Are They Now?*, 43.

123. Mindy Thompson Fullilove, *Root Shock: How Tearing Up City Neighborhoods Hurts America, and What We Can Do About It* (New York: One World Ballantine Books, 2005), 10–11.

124. Ibid., 16–17.

125. *Washington Post Magazine*, "The Inferno and the Aftermath" (April 3, 1988): W23.

126. Charles Tilly agues that even despite numerous studies of the phenomenon, an adequate explanation of the 1960s riots was never developed, because most theories focused on the characteristics of riot participants, rather than the interactions between the armed authorities and civilians. See Bert Useem, "The State and Collective Disorders: The Los Angeles Riot/Protest of April 1992," *Social Forces* 76, no. 2 (December 1997): 357–58. Indeed, David O. Sears contends that no fewer than five types of explanation emerged in the wake of the 1992 Los Angeles riots: social contagion theory (i.e., crowds cause riots); black protest interpretations; a rainbow coalition argument (bringing together a variety of disadvantaged minority groups); the "bladerunner scenario" (the riot was a symptom of a larger breakdown in civilized society); and a theory of multiethnic conflict. Sears concludes that "no simple or single interpretation fits the 1992 events very well" (251). See David O. Sears, "Urban Rioting in Los Angeles: A Comparison of 1965 with 1992," in *The Los Angeles Riots: Lessons for the Urban Future*, edited by Mark Baldassare (Boulder, San Francisco, and Oxford: Westview Press, 1994), 237–54.

127. Dennis R. Judd, *The Politics of American Cities, Third Edition* (Glenview, Ill.: Little, Brown, 1988), 273.

128. Frieden and Sagalyn, *Downtown, Inc.*, 52

129. For an excellent account of how racist housing policy and practices contributed to

the expansion of black ghettos in Detroit, see Thomas J. Sugrue, *The Origins of the Urban Crisis: Race and Inequality in Postwar Detroit* (Princeton: Princeton University Press, 1996). For more on the relationship between urban renewal and the riot in Washington, see Gillette, *Between Justice and Beauty*, 167–69.

130. In Ben W. Gilbert and the Staff of the *Washington Post, Ten Blocks from the White House: Anatomy of the Washington Riots of 1968* (New York: Frederick A. Praeger Publishers, 1968), 165. It seems that *revolution* is the word we use to describe a situation in which oppressed people rise up and succeed in changing the dominant political or economic order, whereas *riot* is the word we use when they do the same thing and fail. (A revolution is a riot with history on its side?)

131. *New York Times* (April 7, 1968): 62.

132. Orville Lee, "Culture and Democratic Theory: Toward a Theory of Symbolic Democracy," *Constellations* 5 (1996): 449. This is not to suggest that this is the only possible interpretation for these events. The civil disturbances in Washington were multivocal in nature, much like the spaces they claimed. The Northwest section of Washington was a thriving black commercial center, whose geographic and psychic boundaries created the conditions of possibility for a tightly knit and productive community while simultaneously serving to reinforce the reality of a segregated city.

133. Virginia Postrel reports that in examining the long-term consequences of the riots, Professors Robert A. Margo and William J. Collins found that cities that experienced riots faced decades of depressed inner-city incomes and property values. Compared to cities that did not experience riots in the decade 1960–70, median black family income, male employment, and the median value of all central city homes dropped significantly. See Postrel, "The Long-term Consequences of the Race Riots in the Late 1960s Come into View," *New York Times* (December 30, 2004): C2.

134. Mindy Fullilove makes this point clearly when describing what she terms the civil insurrection in Newark. Only a month earlier, many of those who would later participate in the insurrection were voicing their concerns—to no avail—over another expansive urban renewal project in the city at public hearings. *Root Shock*, 148–53.

135. Scott, *Seeing Like a State*, 61

136. Interview in Gilbert et al., *Ten Blocks from the White House*, 167.

137. *Washington Post Magazine*, "The Inferno and the Aftermath," (April 3, 1988): W30.

138. Bart Barnes, "Wary Police Keep Lid on in Suburbs," *Washington Post* (April 7, 1968): A8.

139. Just, "City Besieged," A14.

Chapter 5: Millennial Space

1. Quoted in Jay Tolson, "Scenes from the Mall," *U.S. News & World Report* (September 18, 2000): 69.

2. See, for example, Catesby Leigh, "In Memoriam: World War II on the Mall," *The Weekly Standard*, 9, no. 36 (May 31, 2004). See also Paul Goldberger, "Down at the Mall: The New World War II Memorial Design Doesn't Rise to the Occasion," *New Yorker* (May 31, 2004).

3. James Reston Jr., "The Monument Glut," *New York Times Magazine* (September 10, 1995): 48–49.

4. Jürgen Habermas, *The Structural Transformation of the Public Sphere: An Inquiry into a Category of Bourgeois Society* (Cambridge: MIT Press, 1991).

5. Young, *Justice and the Politics of Difference,* 237, 227.

6. Obviously, there are significant differences between these two authors. One clear difference is the kind of city each privileges. In *The Fall of Public Man,* Sennett harkens back to (his versions of) Paris and London at the midpoint of the eighteenth century as the models of public life; through a variety of forces (notably consumerism), this world (according to Sennett) vanished over the course of the eighteenth century and has left us with cities that are urban in population density only. Young, by contrast, embraces the character of our chaotic, (post)modern cities (repr. 1974 New York: W. W. Norton, 1992).

Although the differences between them are surely important, they do not detract from the similarity I am examining here: the role of an urban environment in sustaining democratic life. By arguing for this kind of urban subjectivity, both Sennett and Young differentiate themselves from the work of other democratic urbanists such as Jane Jacobs's *The Death and Life of Great American Cities* (New York: Random House, 1961), whose version of city life (intimate neighborhoods, streets, and sidewalks) more closely approximates the Rousseauian community Young and Sennett critique.

7. Sennett, *Fall of Public Man,* 39.

8. Ibid., 40.

9. Ibid., 300–301.

10. Ibid., 340.

11. Jodi Dean, *Publicity's Secret: How Technoculture Capitalizes on Democracy* (Ithaca: Cornell University Press, 2002).

12. Ibid., 79.

13. From Catesby Leigh, "Our Monuments, Our Selves: What We Build Then, What We Build Now," *Weekly Standard* (March 5, 2001).

14. Reston, "Monument Glut," 48–49; Elaine Sciolino, "Agencies Limit New Memorials on Coveted Washington Mall," *New York Times* (September 7, 2001): A14.

15. National Capital Planning Commission (NCPC), *Museums and Memorials Master Plan* (Washington, D.C.: National Capital Planning Commission, September 2001), 3.

16. The Commemorative Works Act (CWA) of 1986 attempted to standardize memorial placement by distinguishing between Area I memorials and Area II memorials in Washington. Area I, which the CWA designates as the Washington Mall and portions of the city directly adjacent to it, is reserved for commemorative works of "'preeminent historical and lasting significance.'" Memorials in Area II, which lies outside the monumental core, should be the site for works of "'lasting historical significance'" (quoted in National Capital Planning Commission [NCPC], *Museums and Memorials Master Plan,* 5). The CWA did not provide guidelines for the placement of museums in the city.

17. 2004 saw the addition of two significant structures to the Mall: the World War II Memorial and the American Indian Museum.

18. NCPC, *Museums and Memorials Master Plan,* 3–5.

19. Roger K. Lewis, "Washington Monuments: Battles Over the Mall," *Architectural Record* 184, no. 1 (January 1996): 20.

20. Lewis, "Washington Monuments," 20.

21. Martin Kettle, "Capital City's Memorial Fever? Case of Monumental Madness," *Houston Chronicle* (November 9, 1997).

22. Stephen Kliment, "More Monuments?" *Architectural Record* 183, no. 10 (October 1995): 9.

23. Reston, "Monument Glut," 49. These issues have inspired many commentators to weigh in on the proper criteria for and appropriate shape of remembrance. Of course, these questions—how to remember and whom should be remembered—are always inextricably linked. Historian Stephen Ambrose argues that monuments and memorials should be reserved for those "who acted in some positive way for the good of the nation." For this reason, he sees the newly completed Japanese American Memorial as "a terrible idea." See Stephen E. Ambrose, "A Terrible Idea," *National Review* 51, no. 22 (November 22, 1999): 30–31. Ambrose's criteria for memorialization create a spatial narrative of American history that omits or paves over inconsistencies and incongruities, and prohibits the representation of conflicting experiences of citizenship that include honor, grief, pride, and shame. In this blinkered conception of what it means to be heroic, the depths of a more somber national memory are thus buoyed through a kind of historical and architectural Prozac.

24. Kettle, "Capital City's Memorial Fever?"

25. Deborah K. Dietsch, "National Mall is Jam-Packed—and Losing Its Majestic Image," *USA Today* (October 14, 2004): 25A.

26. Lawrence Halprin, *The Franklin Delano Roosevelt Memorial* (San Francisco: Chronicle Books, 1997), 7.

27. Critics have also decried the omission of one of Roosevelt's most frequent accessories from the statues: a cigarette holder.

28. Leigh, "Our Monuments, Our Selves." The issue of the "correct" version of Roosevelt is complicated, though. During his lifetime, Roosevelt went to some lengths to conceal his disability, eschewing his wheelchair, for example, while he was campaigning. The public perception of Roosevelt, moreover, was that of a strong and charismatic (and able-bodied) leader. And the original statue, although concealing the bulk of the wheelchair, is not exactly traditionally "heroic." In it, the lines around Roosevelt's eyes and mouth are pronounced; he looks haggard and wise, rather than especially gallant.

Finally, Roosevelt himself disdained the idea of an elaborate monument in his honor. He said, "If any memorial is erected to me, I should like it to consist of a block about the size of this desk and placed in front of the Archives Building. I want it plain, without any ornamentation, with the simple carving 'In Memory of.'" (Such a stone was placed in front of the Archives Building in the 1960s.) From "F.D.R. Remembered," transcript of PBS NewsHour, May 1, 1997. Accessed at http://www.pbs.org/newshour/bb/remember/1997/fdr_5–1.html.

29. See Michael Rogin, *Ronald Reagan, the Movie and Other Episodes in Political Demonology* (Berkeley: University of California Press, 1987), ch. 2.

30. Leigh, "In Memoriam."

31. Leigh, "Our Monuments, Our Selves."

32. The Joint Task Force on Memorials (JTFM) was formed in 1997 and comprises the NCPC, the Commission on Fine Arts (CFA), and the National Capital Memorial Commission (NCMC). Its mission comes directly out of the NCPC's initial efforts at studying and solving monument glut: a plan titled *Extending the Legacy: Planning America's Capital for the 21st Century,* which was published in 1997. *Legacy's* principal solution is to "[create] opportunities for new museums, memorials and other public buildings in all quadrants

of the city" (NCPC, *Museums and Memorials Master Plan,* 2); the JTFM's directive was to assist in establishing standardized criteria for selection and then identifying specific potential commemorative sites. The Memorials and Museums Master Plan was approved in September 2001.

33. NCPC, *Museums and Memorials Master Plan,* 1.

34. The monuments exempted from the policy include the World War II Memorial (not completed until 2004), the Black Revolutionary War Patriots Memorial, the George Mason Memorial, the U.S. Air Force Memorial, and the Martin Luther King Jr. Memorial.

35. NCPC, *Museums and Memorials Master Plan,* 13.

36. NCPC, *Museums and Memorials Master Plan,* 30.

37. Johnston, "Political Not Patriotic," 2. See also David Harvey, *Justice, Nature, and the Geography of Difference,* esp. 306–10; and Pile, *Body and the City.*

38. See Schirmer, "Nation-building and Nation-Buildings," 144–47.

39. Margaret G. Vanderhyde, quoted in Barbara Saffir, "Plan Outlines where to Place D.C. Memorials and Museums," *Architectural Record* 189, no. 2 (February 2001): 40.

40. Jacobs, *The Death and Life of Great American Cities,* 372–73.

41. Johnston, "Political Not Patriotic."

42. Joel Garreau, *Edge City: Life on the New Frontier* (New York: Doubleday, 1991).

43. Well-known examples of this strategy include Fanueil Hall and Quincy Market in Boston, Harbor Place in Baltimore, Fisherman's Wharf in San Francisco, Navy Pier in Chicago, and South Street Seaport in Manhattan. See M. Christine Boyer, "Cities for Sale: Merchandising History at South Street Seaport," in *Variations on a Theme Park: The New American City and the End of Public Space,* edited by Michael Sorkin (New York: Hill and Wang, 1992).

44. U.S. Senate, *DC Area Monuments and Memorials.*

45. NCPC, *Museums and Memorials Master Plan,* 3, 13.

46. Boyer, "Cities for Sale," 192.

47. William E. Connolly, *Why I Am Not a Secularist* (Minneapolis: University of Minnesota Press, 1999), 89.

48. Again, Washington, D.C., is not unique here, but is at the forefront of national trends. According to the *Washington Post,* 80 percent of nineteen thousand police departments in the United States use closed-circuit television in their jurisdictions, and 10 percent more plan to do so in the future. Spencer S. Hsu, "Video Surveillance Planned on the Mall," *Washington Post* (March 22, 2002): C1. There are as many as two hundred surveillance cameras in Times Square alone. CBS, "Close Watch," April 22, 2002.

Great Britain, however, is the country leading the way in video surveillance, with over two million cameras in place around the nation, 150,000 in London alone. First used to monitor IRA activities, many politicians attribute the noticeable drop in street crime to their presence. According to some estimates, "'The average Londoner is caught on film about 300 times a day.'" Congresswoman Morella, quoted in CBS, "Close Watch". According to a recent estimate, the average citizen of Washington and its environs is caught on camera eight to ten times a day. ABC World News, October 17, 2002.

49. Paul Virilio, "The Virtual Crash," in *CTRL [SPACE]: Rhetorics of Surveillance from Bentham to Big Brother,* edited by Thomas Y. Levin, Ursula Frohne, and Peter Weibel (Cambridge: ZKM and MIT Press, 2002), 109, italics removed from original. Currently,

Joint Operations Command Centers are proposed for many major urban areas, including Los Angeles, Chicago, Atlanta, and New York.

50. Jodi Dean, for example, argues that technoculture and its myriad, private "little brothers" have replaced technocracy and its centralized, government-sponsored "Big Brother." See Dean, *Publicity's Secret,* ch. 3. For discussion of the surveilled character of gated communities, see Bickford, "Constructing Inequalities"; and Teresa Pires do Rio Caldeira, "Fortified Enclaves: The New Urban Segregation," *Public Culture* 9 (1996), 303–28. For discussion of shopping malls, see Margaret Crawford, "The World in a Shopping Mall," in *Variations on a Theme Park: The New American City and the End of Public Space,* edited by Michael Sorkin (New York: Hill and Wang, 1992), 3–20; and Margaret Kohn, "The Mauling of Public Space," *Dissent* 48, no. 2 (Spring 2001): 71–77.

51. See Matthew Brzezinski, "Fortress America" *New York Times Magazine* (February 23, 2003): 43.

52. Young, *Justice and the Politics of Difference,* 227.

53. Georgetown, for instance, has already requested that cameras monitoring its streets and businesses be integrated into the command center's operations. The Benning Ridge neighborhood in Southeast Washington has also requested cameras be installed to curb crime. David A. Fahrenthold, "Crime-Plagued D.C. Neighborhoods Ask for Cameras," *Washington Post* (March 10, 2003): B1 and B6.

54. See Notice of Proposed Rulemaking on Closed Circuit Television Cameras for the MPD at www.dcwatch.com/police/020613.

55. See Crawford, "The World in a Shopping Mall," 3–30.

56. Timothy Druckrey, "Secreted Agents, Security Leaks, Immune Systems, Spore Wars . . ." in *CTRL [SPACE],* edited by Levin et al., 153, his emphasis. Facial recognition software was also used recently in the Convention Center at the WTO ministerial meeting in Cancun.

57. Brzezinski, "The Homeland Security State," 41.

58. Quoted in Virilio, "The Virtual Crash," 109.

59. Mona Domosh, "Those 'Gorgeous Incongruities': Polite Politics and Public Space on the Streets of Nineteenth Century New York City," *Annals of American Geographers* no. 88:209.

60. Jacobs, *Death and Life of Great American Cities,* 35.

61. Petula Dvorak, "Washington Monument Subtly Fortified," *Washingtong Post* (July 1, 2005): A1.

62. *Scopophilia* was a term originally employed by Freud in his essay on sexual aberrations to describe intense sexual pleasure in looking at the object of desire, a normal condition that threatens to morph into perversion when visual stimulation becomes a substitute for copulation. See Sigmund Freud, *Three Essays on the Theory of Sexuality* (New York: Basic Books, 1962), 22–23.

63. Jacqueline Rogers quoted in Peter T. Kilborn, "For Security, Tourists to Be on Other Side of Cameras," *New York Times* (March 23, 2002): 12.

64. Holloway Sparks, "Dissident Citizenship: Democratic Theory, Political Courage, and Activist Women," *Hypatia: A Journal of Feminist Philosophy* 12, no. 4 (1997): 75.

65. Thanks to Joel Olson for this formulation, and for helping me to think through this section of the chapter.

66. See the ACLU Web site, www.aclu.org/privacy/spying/14863res20020225.html.

67. See www.mediaeater.com/cameras/ for a description of the project and the maps.

68. See www.notbored.org/maps-usa.html.

69. See Michel Foucault, "Subject and Power," 208–26. See also William E. Connolly, *Identity\Difference: Democratic Negotiations of Political Paradox* (Ithaca: Cornell University Press, 1991).

70. See the Observing Surveillance Web site at http://observingsurveillance.org/. Observing Surveillance also produces a "tourist map" of camera locations.

71. See Copwatch.com

72. The documentary *This Is What Democracy Looks Like* (Seattle Independent Media Center and Big Noise Films, 2000) is a compilation of footage shot by over one hundred media activists during the antiglobalization protests at the 1999 WTO meeting in Seattle.

73. Most memorably, the network news anchors, city officials, and business leaders express outrage at the "injustice" of protestors breaking a Starbucks window while protestors are being beaten and gassed.

Chapter 6: Building the Body Politic

1. Connolly, *Identity\Difference*, 198.

2. Jacobs, *Death and Life of Great American Cities*, esp. ch. 19.

3. Elizabeth Wilson, "Against Utopia: The Romance of Indeterminate Space," in *Embodied Utopias: Gender, Social Change, and the Modern Metropolis*, edited by Amy Bingaman, Lise Sanders, and Rebecca Zorach (New York: Routledge, 2002), 257.

4. Lefebvre, *Production of Space*, 165.

5. Kirk Savage, *Standing Soldiers, Kneeling Slaves: Race, War and Monument in Nineteenth-Century America* (Princeton: Princeton University Press, 1997), 212.

6. The distinction is Saussure's in Michel de Certeau, *The Practice of Everyday Life* (Berkeley: University of California Press, 1984), 32.

7. For example, in her classic work *The Death and Life of Great American Cities*, Jane Jacobs notes that parks designed for recreation and leisure went unused and were abandoned in favor of playing in alleys. William Whyte, in his landmark study *City: Rediscovering the Center*, found that the points of the most concentrated pedestrian traffic are also the points at which most people stop to talk (instead of moving out of the way, they stand in the centers of the busiest corners in town)—not by inertia, but by choice (New York: Doubleday, 1988).

8. The phrase "unspecified possibility" comes from Wilson, "Against Utopia," 259.

9. Donna J. Haraway, *Modest Witness @ Second Millennium: FemaleMan Meets Onco-Mouse . . .* (New York: Routledge, 1997), 132.

Bibliography

Books and Articles

Anderson, Benedict. *Imagined Communities: Reflections on the Origin and Spread of Nationalism.* London and New York: Verso Press, 1992.

Bachrach, Peter, and Morton S. Baratz. *Power and Poverty: Theory and Practice.* New York and London: Oxford University Press, 1970.

Benjamin, Walter. *Reflections: Essays, Aphorisms, and Political Writings.* New York: Schocken Books, 1978.

Berlant, Lauren. *The Anatomy of National Fantasy: Hawthorne, Utopia, and Everyday Life.* Chicago and London: University of Chicago Press, 1991.

Berman, Marshall. *All That Is Solid Melts into Air: The Experience of Modernity.* New York: Penguin Books, 1998.

Bickford, Susan. "Constructing Inequality: City Spaces and the Architecture of Citizenship." *Political Theory* 28, no. 3 (2000): 355–76.

——. *The Dissonance of Democracy: Listening, Conflict, and Citizenship.* Ithaca and London: Cornell University Press, 1996.

Blakely, Edward J. and Mary Gail Snyder. "Divided We Fall: Gated and Walled Communities in the United States." In *Architecture of Fear,* edited by Nan Ellin, 85–99. New York: Princeton Architectural Press, 1997.

Bondi, Liz. "Gender Symbols and Urban Landscapes." *Progress in Human Geography* 16 (1992): 157–70.

Borchert, James. *Alley Life in Washington: Family, Community, Religion and Folklife.* Urbana and Chicago: University of Illinois Press, 1980.

Bordo, Susan. *Unbearable Weight: Feminism, Western Culture, and the Body.* Berkeley: University of California Press, 1993.

Boyer, M. Christine. "Cities for Sale: Merchandising History at South Street Seaport." In *Variations on a Theme Park: The New American City and the End of Public Space,* edited by Michael Sorkin, 181–204. New York: Hill and Wang, 1992.

Boyer, Paul S. *Urban Masses and Moral Order in America, 1820–1920.* Cambridge: Harvard University Press, 1978.

Braidotti, Rosi. *Nomadic Subjects: Embodiment and Sexual Difference in Contemporary Feminist Theory*. New York: Columbia University Press, 1994.

Brzezinski, Matthew. "Fortress America," *New York Times Magazine*. February 23, 2003, 38–44.

Butler, Judith. *Gender Trouble: Feminism and the Subversion of Identity*. New York and London: Routledge, 1990.

Caldeira, Teresa Pires do Rio. "Fortified Enclaves: The New Urban Segregation." *Public Culture* 8 (1996): 303–28.

Caraway, Nancie. *Segregated Sisterhood: Racism and the Politics of American Feminism*. Knoxville: University of Tennessee Press, 1991.

Carmona, Michael. *Haussmann: His Life and Times, and the Making of Modern Paris*. Chicago: Ivan R. Dee, 2002.

Casey, Edward S. *The Fate of Place: A Philosophical History*. Berkeley: University of California Press, 1997.

Castells, Manuel. *The Informational City: Information Technology, Economic Restructuring, and the Urban-Regional Process*. Cambridge: Basil Blackwell, 1989.

Certeau, Michel de. *The Practice of Everyday Life*. Berkeley: University of California Press, 1984.

Connolly, William E. *The Ethos of Pluralization*. Minneapolis: University of Minnesota Press, 1995.

———. *Identity\Difference: Democratic Negotiations of Political Paradox*. Ithaca and London: Cornell University Press, 1991.

———. *Why I Am Not a Secularist*. Minneapolis: University of Minnesota Press, 1999.

Crawford, Margaret. "The World in a Shopping Mall." In *Variations on a Theme Park: The New American City and the End of Public Space*, edited by Michael Sorkin, 3–30. New York: Hill and Wang, 1992.

Crenson, Matthew. *The Un-Politics of Air Pollution: A Study of Non-Decisionmaking in the Cities*. Baltimore: Johns Hopkins University Press, 1972.

Cruikshank, Barbara. *The Will to Empower: Democratic Citizens and Other Subjects*. Ithaca: Cornell University Press, 1999.

Dahl, Robert A. *Who Governs? Democracy and Power in an American City*. New Haven and London: Yale University Press, 1961.

Davis, Mike. *City of Quartz: Excavating the Future in Los Angeles*. London and New York: Vintage Press, 1992.

———. *Magical Urbanism: Latinos reinvent the US City*. London and New York: Verso Press, 2000.

Dean, Jodi. *Publicity's Secret: How Technoculture Capitalizes on Democracy*. Ithaca: Cornell University Press, 2002.

Digeser, Peter. "The Fourth Face of Power." *Journal of Politics* 54 (1992): 977–1006.

Doherty, R. J. *Social-Documentary Photography in the USA*. Garden City, N.Y.: American Photographic Book Publishing Company, 1976.

Domosh, Mona. "A 'Feminine' Building? An Inquiry into the Relations between Gender Ideology and Aesthetic Ideology in Turn-of-the-Century America." *Ecumene: A Journal of Environment, Culture and Meaning* 3 (1996): 305–24.

———. "Those 'Gorgeous Incongruities': Polite Politics and Public Space on the Streets of Nineteenth Century New York City," *Annals of American Geographers* no. 88:209–26.

Douglas, Mary. *Purity and Danger: An Analysis of Concepts of Pollution and Taboo.* New York and Washington: Frederick A. Praeger, 1966.

Dowler, Lorraine. "'And They Think I'm Just a Nice Old Lady': Women and War in Belfast, Northern Ireland." *Gender Place and Culture* 5 (1998): 159–76.

Dreier, Peter, John Mollenkopf and Todd Swanstrom. *Place Matters: Metropolitics for the Twenty-first Century,* 2d ed. Lawrence: University of Kansas Press, 2004.

Dreyfus, Hubert L. and Paul Rabinow. *Michel Foucault: Beyond Structuralism and Hermeneutics.* Chicago: University of Chicago Press, 1983.

Druckrey, Timothy. "Secreted Agents, Security Leaks, Immune Systems, Spore Wars . . ." In *CTRL [SPACE]: Rhetorics of Surveillance from Bentham to Big Brother,* edited by Thomas Y. Levin, Ursula Frohne, and Peter Weibel, 150–57. Karlsruhe and Cambridge, Mass.: ZKM and MIT Press, 2002.

Dumm, Thomas. *Michel Foucault and the Politics of Freedom.* Thousand Oaks, Calif., London, and New Delhi: Sage Publications, 1996.

———. *united states.* Ithaca and London: Cornell University Press, 1994.

Duncan, James S. *The City as Text: Interpretations in the Kandyan Kingdom.* Cambridge and New York: Cambridge University Press, 1990.

Edkins, Jenny. *Trauma and the Memory of Politics.* Cambridge: Cambridge University Press, 2003.

Ferguson, Kathy. *The Man Question: Visions of Subjectivity in Feminist Theory.* Berkeley: The University of California Press, 1993.

Foucault, Michel. "Body/Power." In *Power/Knowledge: Selected Interviews and Other Writings 1972–1977,* edited by Colin Gordon, 55–62. New York: Pantheon, 1980.

———. *Discipline and Punish: The Birth of the Prison.* New York: Vintage, 1977.

———. "The Eye of Power." In *Power/Knowledge: Selected Interviews and Other Writings 1972–1977,* edited by Colin Gordon, 146–65. New York: Pantheon Books, 1980.

———. "Governmentality." In *The Foucault Effect: Studies in Governmentality,* edited by Burchell, et al., 87–104. Chicago: University of Chicago Press, 1991.

———. "The History of Sexuality." In *Power/Knowledge: Selected Interviews and Other Writings 1972–1977,* edited by Colin Gordon, 183–93. New York: Univeristy of Kansas Press, 1980.

———. *The History of Sexuality,* Vol. 1. New York: Random House, 1990.

———. *Language, Counter-Memory, and Practice: Selected Essays and Interviews.* Edited by Donald F. Bouchard. Ithaca: Cornell University Press, 1977.

———. "Nietzsche, Genealogy, History." In *The Foucault Reader,* edited by Paul Rabinow, 76–100. New York: Pantheon, 1984.

———. "Of Other Spaces." *diacritics,* Spring 1986, 22–27.

———. *The Order of Things: An Archeology of the Human Sciences.* New York: Vintage, 1994.

———. "Questions of Method." In *The Foucault Effect: Studies in Governmentality,* edited by Graham Burchell, Colin Gordon, and Peter Miller, 73–86. Chicago: University of Chicago Press, 1991.

———. "Questions on Geography." In *Power/Knowledge: Selected Interviews and Other Writings 1972–1977,* edited by Colin Gordon, 63–77. New York: Pantheon, 1980.

———. "Space, Knowledge, and Power." In *The Foucault Reader,* edited by Paul Rabinow, 239–56. New York: Pantheon, 1984.

———. "The Subject and Power." In *Michel Foucault: Beyond Structuralism and Hermeneutics,* edited by Hubert L. Dreyfus and Paul Rabinow, 208–26. Chicago: University of Chicago Press, 1983.

———. "Two Lectures." In *Power/Knowledge: Selected Interviews and Other Writings 1972–1977,* edited by Colin Gordon, 78–108. New York: Pantheon Books, 1980.

———. *The Use of Pleasure: The History of Sexuality,* Vol. 2. New York: Random House, 1985.

Fraser, Nancy and Linda Gordon. "Decoding Dependency: Inscriptions of Power in a Keyword of the U.S. Welfare State." In *Reconstructing Political Theory: Feminist Perspectives,* edited by Mary Lyndon Shanley and Uma Narayan, 25–47. University Park: Pennsylvania State University Press, 1997.

Freud, Sigmund. *Civilization and Its Discontents.* Edited and translated by James Strachey. New York and London: W. W. Norton, 1961.

———. *Three Essays on the Theory of Sexuality.* New York: Basic Books, 1962.

Frieden, Bernard J. and Lynne B. Sagalyn. *Downtown, Inc.: How American Rebuilds Cities.* 1989. Reprint, Cambridge, Mass., and London: MIT Press, 1994.

Fullilove, Mindy Thompson. *Root Shock: How Tearing Up City Neighborhoods Hurts America, and What We Can Do About It.* New York: One World Ballantine Books, 2005.

Gandy, O. H. *The Panoptic Sort: A Political Economy of Personal Information.* Boulder: Westview, 1993.

Garreau, Joel. *Edge City: Life on the New Frontier.* New York: Doubleday, 1991.

Gatens, Moira. "Corporeal Representation in/and the Body Politic." In *Cartographies: Poststructuralism and the mapping of bodies and spaces,* edited by Rosalyn Diprose and Robyn Ferrell. North Sydney: Allen & Unwin, 1991.

Gaventa, John. *Power and Powerlessness: Quiescence and Rebellion in an Appalachian Valley.* Urbana and Chicago: University of Illinois Press, 1980.

Gilbert, James. *Perfect Cities: Chicago's Utopias of 1893.* Chicago: University of Chicago Press, 1991.

Gillette, Howard. *Between Justice and Beauty: Race, Planning, and the Failure of Urban Policy in Washington, D.C.* Baltimore: Johns Hopkins University Press, 1995.

Green, Constance McLaughlin. *The Secret City: A History of Race Relations in the Nation's Capital.* Princeton: Princeton University Press, 1967.

———. *Washington: A History of the Capital, 1800–1950.* Princeton: Princeton University Press, 1962.

Grosz, Elizabeth. *Volatile Bodies: Towards a Corporeal Feminism.* Bloomington and Indianapolis: Indiana University Press, 1994.

Gutheim, Frederick. *Worthy of the Nation: The History of City Planning for the National Capital.* Washington, D.C.: The Smithsonian Institution Press, 1977.

Habermas, Jürgen. *The Philosophical Discourse of Modernity.* Translated by Frederick G. Lawrence. Cambridge: MIT Press, 1987.

———. *The Structural Transformation of the Public Sphere: An Inquiry into a Category of Bourgeois Society.* Cambridge: MIT Press, 1991.

Hall, Peter. *Cities of Tomorrow: An Intellectual History of Urban Planning and Design in the Twentieth Century.* Oxford: Basil Blackwell, 1988.

Halprin, Lawrence. *The Franklin Delano Roosevelt Memorial.* San Francisco: Chronicle Books, 1997.

Haraway, Donna J. *Modest Witness @ Second Millennium. FemaleMan© Meets Onco-Mouse*™. New York and London: Routledge, 1997.

———. *Simians, Cyborgs, and Women: The Reinvention of Nature.* New York: Routledge, 1991.

Harstock, Nancy C. M. *Money, Sex and Power: Toward a Feminist Historical Materialism.* Boston: Northeastern University Press, 1983.

Hartwick, M. Jeffrey. *Mall Maker: Victor Gruen, Architect of an American Dream.* Philadelphia: University of Pennsylvania Press, 2003.

Harvey, David. *The Condition of Postmodernity: An Enquiry into the Origins of Cultural Change.* Cambridge: Basil Blackwell, 1989.

———. *Consciousness and the Urban Experience.* Baltimore: Johns Hopkins University Press, 1985.

———. *Justice, Nature & the Geography of Difference.* New York: Routledge, 1996.

———. *Spaces of Hope.* Berkeley and Los Angeles: University of California Press, 2002.

Hayden, Dolores. *The Power of Place: Urban Landscapes as Public History.* Cambridge: MIT Press, 1997.

———. *Redesigning the American Dream: Gender, Housing, and Family Life.* 1984. Reprint, New York: W. W. Norton, 2002.

Hayward, Clarissa Rile. *De-Facing Power.* Cambridge and New York: Cambridge University Press, 2000.

———. "The Difference States Make: Democracy, Identity, and the American City." *American Political Science Review* 97, no. 4 (November 2003): 501–14.

Hénaff, Marcel and Tracy B. Strong, ed. *Public Space and Democracy.* Minneapolis: University of Minnesota Press, 2001.

Isenberg, Alison. *Downtown America: A History of the Place and the People Who Made It.* Chicago: University of Chicago Press, 2004.

Isin, Engin. *Being Political: Genealogies of Citizenship.* Minneapolis: University of Minnesota Press, 2002.

Jacobs, Jane. *The Death and Life of Great American Cities.* New York: Random House, 1961.

Jacoby, Russell and Naomi Glauberman, ed. *The Bell Curve Debate.* New York: Three River Press, 1995.

Jameson, Fredric. *Postmodernism, or the Cultural Logic of Late Capitalism.* Durham: Duke University Press, 1991.

Johnston, Steven. "Political Not Patriotic: Democracy, Civic Space, and the American Memorial/Monument Complex." *Theory & Event* 5, no. 2 (2001).

Jones, Kathleen B. *Compassionate Authority: Democracy and the Representation of Women.* New York and London: Routledge, 1993.

Judd, Dennis R. *The Politics of American Cities: Private Power and Public Policy,* 3d ed. Boston: Addison-Wesley, 1988.

Katarani, Kojin. *Architecture as Metaphor: Language, Number, Money.* Translated by Sabu Kohso, edited by Michael Speaks. Cambridge: MIT Press, 1995.

Kateb, George. "Aestheticism and Morality: Their Cooperation and Hostility." *Political Theory* 28 (2000): 5–37.

Kelly, Charles Suddarth. *Washington, D.C., Then and Now: 69 Sites Photographed in the Past and Present.* New York: Dover Publications, 1984.

Kirby, Kathleen M. *Indifferent Boundaries: Spatial Concepts of Human Subjectivity.* New York and London: The Guilford Press, 1996.

Kohn, Margaret. *Brave New Neighborhoods: The Privatization of the Public Sphere.* New York: Routledge, 2004.

———. "The Mauling of Public Space." *Dissent* 48 (Spring 2001): 71–77.

———. *Radical Space: Building the House of the People.* Ithaca: Cornell University Press, 2003.

Kristeva, Julia. *The Powers of Horror: An Essay on Abjection.* New York: Columbia University Press, 1982.

Larson, Erik. *The Devil in the White City: Murder, Magic and Madness at the Fair that Changed America.* New York: Vintage, 2003.

Lee, Orville. "Culture and Democratic Theory: Toward a Theory of Symbolic Democracy." *Constellations* 5 (1996): 435–55.

Lefebvre, Henri. *The Production of Space.* Oxford and Cambridge : Blackwell, 1991.

Lin, Maya. *Boundaries.* New York: Simon and Schuster, 1999.

Loewen, James W. *Lies Across America: What Our Historic Sites Get Wrong.* New York: The New Press, 1999.

Love, Nancy. "Politics and Voice(s): An Empowerment/Knowledge Regime." *differences* 3, no. 1 (Spring 1991): 85–103.

Lugones, Maria. "Playfulness, 'World'-Traveling, and Loving Perception." In *Haciendo-Caras—Making Face, Making Soul, Creative and Critical Perspectives by Women of Color,* edited by Gloria Anzaldua, 390–402. San Francisco: Aunt Lute Foundation, 1990.

Luke, Timothy W. *Museum Politics: Power Plays at the Exhibition.* Minneapolis: University of Minnesota Press, 2002.

Massey, Doreen. 1994. *Space, Place and Gender.* Minneapolis: University of Minnesota Press, 1994.

Merrifield, Andy. "Between Process and Individuation: Translating Metaphors and Narratives of Urban Space." *Antipode* 29, no. 4 (1997): 417–36.

Miller, Eugene F. "Metaphor and Political Knowledge." *American Political Science Review* 73, no. 1 (1979): 155–70.

Mumford, Lewis. *The City In History: Its Origins, Its Transformations, and Its Prospects.* New York: Harcourt, Brace, & World, 1961.

———. *The Culture of Cities.* 1938. Reprint, New York: Harcourt, Brace & World, 1970.

New York Civil Liberties Union. "Surveillance Camera Project." In *CTRL [SPACE]: Rhetorics of Surveillance from Bentham to Big Brother,* edited by Thomas Y. Levin, Ursula Frohne, and Peter Weibel, 388–71. Karlsruhe and Cambridge: ZKM and MIT Press, 2002.

Nietzsche, Friedrich. 1967. *On the Genealogy of Morals,* translated by Walter Kaufmann. 1967. Reprint, New York: Vintage Books, 1989.

———. "On the Uses and Disadvantages of History for Life." In *Untimely Meditations,* edited by Daniel Breazeale, 57–124. Cambridge: The Cambridge University Press, 1997.

Olson, Joel. "The Democratic Problem of the White Citizen." *Constellations* 8, no 2 (2001): 163–83.

PBS NewsHour. "FDR Remembered" (May 1, 1997).

Peterson, Jon A. "The Nation's First Comprehensive City Plan: A Political Analysis of the McMillan Plan for Washington, D.C., 1900–1902." *Journal of the American Planning Association* 51 (Spring 1985): 134–50.

Pile, Steve. *The Body and the City: Psychoanalysis, Space and Subjectivity.* London and New York: Routledge, 1996.

Poovey, Mary. "The Production of Abstract Space." In *Making Worlds: Gender, Metaphor, and Materiality,* edited by Susan Hardy Aiken, Sallie A. Marston, and Penny Waterstone, 69–89. Tuscon: University of Arizona Press, 1998.

Reps, John. *Monumental Washington: The Planning and Development of the Capital Center.* Princeton: Princeton University Press, 1967.

Roediger, David R. *The Wages of Whiteness: Race and the Making of the American Working Class.* New York: Verso, 1991.

Rogin, Michael. *Ronald Reagan, the Movie and Other Episodes in Political Demonology.* Berkeley: University of California Press, 1987.

Rose, Gillian. "As if the Mirrors Had Bled: Masculine Dwelling, Masculinist Theory, and Feminist Masquerade." In *Bodyspace: Destabilizing Geographies of Gender and Sexuality,* edited by Nancy Duncan, 56–74. London and New York: Routledge, 1996.

———. *Feminism and Geography.* Cambridge: Polity Press, 1993.

Rydell, Robert W. *All the World's a Fair: Visions of Empire at American International Exhibitions, 1876–1916.* Chicago: University of Chicago Press, 1987.

Sanger, P. Steven. "'Power' against Ideology: A Critique of Foucaultian Usage." *Cultural Anthropology* 10, no. 1 (1995): 3–40.

Savage, Kirk. *Standing Soldiers, Kneeling Slaves: Race, War and Monument in Nineteenth-Century America.* Princeton: Princeton University Press, 1997.

Schirmer, Dietrich. "Nation-building and Nation-Buildings: Washington Art and Architecture and the Symbols of American Nationalism." In *Identity and Intolerance: Nationalism, Racism and Xenophobia in Germany and the United States,* edited by Norbert Finzsch and Dietmar Schrirmer. Cambridge: Cambridge University Press, 1998.

Schorske, Carl E. *Fin-de-Siècle Vienna: Politics and Culture.* 1961. Reprint, New York: Vintage, 1981.

Scott, James C. *Seeing Like a State: How Certain Schemes to Improve the Human Condition Have Failed.* New Haven and London: Yale University Press, 1998.

Sears, David O. "Urban Rioting in Los Angeles: A Comparison of 1965 with 1992." In *The Los Angeles Riots: Lessons for the Urban Future,* edited by Mark Baldassare, 237–54. Boulder, San Francisco, and Oxford: Westview Press, 1994.

Sennett, Richard. *The Conscience of the Eye: The Design and Social Life of Cities.* New York and London: W. W. Norton, 1990.

———. *The Fall of Public Man.* 1974. Reprint, New York and London: W. W. Norton, 1992.

Shapiro, Michael J. "Constructing 'America': Architectural Thought-Worlds." *Theory & Event* 7, no. 4 (2004).

Sharp, Joanne P. "Gendering Nationhood: A Feminist Engagement with National Identity." In *Bodyspace: Destabilizing Geographies of Gender and Sexuality,* edited by Nancy Duncan, 97–108. London and New York: Routledge, 1996.

Shields, Rob. *Lefebvre, Love and Struggle: Spatial Dialectics.* London and New York: Routledge, 1999.

Shklar, Judith N. *American Citizenship: The Quest for Inclusion.* Cambridge: Harvard University Press, 1991.

Silber, Ilana Friedrich. "Space, Fields, Boundaries: The Rise of Spatial Metaphors in Contemporary Sociological Theory." *Social Research* 62, no. 2 (1995): 323–53.

Simmel, Georg. "The Metropolis and Mental Life." In *On Individuality and Social Forms: Selected Writings,* edited by Donald Levine, 325–39. 1903. Reprint, Chicago: University of Chicago Press, 1971.

Slotkin, Richard. *Regeneration through Violence: The Mythology of the American Frontier, 1600–1860.* New York: HarperCollins, 1973.

Smith, Neil. "New City, New Frontier." In *Variations on a Theme Park,* edited by Michael Sorkin, 61–93. New York: Hill and Wang, 1992.

Smith, Neil and Cindi Katz. "Grounding Metaphor: Towards a Spatialized Politics." In *Place and the Politics of Identity,* edited by Michael Keith and Steve Pile, 67–83. New York and London: Routledge, 1993.

Soja, Edward W. *Thirdspace: Journeys to Los Angeles and Other Real-and-Imagined Places.* Cambridge: Blackwell, 1996.

Sparks, Holloway. "Dissident Citizenship: Democratic Theory, Political Courage, and Activist Women." *Hypatia: A Journal of Feminist Philosophy* 2, no. 4 (1997).

Sugrue, Thomas J. *The Origins of the Urban Crisis: Race and Inequality in Postwar Detroit.* Princeton: Princeton University Press, 1996.

Taylor, Nigel. *Urban Planning Theory since 1945.* Thousand Oaks, Calif.: Sage, 1998.

Teaford, Jon C. *The Rough Road to Renaissance: Urban Revitalization in America, 1940–1985.* Baltimore: Johns Hopkins University Press, 1990.

This is What Democracy Looks Like. The Seattle Independent Media center and Big Noise Films, 2000.

Useem, Bert. "The State and Collective Disorders: The Los Angeles Riot/Protest of April 1992." *Social Forces* 76, no. 2 (December 1997): 357–58.

Virilio, Paul. "The Virtual Crash." In *CTRL [SPACE]: Rhetorics of Surveillance from Bentham to Big Brother,* edited by Thomas Y. Levin, Ursula Frohne, and Peter Weibel, 108–13. Karlsruhe and Cambridge: ZKM and MIT Press, 2002.

Weisman, Leslie Kanes. *Discrimination by Design: A Feminist Critique of the Man-Made Environment.* Urbana and Chicago: University of Illinois Press, 1992.

White, Stephen K. *Sustaining Affirmation: The Strengths of Weak Ontology in Political Theory.* Princeton: Princeton University Press, 2000.

Whyte, William. *City: Rediscovering the Center.* New York: Doubleday, 1988.

Wilson, Elizabeth. "Against Utopia: The Romance of Indeterminate Spaces." In *Embodied Utopias: Gender, Social Change and the Modern Metropolis,* edited by Amy Bingaman, Lise Sanders, and Rebecca Zoarch, 256–62. London and New York: Routledge, 2002.

———. *The Sphinx in the City: Urban Life, the Control of Disorder, and Women.* Berkeley and Los Angeles: University of California Press, 1992.

Wohlenberg, Ernest H. "The 'Geography of Civility' Revisited: New York Blackout Looting, 1977." *Economic Geography* 58, no. 1 (January 1982): 29–44.

Wolin, Sheldon. *Politics and Vision: Continuity and Innovation in Western Political Thought,* Exp. ed. Princeton: Princeton University Press, 2004.

Wood, Edward M., Sidney N. Brower, and Margaret W. Latimer. "Planners' People." *Journal of the American Institute of Planners* 32 (July 1966): 228–34.

Young, Iris Marion. *Intersecting Voices: Dilemmas of Gender, Political Philosophy, and Policy.* Princeton: Princeton University Press, 1997.

———. *Justice and the Politics of Difference.* Princeton: Princeton University Press, 1990.

Zizek, Slavoj. "Big Brother, or, the Triumph of the Gaze over the Eye." In *CTRL [SPACE]: Rhetorics of Surveillance from Bentham to Big Brother,* edited by Thomas Y. Levin, Ursula Frohne, and Peter Weibel, 224–27. Karlsruhe and Cambridge: ZKM and MIT Press, 2002.

Zukin, Sharon. *Landscapes of Power: From Detroit to Disneyworld.* Berkeley: University of California Press, 1991.

Primary Sources—Books

American Institute of Architects (AIA). *No Time for Ugliness: An Appraisal of the American City by the American Institute of Architects.* Washington, D.C.: American Institute of Architects, 1966.

———. *Of Plans and People: A study of the plan of Washington prepared by the Washington-Metropolitan Chapter of the American Institute of Architects.* Washington, D.C.: The Washington-Metropolitan Chapter of the AIA, 1950.

Editors of *Fortune* Magazine. *The Exploding Metropolis.* Garden City, N.Y.: Doubleday Anchor Books, 1958.

Gilbert, Ben W. and the Staff of the *Washington Post. Ten Blocks from the White House: Anatomy of the Washington Riots of 1968.* New York: Frederick A. Praeger, 1968.

Justement, Louis. *New Cities for Old: City Building in Terms of Space, Time, and Money.* New York and London: McGraw-Hill, 1946.

Moore, Charles. *The Life and Times of Charles McKim.* Cambridge: The Riverside Press, 1929.

Ratigan, Marion. *A Sociological Survey of Disease in Four Alleys in the National Capital.* Washington, D.C.: Catholic University of America Press, 1946.

Robinson, Charles Mulford. *Modern Civic Art or, the City Made Beautiful.* 1903. Reprint, New York: Arno Press, 1970.

Rouse, James W. and Nathaniel Keith. *No Slums in Ten Years: A Workable Program for Urban Renewal,* Washington, D.C.: Report to the Commissioners of the District of Columbia, 1955.

Thursz, Daniel. *Where Are They Now? A Study of the Impact of Relocation on Former Residents of Southwest Washington Who Served in an HWC Demonstration Project.* Washington, D.C.: Health and Welfare Council of the National Capital Area, 1966.

Weller, Charles Frederick. *Neglected Neighbors: Stories of Life in the Alleys, Tenements, and Shanties of the National Capital.* Philadelphia: John C. Winston Company, 1909.

Primary Sources—Newspaper and Magazine Articles

Adams, John Coleman. "What a Great City Might Be—A Lesson From the White City." *New England Magazine* 14 (1896): 3–13.

Ambrose, Stephen E. "A Terrible Idea." *National Review* 51, 22 (November 1999): 30–31.

American City. "Everyone Pays for Blight." May 1947, 102.

Baker, Donald P. "Controversy Aside, Ashe Statue Is a Hit." *Washington Post* (April 19, 1996): sec. D.

Baker, Russell. "Capital Planning City within a City." *New York Times* (January 2, 1956): 23.

Barnes, Bart. "Wary Police Keep Lid on in Suburbs." *Washington Post* (April 7, 1968): A8.

Burnham, Daniel H. "White City and Capital City." *Century* 63 (1902): 619–20.

Bush-Brown, H. K. "New York City Monuments." *Municipal Affairs* 3 (1899): 602–12.

Caemmerer, H. Paul. "Washington Has Local Problems, Too." *The American City* (June 1947): 73–75.

CBS. "Close Watch." April 22, 2002.

Century. "Civic Improvement a Phase of Patriotism." *The Century* 63 (1902): 793.

Charities. "A Capital City of Broad Streets but Evil Alleys." *Charities* 10 (1903): 585.

———. "To Wipe Washington Alleys off the Map." *Charities* 13 (1905): 960.

Clopton, William. "Four Thousand Troops Move into District after Day of Looting and Arson." *Washington Post* (April 6, 1968): sec. A.

Clymer, Adam. "Big Brother vs. Terrorist in Spy Camera Debate." *New York Times* (June 19, 2002): 16.

Dietsch, Deborah K. "National Mall Is Jam-Packed—and Losing Its Majestic Image." *USA Today* (October 14, 2004): 25A.

Dodd, Matthew. "Remembrance Days." *New Statesman* (July 29, 2002).

Dvorak, Petula. "Washington Monument Subtly Fortified." *Washington Post* (July 1, 2005): A1.

Evening Star. "Bill Provides Land Agency," (April 16, 1946).

———. "Decision on Slabs," (September 23, 1966).

———. "The Future Capital," (February 23, 1900).

———. "Group Forms to Stimulate 'Orderly' City Rebuilding," (November 22, 1946).

———. "Improved Park System: Senate District Committee Submits Report," (January 15, 1902).

———. "NCHA Reports on the Number of Unfit D.C. Dwellings to Congress," (April 16, 1946).

———. "An Overdue Master Plan," (September 27, 1947).

———. "Planning Group Hopes to Outline Southwest Program This Week," (October 23, 1952).

———. "Plan of New Capital," (January 16, 1902).

———. "Southwest's Dwellings Mostly Substandard, Planners Declare," (November 11, 1952).

Fahrenthold, David A. "Crime-Plagued D.C. Neighborhoods Ask for Cameras." *Washington Post* (March 10, 2003): B1 and B6.

Flor, Lee. "Shouting Flares at Cardozo Meeting on Riots." *Evening Star* (April 13, 1968).

Frankel, Godfrey and Laura Goldstein. *In the Alleys: Kids in the Shadow of the Capitol.* Washington: Smithsonian Institution Press, 1995.

Goldberger, Paul. "Down at the Mall: The New World War II Memorial Doesn't Rise to the Occasion." *New Yorker,* accessed at www.newyorker.com/archive/2004/05/31/040531crsk_syline.

Hsu, Spencer S. "Video Surveillance Planned on Mall." *Washington Post* (March 22, 2002): 1 and 8.

Ivy, Robert. "Keep Off the Grass." *Architectural Record* 188, no. 10 (October 2000): 19.

———. "Neo-Memorial." *Architectural Record* 192, no. 6 (June 2004).

Just, Ward. "The City Beseiged: A Study in Ironies." *Washington Post* (April 6, 1968): sec. A.

Kettle, Martin. "Capital City's Memorial Fever? Case of Monumental Madness." *Houston Chronicle* (November 9, 1997).

Kilborn, Peter T. "For Security, Tourists to Be on Other Side of Cameras." *New York Times* (March 23, 2002): 12.

Kliment, Stephen. "More Monuments?" *Architectural Record* 183, no. 10 (1995): 9.

Kriehn, George. "The City Beautiful." *Municipal Affairs* 3 (1899): 594–601.

Leigh, Catesby. "In Memoriam: World War II on the Mall." *Weekly Standard* (May 31, 2004).

———. "Our Monuments, Our Selves: What We Built Then, What We Build Now." *Weekly Standard* (March 5, 2001).

Lewis, Roger K. "Washington Monuments: Battles over the Mall." *Architectural Record* 184, no. 1 (January 1996): 17–21.

Moore, Charles. "The Improvement of Washington City, First Paper." *The Century* 63 (1902): 621–28.

———. "The Improvement of Washington City, Second Paper." *The Century* 63 (1902): 747–57.

———. "The Transformation of Washington: A Glance at the History Along the Vista of the Future of the Nation's Capital." *National Geographic Magazine* 63 (1923): 569–95.

New York Times. "D.C. Hotels Report Tourists Avoiding the Capital Area," (April 7, 1968): A62.

———. "Gala Day for Washington," (December 9, 1900).

———. "The Nation's New Capital," (January 19, 1902).

———. "Project to Erase Washington Slum," (January 8, 1957): 49.

———. "Rebuilding Plans Gain in Capital," (June 8, 1956): 57.

———. "To Beautify Washington," (April 3, 1902).

———. "Video Surveillance Planned for Capital," (March 22, 2002): 13.

———. "Zeckendorf Acts on Capital Slums," (March 15, 1954): 14.

Postrel, Virginia. "The Long-Term Consequences of the Race Riots in the Late 1960s Come into View." *New York Times* (December 30, 2004): C2.

Proctor, John Clagett. "Landmarks and Odd Names Guided Searching Efforts in Early Washington." *Evening Star* (February 26, 1939).

Reston, James. "L'Enfant's Capital—and Boomtown, Too." In *Modern American Cities*, edited by Ray Ginger, 35–41. 1941. Reprint, Chicago: Quadrangle Books, 1969.

Reston, Jr., James. "The Monument Glut." *New York Times Magazine* (September 10, 1995): 48–49.

Roberts, Chalmers M. "Capital's Problem Area Pronounced Ripe for Redevelopment." *Washington Post* (February 12, 1952): B1.

———. "It's Costly and Dangerous for District to Maintain Slum Area." *Washington Post* (January 30, 1952): B1.

———. "One 'Super-Block' Could Replace Four Blocks of D.C. Slums." *Washington Post* (February 12, 1952): B1.

———. "Progress or Decay? Washington Must Choose." *Washington Post* (January 27, 1952): B1.

Saffir, Barbara J. "Plan Outlines Where to Place D.C. Memorials and Museums." *Architectural Record* 189, no. 2 (February 2001): 40.

Safire, William. "The Great Unwatched." *New York Times* (February 18, 2002): 15.

Sciolino, Elaine. "Agencies Limit New Memorials on Coveted Washington Mall." *New York Times* (September 7, 2001): A14.

Sternberg, George M. "Housing Conditions in the National Capital." *Charities* 12 (1904): 762–64.

Tirana, T. W. "The New People of Southwest." *Evening Star* (September 23, 1962).

Tolson, Jay. "Scenes from the Mall." *U.S. News & World Report* (September 18, 2000): 69.

Washington Post Magazine. "The Inferno and Its Aftermath," (April 3, 1988).

Washington Times. "Capitol Slave Labor Studied," (June 1, 2005.)

Wheeler, Linda. "Broken Ground, Broken Hearts—Urban Renewal Cost Homes." *Washington Post* (June 21, 1999).

———. "On U. Street, Blacks Created a Powerful Symbol." *Washington Post* (January 19, 1999).

Wood, Edith Elmer. "Four Washington Alleys." *Survey* 31 (1913): 44–46.

Zueblin, Charles. "The White City and After." In *A Decade of Civic Development,* edited by Charles Zueblin, 59–82. Chicago: University of Chicago Press, 1905.

Primary Sources—Government Documents

Moore, Charles, ed., 1901. *The Embellishment of Washington: Preliminary Report of the Senate Committee on a Plan for the Improvement of the District of Columbia.* Published in *Municipal Affairs* 4:909–16.

National Capital Park and Planning Commission (NCPPC). *Washington: Present and Future: A General Summary of the Comprehensive Plan for the National Capital and Its Environs.* Washington, D.C.: National Capital Park and Planning Commission, 1950.

National Capital Planning Commission (NCPC). *Museums and Memorials Master Plan.* Washington, D.C.: National Capital Planning Commission, 2001.

· Schorr, Alvin L. *Slums and Social Insecurity: An Appraisal of the Effectiveness of Housing Projects in Helping to Eliminate Poverty in the United States.* Washington, D.C.: U.S. Government Printing Office, 1963.

Sternberg, George. *Report of Committee on Building of Model Homes.* Washington, D.C.: The President's Homes Commission, 1908.

U.S. Congress. House of Representatives. *Certain Alleys in the District of Columbia: Hearing before House Committee on the District of Columbia.* 63d Cong., 2d sess., 1914.

———. *Public Buildings—Southwest Redevelopment—D.C.: Hearings before the Subcommittee on Public Buildings and Grounds and the Committee on Public Works.* 83d Cong., 2d sess., 1954.

U.S. Congress. Senate. *Construction of Certain Government Buildings in the District of Columbia: Hearings before a Subcommittee of the Committee on Public Works.* 84th Cong., 1st sess., 1955.

———. *DC Area Monuments and Memorials: Hearing before the Subcommittee on National Parks, Historic Preservation and Recreation of the Committee on Energy and National Resources.* 106th Cong., 2d sess., 2000.

———. *Hearing on the Bill (S. 3244) Creating a Commission for the Condemnation of Insanitary Buildings in the District of Columbia.* 57th Cong., 1st sess., 1902.

———. *Inhabited Alleys in the District of Columbia: Hearing of the United States Senate Subcommittee on the District of Columbia.* 63d Cong., 2d sess., 1914.

———. *Investigation of the Program of the National Housing Authority: Hearings before a Subcommittee of the Committee on the District of Columbia.* 78th Cong., 1st sess., 1943.

———. *Low-Cost Housing in District of Columbia: Hearings before a Subcommittee of the Committee on the District of Columbia.* 79th Cong., 1st sess., 1945.

———. *Report of the Senate Committee of the District of Columbia on the Improvement of the Park System of the District of Columbia.* 57th Cong., 1st sess., 1902.

Index

MARGARET E. FARRAR is associate professor of political science at Augustana College (Illinois). Her articles have appeared in *Politics & Gender* and *Polity.*

The University of Illinois Press
is a founding member of the
Association of American University Presses.

Composed in 10.5/13 Minion
with Minion display
by Celia Shapland
at the University of Illinois Press
Manufactured by Thomson-Shore, Inc.

University of Illinois Press
1325 South Oak Street
Champaign, IL 61820-6903
www.press.uillinois.edu